GERMAN COLONIALISM

Germany was a late-comer to the colonial world of the late nineteenth century, but this history of German colonialism makes clear the wide-reaching consequences of Germany's short-lived colonial project. Sebastian Conrad charts the expansion of the empire from its origins in the acquisition of substantial territories in present-day Togo, Cameroon, Namibia, and Tanzania to new settlements in east Asia and the Pacific, and reveals the colonialist culture which permeated the German nation and its politics. Drawing on the wider history of European expansion and globalization he highlights the close interactions and shared vocabularies of the colonial powers and emphasizes Germany's major role in the period of high imperialism before 1914. Even beyond the official end of the empire in 1919 the quest for *Lebensraum* and the growth of the Nazi empire in eastern Europe can be viewed within a framework of colonialism whose effects resonate to the present day.

Sebastian Conrad is Professor of Modern History at the Free University of Berlin. His previous books include *Globalisation and the Nation in Imperial Germany* (Cambridge, 2010) and *The Quest for the Lost Nation: Writing History in Germany and Japan in the American Century* (2010).

GERMAN COLONIALISM:
A SHORT HISTORY

SEBASTIAN CONRAD
TRANSLATED BY SORCHA O'HAGAN

CAMBRIDGE
UNIVERSITY PRESS

CAMBRIDGE
UNIVERSITY PRESS

University Printing House, Cambridge CB2 8BS, United Kingdom

Cambridge University Press is part of the University of Cambridge.

It furthers the University's mission by disseminating knowledge in the pursuit of education, learning and research at the highest international levels of excellence.

www.cambridge.org
Information on this title: www.cambridge.org/9781107400474

Originally published in German as *Deutsche Kolonialgeschichte* by Verlag C. H. Beck oHG, Munich 2008

© Verlag C. H. Beck oHG, Munich 2008

First published in English as *German Colonialism: A Short History* by Cambridge University Press, 2012

English edition © Cambridge University Press 2012
Reprinted 2012

A catalogue record for this publication is available from the British Library

Library of Congress Cataloguing in Publication data
Conrad, Sebastian.
[Deutsche Kolonialgeschichte. English]
German colonialism: a short history / Sebastian Conrad; translated by Sorcha O'Hagan.
p. cm.
"Originally published in German as Deutsche Kolonialgeschichte by Verlag C. H. Beck oHG, Munchen 2008" – T.p. verso.
ISBN 978-1-107-00814-4 – ISBN 978-1-107-40047-4 (pbk.)   1. Germany – Colonies – History.   2. Germany – Foreign relations – 1871–1918.   I. Title.
JV2017.C6613   2011
325′.343–dc23
2011025088

ISBN 978-1-107-00814-4 Hardback
ISBN 978-1-107-40047-4 Paperback

Contents

Illustrations

Maps

Acknowledgements

I am grateful for helpful and stimulating comments on parts of the manuscript by Andreas Eckert, Geoff Eley, Minu Hashemi Yekani, Christoph Kalter, Dörte Lerp, Bradley Naranch, Tim Opitz, and Ulrike Schaper. My thanks go to Stefanie Senger for procuring the images, to Kelly Mulvancy for compiling the index, and to Matthias Thaden for help with the page proofs. This work was supported by a grant from the Academy of Korean Studies funded by the Korean Government (MEST) (AKS-2010-DZZ-3103).

CHAPTER I

Introduction

The German colonial empire lasted a mere thirty years, and is thus one of the most short-lived of all modern 'colonialisms'. Consequently, it has not occupied centre-stage in most accounts and overviews of German history. The colonial experience was deemed marginal and insignificant, compared both to the long histories of the British and French empires, and also to the towering impact, on German history and beyond, of subsequent events: the First World War, the Weimar Republic and the rise of National Socialism, the Third *Reich* and the Holocaust. In recent years, however, interest in Germany's colonial past has made a remarkable comeback, both in academia and in the wider public sphere, and this mainly for three reasons.

Firstly, Germany's colonial project may have lasted only three decades, but it was a significant and integral part of the period of high imperialism before the First World War. For anyone interested in a comparative and global perspective on modern empires, the German example is in many ways an instructive and illuminating case. Germany was a colonial late-comer. Only after unification in 1871, which replaced the thirty-eight sovereign German states with a unified nation-state under the leadership of Prussia and Chancellor Bismarck, did the acquisition of colonies emerge as a realistic political project. Powerful pressure groups as well as reckless colonial pioneers in Africa forced Bismarck, to some extent against his will, into government support for the occupation of the first colonial territories in 1884. In the autumn of that year, Bismarck invited the European powers to the Berlin Conference: this in many ways formalized the scramble for African possessions. In 1884/85, Germany acquired large territories in Africa in today's Togo, Cameroon, Namibia, and

Illustration 1 In the late nineteenth century, colonial discourse was premised on the assumption of marked differences between the politics of colonizing nations. The image

Tanzania. In the late 1890s, smaller possessions in East Asia (Shandong province in China) and the Pacific (Samoa, New Guinea, and a number of Pacific Islands) were added. After those of Britain, France, and the Netherlands, this was the fourth largest colonial empire at the time.

In its basic structures, the German empire resembled the other empires of the time. It was built on ideological foundations that were shared by the other imperial powers, namely the civilizing mission promising modernization to the colonized populations under the tutelage of the colonizers. German colonialism also shared the general assumption that the world was ordered along racial lines, and belief in colonies as an outward proof of the power of the nation-state. As elsewhere, the colonial project was driven by the calculations of economic benefit, by the attempt to export social conflicts abroad, and by the expectation of creating large settler communities and thus of establishing 'New Germanies' overseas. German colonialism, in other words, was part and parcel of the larger European colonial project (see Illustration 1). This was not so much a matter of parallel developments, but rather of close interactions and shared vocabularies. More than that, European colonial powers closely collaborated with each other; while popular sentiments and *raison d'état* may have produced a rhetoric of national differences, German and British colonial officers on the ground agreed and cooperated on a variety of issues.

Beyond these commonalities and shared characteristics, however, historians have also suggested ways in which German colonialism may have been unique. They point, for example, at the degree of racial

---

Caption for Illustration 1 (cont.)
of Germany as a peaceful colonizer, for example, was part of the propaganda of colonial lobby groups and pitted against the allegedly less benevolent French and English. In this critical drawing in the satirical magazine *Simplicissimus* (in 1904), Thomas Theodor Heine (1867–1948) drew on national stereotypes to portray the colonizing efforts of the great powers. The Germans (top) are shown to fetishize law, order, and discipline (the sign on the palm tree reads: 'No tipping or dumping of snow'); the English (middle) corrupt the African population with whisky and a dose of Christianity while the real purpose is economic exploitation; the French (bottom left) are depicted as sexually engaging with the colonized, an allusion to the politics of assimilation pursued in the French colonies; and the Belgians are lambasted for their brutal reign in the Congo.

segregation, a feature found in all colonial systems but leading to legal prohibitions of intermarriage only in the German empire. Another case in point is the relative violence of Germany's colonial wars as manifest in the genocidal strategies of warfare against the Herero and Nama in 1904. Also, the contemporary claim that Germany's colonial policy, as also the Japanese, was more 'modern' as it was built on a scientific approach and the systematic study of territories and populations, would lend itself to comparative analyses. In short, for comparative and global historians, German colonialism offers a rich and revealing case study.

Secondly, colonialism also had a more significant role to play within German history than has long been assumed. Colonial interactions left their imprint on German society, and the impact of the colonial experience continued after the formal end of the empire. On the one hand, as recent scholarship has amply shown, colonialism was not confined to the colonized territories. Rather, it reached deep into metropolitan society and penetrated Germany in a variety of ways. Colonialism left its imprint on the debates of the *Reichstag* and on the press; on the realm of representation, from the huge colonial exhibition in 1896 to the arts and popular culture; on the structure of trade and migration regimes; and on the order of knowledge, as many disciplines, including anthropology and geography, were deeply implicated in the colonial project. Moreover, key ideological notions that would continue to be influential beyond the end of empire, such as *Lebensraum* and race, emerged and developed in the context of colonialism.

On the other hand, colonialism was not limited to the period of formal territorial rule that ended with the treaty of Versailles in 1919. This is mainly true for the colonies that continued to be shaped, and hampered, by decisions and paths taken in colonial times. But it also applies to Germany. The Nazi empire in eastern Europe, for example, needs to be placed within a history of German colonialism broadly defined. And a vibrant scholarly debate has dwelt on the question to what extent the origins of the genocidal politics of the Nazis must be located in the brutal colonial wars in Africa.

Thirdly, the colonial past is still very much with us. Indeed, it is almost ubiquitous, and not just in the former colonies. The legacy of colonialism is equally evident in the metropoles, and colonial issues continue to be central to present-day political conflicts. In Europe, reminders of the colonial era are everywhere, from the ban on the *hijab* in French schools and apologies for slavery in Britain to debates on Dutch 'excesses' in Indonesia. In 2005, the French parliament decided that schools must make a deliberate effort to emphasize the 'positive aspects' of colonial rule. Simultaneously, uncritical interpretations of colonialism presented in Japanese schoolbooks were provoking violent demonstrations in Beijing and Seoul. The claim for reparations launched by the Herero of Namibia against the Federal Republic of Germany brought the colonial past onto the agenda in German society, too. Across Germany, debates are under way about whether streets with names referring to certain inglorious episodes from the German colonial era should be renamed.

The current interest in colonialism, both in the media and in politics, needs to be closely correlated to the present-day processes of globalization. The issue of possible links between colonialism and current global integration is the subject of intense debate. Phrases such as 'neo-imperialism' and 'colonization of the mind' have become commonplace. Since 9/11 and the debate about an American empire, the question of how colonialism and imperialism should be viewed, in both political and moral terms, has been the subject of ongoing discussion.

The heightened interest in German colonial history must also be seen in this context. It is important to recognize that with this renewed attention, the perspective on the colonial past has been transformed. The issues that we are facing today have also changed the way in which we look at the colonial era. This is true for public discourse, but it also applies to historians and historiography. In the next section, I will present a short historiographical overview in order to reveal the extent to which priorities and areas of interest have changed since the German colonial empire officially came to an end in 1919. It is possible to identify a number of different phases that differ considerably in terms of the issues and questions investigated and also in terms of the methodological approaches taken. To generalize somewhat, we can identify three main strands: a politically revisionist strand during the 1920s, a reaction to the end of the colonial empire; a highly critical social history perspective in the late 1960s and 1970s, in the context of decolonization; and finally post-colonial historiography from the 1990s onward, shaped by present-day globalization.

After the Treaty of Versailles, which transferred Germany's overseas holdings to the mandate powers, most German historians, like the majority of the German population, were dismayed at the loss of the colonies. In fact, opinion about colonialism was probably more united during the Weimar Republic era than before the First World War; there was consensus across the political spectrum on the necessity to recover the colonial territories for Germany. This was a debate conducted primarily in the political arena and the press, and historians contributed only marginally to the discussions. The most important publications on the issue were written by veterans of the colonial service. An example is the *Deutsches Kolonial-Lexikon*, put together by the former Governor of German East Africa, Heinrich Schnee.[1] The purpose of works such as these was primarily to thwart the Versailles dictum of German colonial crimes, and the charge that Germans had ruled their colonies in a violent, 'uncivilized' manner. Heinrich Schnee tried to play down such accusations by referring to them as the 'colonial guilt lie' (*Kolonialschuldlüge*) (see Illustration 2). Most of the works published in the 1920s can thus be read as part of an attempt to draw attention to the achievements of German colonial rule, in order to support the argument for a return of the colonies to German ownership. One of the consequences of this revisionist concern was that little attention was paid to contemporary international research, mainly in English, on German colonialism.[2]

Germans began to examine the colonial era in a critical light only in the late 1960s. For several decades, little attention had been paid to the issue. But the global process of decolonization and public interest in campaigns for national independence in the Third World brought the colonial past back to the forefront of public attention. This reassessment of German colonialism drew some of its force from the

[1] Heinrich Schnee (ed.), *Deutsches Kolonial-Lexikon*, 3 vols., Leipzig (Quelle & Meyer) 1920.
[2] Most notably Mary E. Townsend, *The Rise and Fall of Germany's Colonial Empire 1884–1918*, New York (Macmillan) 1930.

Illustration 2 In 1924, Heinrich Schnee, the last governor of German East Africa, published his account of the *Kolonialschuldlüge* (colonial guilt lie). The book was intended to counter the verdict of the Allied powers, formulated during the peace treaty negotiations in Versailles, that 'Germany's failure in the field of colonial civilization . . . has become all too apparent to leave thirteen to fourteen million natives again to the fate from which the war had liberated them.' The Allied position relied heavily on the debates conducted in the *Reichstag* before 1914, led by such critical voices as Matthias Erzberger and Gustav Noske. Schnee's book was intended to prove the Allied accusations wrong by demonstrating that colonial rule by other European powers was much less benevolent than Germany's. As one of the major civilized nations, Germany had the right, as Schnee saw it, to continue participating in the colonizing project.

nascent criticisms of the traditions of German historiography that were seen as implicated in German nationalism and imperialism.[3] Another impulse was the challenge by historians in the German Democratic Republic (GDR) who in the 1970s developed a perspective critical of imperialism that their West German colleagues could not completely ignore. Publications by American historians were another factor. And in Tanzania (formerly German East Africa), source material still in storage in Dar es Salaam was accessed to create some important studies about the colonial era, written mainly from the point of view of the new post-colonial state.

While earlier research had concentrated on foreign policy and military conflicts, historians were now focusing their attention on social history. Many of the issues that had been of interest to earlier generations were put aside, for example the question of why Bismarck seemed to change his mind in 1884 about whether Germany should acquire colonies. Instead, the focus was on social, political and economic development. Many important studies were written during this period on the social history of the colonial movement, on the role of political parties and associations, on economic imperialism, on the missions and educational systems, and on state rule and local resistance. The evident interest in local opposition and resistance was, in part, the result of an explicitly anti-imperialist approach inspired by contemporary groups and movements focused on the Third World.

This new perspective increasingly produced historical work that drew not only on colonial archives but also on a wider knowledge of African history. German East Africa, in particular, was the subject of many studies of administration and resistance, economic development and exploitation. The periods of German rule in Cameroon and German South-West Africa (in the case of the latter, focusing on the Herero war) were also the subject of considerable study. Given the background of 1960s and 1970s decolonization, the majority of these writings focused on Africa. By contrast, the German presence in the Pacific islands and in China received very little attention.

---

[3] This refers mainly to the so-called Fischer controversy. For a good overview, see Georg G. Iggers, 'Introduction', in: Iggers (ed.), *The Social History of Politics: Critical Perspectives in West German Historical Writing since 1945*, Leamington Spa (Berg) 1985, 1–48; Stefan Berger, *The Search for Normality: National Identity and Historical Consciousness in Germany since 1800*, Providence (Berghahn) 1997, 56–76.

Much of the research during this period was shaped by a sense of empathy with the colonized and an interest in native 'agency'. Yet most of these authors still implicitly saw the colonial encounter as a one-way street. They assumed that the most important decisions were taken in Germany and that the most important factors affecting German expansion and rule were to be found in Berlin. Thus viewed, colonialism remained a largely European affair. One good example of this tendency is Hans-Ulrich Wehler's influential study *Bismarck und der Imperialismus*. In this work, Wehler argued that colonialism should be read as social imperialism. The objective of the colonial project, he suggested, was not merely to secure access to resources needed for the expansion of the German economy, but rather, 'by means of mastering extremely difficult tasks, to make Bismarck's charismatic system of rule seem even more successful'.[4] Foreign expansion (overseas), according to this interpretation, was used to win over oppositional groups, primarily the working class, to a new national project, thus distracting them from pressing social and material conflicts at home. By pushing internal problems overseas in this way, the glory of empire had become a 'counter-utopia' (*Gegenutopie*), one that facilitated the political integration and social disciplining of the lower classes.

Wehler was thus using colonial policy to discuss the social conflicts and antagonisms of Wilhelmine society; his focus was, ultimately, not on Togo or on Cameroon but on the structural problems of the *Kaiserreich*. This perspective was typical of much of the research of the 1970s. Colonial policy and colonial politics were a sub-division of German or European politics, albeit 'via an African detour'.[5] The famous figure of Bismarck pointing to a map of Europe – 'That is *my* map of Africa' – remained the model for German interpretations of colonialism, and most historians seemed to have internalized this Prussian mental map. Although many of the studies were purportedly located in the colonies, their main concern was often the ongoing

---

[4] Quote from Hans-Ulrich Wehler, *Deutsche Gesellschaftsgeschichte, vol. III: 1849–1914*, Munich (C. H. Beck) 1995, 986. See also Hans-Ulrich Wehler, *Bismarck und der Imperialismus*, Cologne (Kiepenheuer & Witsch) 1969.

[5] Quoted from Klaus Hildebrand, *Deutsche Außenpolitik 1871–1918*, Munich (Oldenbourg) 1989, 16. Unlike Wehler's, however, Hildebrand's perspective is more traditional and focuses not on internal class conflicts, but rather on the European system of foreign policy.

structural deficits of German society. The use of terms such as 'militarism', 'imperialism' and 'class interests' allowed the history of colonialism to be subsumed into the grand narrative of the German *Sonderweg* and Germany's failure to attain modernity.

Between the mid-1970s and the mid-1990s, the popularity of colonialism as an object of inquiry declined again. The anti-imperialist rhetoric of the Left had lost much of its power and colonial history was not high on the academic agenda. The German overseas empire was regarded as only a minor, ephemeral part of German history. The Nazi era and the Holocaust had firmly taken centre-place in national remembrance, and one consequence was that the colonial experience was pushed into the background. And because there had been very little migration from the former colonies to Germany, there were no influential groups within the German population who could demand that attention be paid to the country's colonial past.

It was only in the 1990s that colonial history re-emerged as a major concern, primarily as a result of globalization and an interest in the pre-history of present-day global interlinkages. In academia, this interest coincided with the rise of post-colonial studies as a major trend in the humanities. These approaches emphasized the role of colonial discourses and colonial forms of knowledge, but also the repercussions of the colonial encounter; they pointed out that colonialism had left its mark on Europe and not just on the colonized regions themselves. While research in the 1970s had largely focused on social history, many of the more recent studies have been inspired by trends in cultural history. As such, the interpretation of the colonial era was once again an integral part of the paradigm change in historiography.

Although a wide variety of approaches have been taken, it is possible to identify four major strands in recent scholarly work on colonialism. The first is an investigation into colonial discourses and questions of representation. Taking post-colonial studies and the call for a 'decolonization of the mind' as a starting-point, many recent works have focused on reconstructing the rhetorical and discursive patterns that structured the colonial project. Objects of inquiry have included ethnographic shows and panoramas, colonial patterns in popular culture and literature, and the language used by those involved in politics and policy-making. These analyses of 'imperial fantasies' are intended to show that colonial expansion was not just based on military, political and economic strategies, but must also be seen as the product of a colonialist culture. A second, closely linked strand of research focuses on the importance of colonial knowledge, that is knowledge generated about the colonial territories and populations. The sciences, for example anthropology or medicine, played an important role in the acquisition and conquest of colonial territories. In these studies, knowledge is not merely a precondition for European supremacy but, following Foucault,[6] an inherent part of colonial power structures.

The third strand investigates the construction of subjectivities under the conditions of colonial asymmetry. Colonial discourse was founded on a series of binary oppositions, for example the strict binary opposition between 'whites' and 'blacks'. These differentiations helped to make ideas about 'race', class, nation, gender, and sexuality seem natural. But colonial practice, which was characterized by a multiplicity of hybrid forms, continually put such categories in question and undermined the Manichaean order of colonial discourse. Fourthly, remembrance and memories of the colonial past are at the centre of a number of studies that examine the after-effects of a history of repression and violence and the biographical tensions and traumas involved.

These approaches, all founded in cultural history, have made a major contribution to reconstructing the many-faceted reality of colonial experiences and to liberating it from oversimplified dichotomies. But they have also been subject to criticism, which has come in two main forms. The first criticism is levelled at the post-colonial and post-structuralist perspectives in general, and is not confined to the German empire. Critics have suggested that the fixation on discourse and representation can sometimes lead historians to ignore structural factors and the role of interests. This is indeed a real danger in those works that are particularly strongly influenced by cultural and literary studies. Studies of colonial history must ensure that analyses of cultural history are grounded and contextualized in the political and economic structures of the period.

---

[6] Michel Foucault, *Power/Knowledge: Selected Interviews and Other Writings, 1972–1977*, ed. and trans. Colin Gordon, Brighton (Harvester) 1980.

The second criticism is more specific and suggests that the importance of the colonial era for German history as a whole is overestimated. The period of German rule in Africa and eastern Asia was very short and therefore, these critics claim, the colonial encounter was far less important for the *Kaiserreich* than were Germany's relationships within Europe. There is a kernel of truth in this criticism as well. Undoubtedly, the colonial empire was less important for Germany than for countries with a longer imperial history such as the Netherlands, France or Japan, not to mention Britain. Until 1914, and even afterwards, Europe remained Germany's foremost point of reference. At the same time, however, it is important to recognize that Europe as a whole was increasingly shaped by its colonial links. And it is impossible to understand late-nineteenth-century colonialism without taking into account the more general increase in transnational links. The global integration of the world around 1900 cannot be understood outside of the colonial structures that shaped global politics and the global economy, migration and cultural exchange. To the extent that this process of globalization affected Germany, the colonial world order was thus of crucial importance for Germany too, even beyond the boundaries of its own colonial empire.

WHICH COLONIAL HISTORY?

These new views on colonialism have also helped to redefine the concept of colonialism itself. For a long time, scholarly research defined the term in a very narrow way to mean a power relationship defined in territorial terms (generally 'overseas') that used violence to impose the direct and formal dependence of the occupied region and control over the indigenous population. Within this definition, it was possible to differentiate between three ideal types of colony: dependencies (such as British India or, for Germany, Togo), trading posts or military bases (Hong Kong, or, for Germany, Kiaochow), and settlement colonies (Algeria; for Germany to some extent German South-West Africa).

This definition is still useful in analysing colonial empires. But any attempt to define colonialism in general and universal terms needs to be cognizant of the fact that the colonial reality was extremely varied and diverse. Kiaochow, an urban centre managed by the German

Navy on the basis of bureaucratic rules, had almost nothing in common with the rural regions of eastern Africa where the illness of a single officer could bring administrative activity to a standstill for months on end. The climatic and geographical conditions, the structures of the indigenous societies, the mechanisms of economic exploitation, the ambitions and objectives of the colonizers, and the reactions of local societies often differed to such an extent that it would be more appropriate to talk of colonialisms in the plural.

This also implies that attempting to differentiate cleanly between imperialism (emphasizing informal control without territorial conquest) and colonialism is not always helpful in describing local realities. To take Egypt as an example: until 1914, it was officially ruled by the Khedives and was nominally under Ottoman sovereignty. But although this arrangement seems like the perfect example of informal empire, the British Consul-General, formally an adviser, was the *de facto* ruler of the country and had an array of powers that exceeded those of almost any colonial governor. The dividing-lines between formal territorial control and various forms of indirect rule, economic control and imperialist infiltration were thus frequently in flux and indistinct. The same applies to the end of colonial rule. Colonial relationships did not suddenly cease to exist with the creation of formal independence. There are thus a number of reasons to consider defining colonialism more broadly. This would imply generating an encompassing notion of colonialism, extending beyond the established colonial empire and covering interactions as diverse as German influence on the Ottoman empire, German colonial fantasies and colonial imagination, the *Kaiser's* travels in the Orient, and colonial structures of rule in eastern Europe.

Of course, implicit in such a broadening of the concept is the danger that it might become overextended, of 'imperial overstretch' on the level of terminology. If not limited to state rule over a territorially defined region, the concept may become imprecise and lose much of its analytical purchase. If almost any kind of asymmetrical relationships imply a 'colonial' dimension the term loses its specificity and is almost identical to more general concepts of rule or power. For this reason, it is useful to describe colonial interactions as being characterized by the fact that imperial and colonized societies (1) have different socio-political orders, (2) have different pre-histories and (3) are differentiated, in the minds of the colonizers, by a belief that they are at different stages of development. This minimal definition does not, however, assume territorial control, geographical distance or the legal status of a colony.

By widening the definition of colonialism in this way, and by including the cultural dimensions of colonialism beyond its immediate political import, it becomes possible to describe more clearly the colonial character of the decades leading up to the First World War. The German empire's engagement in global contexts – global politics and the global economy, human migration and cultural exchange – was shaped by colonial structures. The German possessions were of only limited importance in this regard. German trade with Africa, for example, linked the empire not primarily to its colonies but to South Africa, Morocco and Egypt. When German geographers travelled the continent, they did not confine their journeys to German territories, nor did the 'primitive' African art that became a source of inspiration for German artists necessarily originate in Togo or Cameroon. In other words, the history of German colonialism is more than the history of the German 'protectorates', of the *Schutzgebiete*.

The present account is based on an understanding of colonial history that takes the territorial colonial empire as its starting point but also investigates the broader question of colonial relationships outside 'New Germany'. This means that attention is not limited to the thirty-year era of formal German colonialism but extends both to pre-colonial fantasies and projects, and to later memories of the colonial experience. In spatial terms, this account focuses initially on Germany's official colonial holdings, but it then moves further afield to investigate Germany's links to other colonies and to describe the extent to which late-nineteenth-century colonialism was a pan-European project. In addition, it will become clear that colonial relationships had effects not only outside Europe, but also within it, and that they shaped and transformed, at least in part, German society too. Finally, particular emphasis is placed on investigating the extent to which Germany's embeddedness in the process of globalization before the First World War was based on colonial structures.

CHAPTER 2

Colonialism before the colonial empire

PRE-HISTORIES

Any retelling of German colonial history usually begins with an introduction that traces the history of overseas possessions back as far as the
early modern era. Such accounts assume that demonstrating that there
was already a tradition of German expansion can help to explain the
development of colonialism from the 1880s onward, whether in terms
of continuities of ideas or continuities in the social groups involved.
More recently, Susanne Zantop has suggested a similar link on the level
of cultural and discursive history. In an examination of the eighteenth-
and early-nineteenth-century German literature on Latin America –
before the expansion of the German empire, in other words – she
attempts to identify 'unconsciously expressed colonial fantasies' which
she sees as the root of the desire for expansion. For Zantop, these literary
representations acted almost like a set of instructions for the colonial
movement of the 1880s: 'Imaginary colonialism anticipated actual
imperialism, words, actions. In the end', she summarizes, not without
exaggeration, 'reality just caught up with the imagination'.[1]

In fact, there was a history of German possessions in foreign
territories, and there were many more such plans and projects, mostly
of ephemeral character. They included the colonial experiments in
Venezuela, initiated by the Welser, an important family of merchants
and bankers in Augsburg, between 1528 and 1556. Large land concessions granted by the Spanish emperor Charles V enabled the Welser to
participate in the exploitation of raw materials (the main objective was

---

[1] Susanne Zantop, *Colonial Fantasies: Conquest, Family, and Nation in Precolonial Germany,
1770–1870*, Durham (Duke University Press) 1997, 9.

gold), slavery, and long-distance trade of luxury goods characteristic of colonialism in the sixteenth century. Another example of the mercantilist variety of colonialism was the foundation of 'Gross Friedrichsburg' on the west African coast (in present-day Ghana) by the Great Elector in 1683. As the state of Brandenburg was also able to secure possession of St Thomas, one of the Antilles islands, it succeeded in participating in the triangular trade between Europe, Africa, and the Americas. But the African holdings, which were gradually extended, were sold to the Dutch in 1717 as Brandenburg was not equipped to compete with the maritime powers of the day and thus not able to safeguard its possessions. For most of the seventeenth and eighteenth centuries, the German states did not participate in colonial expansion. This was a peculiarity among the European countries and a result not least of the relatively minor role the various German states played in European power politics.

Only from the 1840s was there again an increased interest in obtaining settlement colonies, sustained by a liberal bourgeoisie that dreamed of national glory. Various schemes aiming at different locations were discussed in the public sphere and in the liberal press. The best-known such project was the 'Texas Society', *Texasverein*, an association made up of aristocratic army officers who sent more than 7,000 emigrants to Texas, hoping to buy enough land there to create a German community, and possibly even an independent territory. The poorly organized initiative ended in massive failure, as more than half of the migrants died, and was abandoned after the annexation of Texas into the United States in 1845. The project – along with many others that frequently did not proceed beyond the planning stage – must be understood in the context of German overseas migration and the fear of a loss of 'national energy' entertained by a patriotic bourgeoisie, and was spawned by the economic interests of the large shipping companies and merchant houses.

It is important to recognize, however, that the active phase of German colonialism, from 1880 onwards, did not develop, in linear fashion, out of such episodes. This is not just because the majority of these visions and plans were never realized. What is more important is that they had developed in an entirely different global political context. One crucial factor that changed the situation was German unification in 1871, which generated a national desire to catch up with other countries in many areas, including colonial policy. Another was that the infrastructural revolution that made modern imperialism possible had not yet taken place, nor had industrialization given the European powers the capabilities to extend their reach in unprecedented ways. German colonialism as it developed after 1880 was an integral part of late-nineteenth-century high imperialism. It was linked to global economic competition and the hunt for raw materials and new markets for the industrializing countries, to global political conflicts between the European powers, and to the ideologies of evolutionism and Social Darwinism, which were increasingly linked to discourses of racial differences. This global framework is much more important for any attempt to explain colonial expansion than continuities with a German pre-history.

Thus, the real importance of these pre-colonial experiments lay elsewhere, and it can be assessed mainly on three levels. Firstly, they were retrospectively adopted by the colonial movement during the 1880s and were pronounced to be the pre-history of contemporary expansionist plans. The main vector of continuity, in other words, pointed back into the past. Through the eyes of colonial enthusiasts in the Bismarck era a few isolated episodes could become a genealogy that would legitimize their own claims. These proponents of colonialism looked back not only at the Welsers and the Texas Society, but also at Alexander von Humboldt, whose 'peaceful conquest' of Latin America was portrayed as a specifically German colonial tradition and described as a contrast to the violent conquests initiated by Columbus.

NATION AND COLONIALISM

The second way in which these projects and visions were important was that they were one of the ways in which the German nation was imagined during the nineteenth century. Because the German-speaking region was broken up into small states for most of the century, and the national movement experienced a series of disappointments and setbacks, the nation's (fictitious) colonial empire served as a screen onto which ideas about national unity and national greatness could be projected. 'We will sail in ships across the sea and here and there set up a new Germany', in the words of Richard Wagner in 1848; 'we will do better than the Spanish, for whom the New World became a cleric-ridden slaughterhouse, and differently from the English, for whom it became a treasure-trove. We will do it in a wonderful, German way.'[2] Susanne Zantop has demonstrated how a vision of the nation was created at the colonial periphery, a vision in which the 'civilizing mission', racial stereotypes, sexuality and gender roles interacted in a very specific way. These links show that even in the early nineteenth century the politically imagined nation had to be located in a context that reached beyond Germany's antagonism to France as the 'Fatherland of the Enemies' and even beyond Europe.[3]

One of the most important mid-nineteenth-century proponents of colonialism in Germany was the economist Friedrich List. 'The crowning success of manufacturing industry', he wrote, 'of internal and external trade, of an active coasting trade, of distant navigation, and great maritime fisheries – in a word, of a respectable naval power, lies in the possession of colonies'.[4]

The increasingly nationalist tone of colonial projects can be well observed in the semantic shift in the way migration was understood – migration that was often not clearly distinguishable from formal colonization. During the early years of mass German 'overseas' migration, which, by mid-century, had increased to 250,000 people per year, those leaving were described as 'emigrants'. But in the mid nineteenth century the terminology began to change. Instead, emigrants and émigrés were usually described as 'overseas Germans' (*Auslandsdeutsche*). This term was linked to the media and political debate about a 'Greater Germany' or 'Lesser Germany' as the solution to the German question. The idea of 'overseas Germans' acted as a kind of *Ersatz* national community, outside the physical boundaries of the German states, through which Germans could 'invent' themselves as a nation. This imagined nation was widely dispersed and by no means a single community, but nevertheless it formed part of an integrated cultural imagination.

---

[2] Quoted from Horst Gründer (ed.), '. . . *da und dort ein junges Deutschland gründen': Rassismus, Kolonien und kolonialer Gedanke vom 16. bis zum 20. Jahrhundert*, Munich (DTV) 1999, 51.

[3] Zantop, *Colonial Fantasies*. The term 'Fatherland of the Enemies' is from Michael Jeismann, *Das Vaterland der Feinde: Studien zum nationalen Feindbegriff und Selbstverständnis in Deutschland und Frankreich 1792–1918*, Stuttgart (Klett-Cotta) 1992.

[4] Friedrick [sic] List, *National System of Political Economy*, trans. G. A. Matile, Philadelphia (J. B. Lippincott) 1856, 351.

The concept of 'overseas Germans' expressed social and cultural fears that had been triggered by increasing human mobility and by the global expansion of European power. Since membership of the German nation was closely linked to the idea of being rooted in German soil, emigrants would necessarily risk losing their national identity. The term 'emigrant' thus emphasized the centrifugal character of migration and assumed that those involved were leaving the Fatherland for good; the emergence of the term 'overseas Germans' marked a major semantic shift. The new terminology emphasized the timelessness, the permanency, of membership of the German nation, now understood in cultural and linguistic terms. The experience of a caesura and of a deep chasm between the homeland and abroad was connected discursively with the belief that a national identity understood in terms of the cultural and, increasingly, the *völkisch* – that is, stressing the notion of an organic German ethnic community – could not be cast aside; it, at least, would endure.[5]

ORIENTALISM

Thirdly, the link between pre-colonial projects and visions, and the nation-state, has been discussed for Germany in another context. In his famous book of 1978, Edward Said explicitly exempted German orientalism from the criticism he was making of French and English culture and societies. For Said, German engagement with the Orient during the first half of the nineteenth century – in literature, painting, linguistics and scholarly studies – was *not* part of a knowledge/power complex in which academic study and colonial rule correlated and were merged in a shared discourse. This was because no German nation-state yet existed during that period, and thus there could have been no national colonial project. '[A]t no time in German scholarship during the first two-thirds of the nineteenth century could a close partnership have developed between Orientalists and a ... *national* interest in the Orient.'[6]

---

[5] See Bradley D. Naranch, 'Inventing the *Auslandsdeutsche*. Emigration, Colonial Fantasy, and German National Identity 1848–71', in: Eric Ames, Marcia Klotz, and Lora Wildenthal (eds.), *Germany's Colonial Pasts*, Lincoln (University of Nebraska Press) 2005, 21–40.

[6] Edward W. Said, *Orientalism*, New York (Pantheon Books) 1978, 19; original emphasis.

Said's statement is based on an important observation: German orientalist scholarship, which did not focus on the Middle East but mainly on India, was influenced by the requirements of colonial power to a much lesser extent than its counterparts in England and France, then the great colonial powers. Studying Indian languages and cultures at Fort William College in Calcutta could lead directly to a career as a civil servant in the British Empire; but all such a student could hope for in Germany was a lecturing post. But Said's statement 'the German Orient was almost exclusively a scholarly, or at least a classical, Orient'[7] was an over-simplification. There were fantasies of seizing power and of territorial control in Germany too.

And it is important to note that in the German case, the thrust of Orientalist projections was not only external. The American anthropologist Sheldon Pollock has argued, using the discipline of Indology as an example, that Orientalism (in Said's sense) in Germany was focused less on India than on groups within Germany. The antithesis between the 'Indo-Germanic' and 'Semitic' people that was supported by German oriental studies allowed a cultural self-view to emerge, he argues, that was based on shared racial and linguistic characteristics and seemed to have older roots than German links with Latin and Christian cultures. The victory of the concept of the 'Indo-Germanic' and the linked mythos of the 'Aryans' was, Pollock believes, a reaction to the increasing political, social, and economic emancipation of Jews. The 'Orientalist' gaze towards India was thus linked in a number of complex ways with anti-Semitism and with processes of social and cultural exclusion within Germany. Pollock's polemic against the history of the discipline even leads him to suggest that German Indology contributed, during the Third *Reich*, to legitimizing genocide.[8]

---

[7] Ibid., 19.

[8] Sheldon Pollock, 'Deep Orientalism? Notes on Sanskrit and Power Beyond the Raj', in: Carol A. Breckenridge and Peter van der Veer (eds.), *Orientalism and the Postcolonial Predicament: Perspectives on South Asia*, Philadelphia (University of Pennsylvania Press) 1993, 76–133. A critique of Pollock from a traditional orientalist perspective is Reinhold Grünendahl, 'Von der Indologie zum Völkermord: Die Kontinuitätskonstrukte Sheldon Pollocks und seiner Epigonen im Lichte seiner Beweisführung', in: Ute Hüsken, Petra Kieffer-Pülz, and Anne Peters (eds.), *Jaina-Itihāsa-Ratna. Festschrift für Gustav Roth zum 90. Geburtstag*, Marburg (Indica-et-Tibetica-Verlag) 2006, 209–36.

CHAPTER 3

Pressure groups, motivations, attitudes

Between 1884 and 1899, the German empire acquired colonies in Africa, in north-eastern China and in the Pacific. By the end of the process it was the fourth-largest European empire. For a long time such a development had seemed very unlikely. Chancellor Bismarck, in particular, had declared his opposition to the acquisition of colonies on many occasions, because he felt they involved immeasurable risks for both Germany's foreign policy and its finances. 'For as long as I remain Chancellor', he declared as late as 1881, 'we will not become involved in colonialism'.[1] (see Illustration 3.) Given this background, the question of most interest to historians was for many years: why did Bismarck change his mind in 1884? Explanations offered include psychological interpretations of the desire of the 'Iron Chancellor' for expansion, responses to the power of public pressure, and a desire to create a conflict with England with the intention of frustrating the policies that Friedrich III, next in line to the imperial throne, and believed to be a liberal Anglophile, was expected to pursue. The most prevalent view taken, however, was that Bismarck was attempting to bring his country closer to France; he hoped that shared colonial interests in expanding and preventing English supremacy would prevent France from plotting revenge against Germany. By contrast, the theory of 'social imperialism' proposed by historians like Hans-Ulrich Wehler denied the primacy of foreign policy and focused on economic policy and, most importantly, on the goal of redirecting domestic social tensions to the colonies.

---

[1] Quoted from Heinrich von Poschinger (ed.), *Fürst Bismarck und die Parlamentarier, vol. III: 1879–1890*, Breslau (Trewendt) 1896, 54.

Illustration 3 In Bismarck's mental map, the colonies were to a large extent a lever that helped him manoeuvre foreign policy conflicts between the European powers. This cartoon in the satirical magazine *Kladderadatsch* in July 1884 is entitled: 'The Pacific is the Mediterranean of the future.' It shows Bismarck comfortably studying a book on social reforms while the other powers compete for possessions in Asia. 'That is fine with me', Bismarck is reported as saying, 'as long as the others are busy down there, one can finally have some peace up here'.

However, Bismarck's supposed change of heart was not really a radical change in direction at all. His ideal overseas policy was one based on private commercial initiatives, which would be supported by the state only in the form of coaling stations and trade bases, and only where Germany's foreign policy interests allowed. His model was the British East India Company rather than French settlement colonies such as Algeria. For this reason, he referred explicitly to 'protectorates' (*Schutzgebiete*) and avoided using the term 'colony', which implied territorial claims and state involvement. The support provided to private colonial groups in 1884 that marked the start of German colonial expansion was well within Bismarck's traditional limits.

PRESSURE GROUPS AND AGENTS

But even when we move away from the idea that history is made by 'great men' and look at more general drivers of social change, we can see that the start of formal German power in Africa was less an abrupt change than part of a continuity. A broad coalition of actors and institutions called for overseas expansion, for a variety of motives. An important influence was exerted by the geographical societies that had been contributing, since the mid nineteenth century, to the scientific 'discovery' of the continent, and also to emigration projects. Particularly in the case of Africa, they helped finance exploration into uncharted territories. Among them were the likes of Heinrich Barth (1821–65), who reached Timbuktu and Cameroon and learned several African languages; Gerhard Rohlfs (1831–96), the first European to cross Africa from north to south (see Illustration 4); and Gustav Nachtigal (1834–85), a doctor in the personal service of the Bey of Tunis, whose famous five-year travels through the central Sahara and the Sudan earned him the position of president of the Geographical Society in Berlin. In specialized journals such as *Globus* and *Petermanns Geographische Mitteilungen*, as well as in the broader bourgeois press, these trips were represented and celebrated as German national accomplishments, even though they were possible only within the transnational context of scientific expeditions, mostly under British leadership, and through the help and agency of African mediators.

A second group that helped fire the colonial imagination were the missionaries. In their case, too, transnational activities were celebrated in national terms; Catholic missionaries in particular were involved in French and Belgian societies as Catholic mission societies did not exist in Germany and furthermore had been prohibited by the

Illustration 4 Before Gerhard Rohlfs was employed by the Bremen Senate and the Prussian government in the late 1860s, he had pursued a transnational career. Rohlfs had served in the French Foreign Legion, as court surgeon to the Grand Sherif of Morocco, and had been an adventurous traveller across the Sahara, frequently trying to pass himself off as a converted Muslim. In spite of his Muslim attire, his travel journals show him to harbour critical views and even hatred towards Muslims, whom he saw enslaving the African population. Instead, he favoured Europe's colonial expansion to facilitate Christian conversion among the Africans. His travel writings, serialized in *Petermanns Geographische Mitteilungen*, made a deep impression on the German public. This image shows him together with Gustav Nachtigal on the eve of their expedition to the central African kingdom of Bornu in 1870.

anti-Catholic legislation of the *Kulturkampf* (culture wars) since the early 1870s. The missionary project had a huge impact on metropolitan society as it popularized the colonial idea among social milieux that remained at a distance from expansionist projects. In addition, staunch defenders of the colonizing project such as the pamphleteer Friedrich Fabri derived their knowledge of overseas territories to a great degree from missionary publications. The countless missionary letters and journals acquainted broad segments of the population with foreign lands, customs and religions, and thus helped make the civilizing mission, the racial order, and the 'white man's burden' appear natural.

A third group that connected the overseas ambitions of the early nineteenth century with the later colonial project of the *Kaiserreich* were the transnational merchant networks. The Hanseatic merchant families, in particular, had established extensive trade links across the globe long before German unification. In 1866, Hamburg alone maintained a global network of 279 consular outposts around the world, particularly in Latin America, where Hamburg merchants had seized the opportunity presented by the end of European imperial rule in the 1820s to negotiate commercial treaties with the newly formed independent states. Until recently, the Hanseatic merchants have been characterized as free-trade cosmopolitans and thus opposed to the nationalist, imperialist drive characteristic of the 1880s. But in various ways, these networks did prepare the ground for later colonial interventions. They did this both by establishing trade links and conquering markets, and also by disseminating information, images, and ideas about foreign lands throughout Germany.[2]

From the 1870s onward, after the founding of the German *Kaiserreich*, popular pressure accelerated. National unification sparked high hopes in the global reach of German language, culture, and political influence, and in the establishment of world markets for the new nation. Under these conditions, a colonial movement grew up in Germany that was small in numerical terms but relatively influential. Its members were mainly educated, liberal (and nationalist) members of the bourgeoisie, but it was also supported by some of the nobility, missionaries and merchants. Several of them briefly became well-known public figures. They included men as diverse as the above-mentioned pamphleteer Friedrich Fabri, a former missionary and an adviser to Bismarck, who set the political agenda with his widely read 1879 text entitled *Does Germany Need Colonies?*, Adolph Woermann, a Hamburg-based merchant and National Liberal member of the *Reichstag*, whose arguments focused on commercial benefits and whose company dominated trade in western Africa, and Carl Peters, a brutal pioneer of colonial expansion (see Illustration 5). Quantitatively speaking, this organized colonial movement remained

---

[2] For colonial activities before formal colonialism, see Bradley D. Naranch, *Beyond the Fatherland: Colonial Visions, Overseas Expansion, & German Nationalism, 1848–1885*, Ph. D. diss., Johns Hopkins University 2006.

Illustration 5 Carl Peters (1856–1918), here depicted on a colonial postcard, was one of the
icons of the colonial movement. Peters held a Ph.D. in history, was a passionate admirer of
the British empire and saw himself as the German Cecil Rhodes. Officially in the service of
the private, but state-backed 'Society for German Colonization', Peters claimed large
territories in East Africa. 'With this coup I will not only secure a grand future for
myself', he confided to his mother, 'but will also fulfil a grand patriotic deed and carve
my name once and for all into German history'. Peters had to leave Africa as a result of the
murder of two Africans in a domestic dispute but was soon rehabilitated and continued
to be a symbol of Germany's colonial aspirations well into the twentieth century. The
Nazis saw Peters as an example of the master race they envisioned, and he was the subject
of a major propaganda film in 1941 (in which his role was played by the famous actor
Hans Albers).

a minority activity. The German Colonial Society never achieved a
membership of more than 43,000 – a tiny number in comparison to
the mass phenomenon that were the *Kriegervereine* – more than 29,000
local patriotic associations (with a total of 2.8 million members)
that kept alive the memory of the wars of unification – and the
Flottenverein (Navy League), highly influential through its media
campaigns. But the colonial enthusiasts' arguments resonated widely,

not least because a number of quite different interests and arguments came together, allowing coalitions to be formed across political and social boundaries.

' FACTORS AND MOTIVATIONS

In addition to foreign-policy considerations, which were important mainly to those at the upper echelons of political decision-making, we can identify four main arguments for colonial expansion. In varying intensity and composition, they are characteristic of all European colonialisms of the time. Firstly, trade interests: colonies would, it was believed, provide resources while simultaneously acting as markets for products manufactured in Germany. In addition to the partisan interests of merchants and industrialists, it was hoped that colonies would help to balance out regularly recurring crises of over-production, and allow economic cycles to be better managed. One such crisis during the recessionary phase of 1882–6 had considerably dampened economic growth in Germany and lent further credence to the call for colonies as a remedy.

The second major argument for the acquisition of colonies had to do with human mobility. A third major wave of German emigration (following those of 1846–7 and 1864–73) had begun in 1880, with total emigrants numbering over two million. Consequently, there was considerable interest in finding suitable locations for new German settlements abroad. The main motivation was to prevent those interested in emigrating from leaving for the United States, by inducing them to settle in a colonial 'New Germany' – so that Germans would remain Germans, albeit overseas, and not deteriorate into what was called 'fertilizer of the peoples' (*Völkerdünger*) in contemporary parlance. The result was, mainly on the nationalist fringe, a discourse of Germanness (*Deutschtum*) and a call for a politics of Germanification in places of German settlement. The fear of rapid assimilation in the North American 'melting pot', where German migration was primarily headed, eventually led to attempts to redirect the flow of German emigrants elsewhere, in particular to Africa, but also to Latin America, the Levant, and Australia. Here, the reasoning went, Germans did not dissolve into the majority population, but were able to retain and even foster their German national characteristics. As the historian

Heinrich von Treitschke pronounced in 1884, '[f]or a people who suffer from constant overproduction and each year send some 200,000 of their children overseas, colonization has become a question of survival'.[3]

The third important motivation was to overcome domestic tensions and to use colonies as a valve for the release of conflicts and antagonisms. Historians have termed this the strategy of social imperialism: it meant declaring colonial expansion to be a task for the nation as a whole, thus pushing material needs and social tensions into the background. It was precisely this alleviating effect that Bismarck had in mind when he saw the primary 'opportunist side' of his imperialism as 'the provision of a new objective for the Germans, one capable of filling them with enthusiasm after the popularity of the government had begun to wane'; he aimed 'to steer the Germans towards new paths' abroad, away from the numerous problems in the domestic sphere.[4]

In some cases, however, this export of potential conflict was actually taken very literally, and then meant extradition of the individuals involved. Earlier colonial propaganda material, in particular, often included suggestions about how the revolutionary potential of social democracy could be exported by setting up penal colonies. Ernst von Weber, the owner of large landholdings in Saxony, even demanded 'broad drainage channels' for the 'proletarian masses that every year grow more numerous and more dangerous' as otherwise Germany would be 'moving in enormous steps towards a revolution'.[5] Felix Friedrich Bruck, a professor of law at the University of Breslau, published a number of writings from the 1890s onward demanding the deportation of the 'work-shy' and of 'vagabonds' to German South-West Africa. These plans never materialized, but their grip on the imagination persisted: this period also saw the first suggestions

[3] Heinrich von Treitschke, 'Die ersten Versuche deutscher Kolonialpolitik', in: Karl Martin Schiller (ed.), *Aufsätze, Reden und Briefe*, Meersburg (Hendel) 1929, 665–76, quote on p. 670.
[4] Quotes from Hans-Ulrich Wehler, 'Bismarck's Imperialism 1862–1890', *Past & Present* 48 (1970), 119–55, quote on p. 142.
[5] Ernst von Weber, *Die Erweiterung des deutschen Wirtschaftsgebietes und die Grundlegung zu überseeischen deutschen Staaten*, Leipzig (Twietmeyer) 1879, 50–1.

that Jews should be forced to emigrate, ideas that were to live on to become the Nazis' 'Madagascar Plan'.

Fourthly and finally, colonization was legitimized in cultural terms and was ideologically underpinned by the idea that Germany had a 'civilizing mission'. The 'elevation' (*Hebung*) of the colonized was a project that brought together widely different groups and won people over to the colonial cause who would otherwise have been opposed to it. This 'improvement' was expressed, according to the preferences of those involved, in terms of educating, Christianizing, or 'educating to work'. Although the belief in a particular 'mission' for the German empire played a role, in contrast to the movements in England and France, this belief in a civilizing mission was shared by all the colonizing countries, fed by a unique mixture of the Enlightenment promise of emancipation and the Social Darwinist theory of hierarchies.

Overall, it must be emphasized that the colonial expansion of the German *Reich* was an integral part of the phase of European (and soon, American and Japanese) high imperialism. Internal factors and domestic interests alone, therefore, cannot adequately explain it. German colonialism participated in the territorial reorganization of the world from about 1880 onwards, of which the 'scramble for Africa' and financial imperialism in eastern Asia after the turn of the century were important chapters. The increase in global economic competition, the development of competing political and economic blocs, the debates about global empires and the global integration of markets in goods and in labour were all part of the context of turn-of-the-century colonialism, as were beliefs about evolution and 'racial' differences. Any viewpoint that restricts itself to analysing the forces in the respective imperial metropoles runs the risk of ignoring these global contexts.

But empires were not only the effect of global structures; they were also made locally. Beyond the motivations and ambitions within Germany, and beyond the level of geopolitics, it is important to recognize the impact of local circumstances in the individual colonies on the emerging patterns of conquest and rule. Two aspects, in particular, are worth mentioning here. The first is a phenomenon that historians have labelled 'sub-imperialism': particularly in the early years, German colonial pioneers and activists, on their own initiative and indeed frequently against the will of the German government, made forays deep into territories not yet claimed by European powers. One example is the young explorer and trader Eugen Zintgraff, who in 1891 recruited several thousand local troops and invaded deep into the hinterland of Cameroon, subdued the local population and declared it to be under German rule. These solo efforts by 'men on the ground' played an important role in the dynamics of the colonial expansion.

Secondly, territorial conquest was always dependent on the activities of locals. In the long run, to be sure, the material superiority of German troops could not be ignored. But in the early stages of the colonial endeavour, this was not yet an important factor. German colonizers therefore depended on the support, help, and collaboration of local mediators. Moreover, the first contracts made by Germans in the African coastal regions were with local power-holders who were pursuing their own interests and attempting to increase their influence over their competitors in the region. And even later on, indigenous potentates made use of the massive changes wrought by colonialism to achieve their own aims, even within the regions that were officially claimed by the German empire. Again, Cameroon provides a good example: the Islamic sultanate of the Fulbe in the northern hinterland, where the power of German rule was largely symbolic, strategically used the sparse German military presence against local opponents to further its own imperialistic projects.

ATTITUDES WITHIN GERMANY TOWARDS GERMAN COLONIALISM

At no point was there ever one uniform view within Germany of the country's colonial policies. Colonization was both welcomed and criticized by different social milieux and political groups. It is fair to say that the majority of the population was fascinated by the promises of colonialism and supported the policy of expansion. The motives to do so, however, and the concerns and hopes connected with the colonial project varied, as different social milieux were affected by these developments in very different ways. It is important to take these different actors and interests into account; engagement with the colonial world was always of a contested nature.

The educated classes – university professors and school teachers, journalists and the free professions – were particularly quick to respond to the colonial challenges. While the *Bildungsbürgertum* was a minority, its influence in shaping the appropriation of the world went well beyond the confines of its constituency. The commitment to secure access to world markets also enlisted the support of industrialists and entrepreneurs. The large merchant houses and trading companies benefited from Germany's presence overseas, even if many of them would have preferred informal ties to territorial conquest. Contrary to the nationalist overtones with which the educated classes voiced their colonial ambitions, they were not interested in imperialist rivalries among the powers. German companies with branches in British Hong Kong such as Siemssen and Melchers, for example, avoided the local branch of the *Deutsche Bank* established in the 1870s and remained with British banks instead. The churches' investment in colonialism was primarily through the missionary project. They helped to transmit the desire for tangible and spiritual acquisitions in exotic regions to social classes that might otherwise not have found it in their interest to support them.

Presumably least affected by intensifying global exchange were the petty bourgeoisie and the lowest social strata. The working class, however, increasingly felt the dependency upon global demand structures, and within the trade unions there were highly emotional debates about the internationalization of the labour market. The thorny issue of immigration and the conflict between proletarian internationalism and the need to represent the interests of workers at home was hotly debated in Germany and at international socialist congresses. At the 1904 Socialist Congress in Amsterdam, a motion that immigration by 'workers of backward races (such as Chinese, Negroes, etc.)' should be restricted as they would 'prevent the progress and the possible realization of socialism' triggered a conflict between representatives of the countries from which emigrants were originating (such as Italy, Hungary, Poland, and Japan) and those to which they were headed (North and Latin America, Australia, and South Africa). The positions taken by German representatives were ambivalent, as the delegates had to balance their reservations about the possible influx of Chinese workers with their duty to represent Polish seasonal workers in Prussia. The effects of the colonial world order and the new flows of labour it facilitated thus posed a challenge to internationalist ideology.[6]

In public debate, the generally positive view of the colonial project was put to the test primarily on the occasion of warfare and colonial scandals. Two of the most infamous scandals involved Carl Peters and Heinrich Leist. Leist (1859–95), vice-governor of Cameroon in 1893, ordered African women who resisted harsh working conditions to be flogged in front of their husbands. The judicial case that eventually stripped him from office was accompanied by broad media attention. Carl Peters (1856–1918) was one of the most influential activists of the colonial movement and a ruthless pioneer who helped establish German rule in East Africa. In 1897, he was dismissed from public office after shooting his African concubine and her lover (only to be pardoned by Emperor Wilhelm II in 1905). The case was turned, by critics of German colonial policy, into a symbol of the brutality of colonial exploitation.

Beyond individual scandals, it was above all the violence of colonial warfare that attracted criticism in the public sphere. On the occasion of the Boxer war in China (1900), Social Democrat papers such as *Vorwärts* collected and published the so-called *Hunnenbriefe* (letters from the Huns), soldiers' letters home with first-hand accounts of atrocities committed by German soldiers in China. August Bebel quoted freely from these letters in a famous speech in the *Reichstag*. They were also picked up broadly in the general press, and indignation at the acts of cruelty committed by Europeans was mixed with a rhetoric of Germany's moral obligation to civilize the 'backward' and also its duty to punish the 'barbaric'. The most vehement debates took place over the issue of the colonial war in German South-West Africa. Journals such as the satirical weekly *Simplicissimus* carried scathing criticisms of the campaign. Subsequently, the Social Democrats (SPD) and the Centre Party refused to support a supplementary budget for colonial policy. This led to the dissolution of the *Reichstag* in 1906.

This brings us to the conflicting attitudes among the political parties, none of which gave colonial expansion their full and unequivocal support; at the same time, all of them operated within the

---

[6] Quotes from Johannes Nichtweiß, *Die ausländischen Saisonarbeiter in der Landwirtschaft der östlichen und mittleren Gebiete des Deutschen Reiches: Ein Beitrag zur Geschichte der preußisch-deutschen Politik von 1890 bis 1914*, Berlin (Rütten & Loening) 1959, 154–74.

framework of a larger colonialist logic. Strong backing came primarily from the National Liberals (*Nationalliberale*), the 'spearhead of imperialist agitation', dominated by the Protestant educated classes and bourgeoisie.[7] Some of its most influential politicians such as Rudolf von Bennigsen and Johannes von Miquel occupied leading positions in the colonial movement. But the party also included a strong faction that insisted on *laissez-faire* trade and was averse to territorial possessions. The two conservative parties, the German Conservative Party (*Deutsch-Konservative Partei*) and the Free Conservatives (*Freikonservative Partei*), were rather sceptical, even though the latter – Bismarck's political base – supported expansion when the Chancellor embraced it from 1884 onwards.

The attitudes of the other political parties were highly ambivalent. On a number of occasions, for example, members of the Catholic Centre Party (*Zentrumspartei*) expressed criticism of colonial adventurers and capitalist exploitation. But they, too, supported the idea of the missionary project and believed in Europeans' 'Christian duty' to ensure the gradual cultural 'elevation of the natives'. For that reason, the Centre Party generally supported the government's colonial policy – not least in the hope that this support would help alleviate the marginal position of Catholics in the wake of the *Kulturkampf.* These arguments for a 'Christian colonialism' also allowed groups who initially would not have supported it to identify with imperialist policy.

Left Liberals and the Social Democrats criticized the colonial project in much stronger terms (see Illustration 6). For the small Left Liberal Party (*Linksliberale Partei*), the acquisition of foreign territory stood in contradiction to the doctrine of free trade. 'We want trade and not dominion', Ludwig Bamberger stated to his liberal counterparts in England.[8] But the idea of the cultural mission gradually led its members to support colonial measures. Like the Centre Party, the SPD was mainly concerned with exposing the

---

[7] Quote by the National Liberal Gustav von Stresemann in 1908, cited in Wolfgang Mommsen, *Imperialismus: Seine geistigen, politischen und wirtschaftlichen Grundlagen*, Hamburg (Hoffmann und Campe) 1977, 137.

[8] Bamberger in the *Reichstag* in 1884, cited in Michael Schubert, *Der Schwarze Fremde: Das Bild des Schwarzafrikaners in der parlamentarischen und publizistischen Kolonialdiskussion von den 1870er bis in die 1930er Jahre*, Stuttgart (Steiner) 2003, 165.

Illustration 6 Critical perspectives on the excesses of colonial rule were not infrequent in the liberal and Social Democratic press. This image appeared in May 1904 in the satirical journal *Simplicissimus*. Entitled 'Modern apostles', it scathingly attacks the violence and murder committed in the name of conversion to Christianity and the civilizing mission. The image was also a comment on the Herero war that had begun in January 1904. Critical positions such as this did not fundamentally challenge the colonial project as such, but they offered important dissenting voices that sometimes had immediate consequences for colonial politics.

use of repression and violence in the colonies and with criticizing exploitation that benefited only the capitalist class. In addition, the SPD expressed a more fundamental criticism, going beyond individual excesses and atrocities. The Social Democrat Wilhelm Liebknecht, father of the famous socialist Karl Liebknecht, denigrated colonialism as 'the export of the social question', and in 1889, August Bebel stated that 'the substance of all policies of colonization is to exploit a foreign population to the highest degree'.[9] On a number of individual issues, for example after the brutal suppression of the Chinese 'Boxer war' in 1900, the criticism expressed in the *Reichstag* and the press could hardly have been more vehement. Yet there was no question of even the SPD actually opposing colonization as such. Especially amongst the reform-oriented section of the party, which became increasingly influential from the turn of the century onward, members of the SPD criticized the methods of colonization employed but not the project itself. In 1906, August Bebel addressed the *Reichstag* as follows:

Gentlemen, the fact that a policy of colonialism is pursued is, in itself, not a crime. In certain circumstances, being engaged in colonial policy can be a cultural act . . . If the representatives of cultured and civilized peoples . . . come to foreign peoples as liberators, . . . as helpers in their hour of need, to bring to them the achievements of culture and civilization, to educate them to become civilized individuals, and if this is done with this honourable purpose and in the proper way, then we Social Democrats will be the first to support such a form of colonization as a great cultural mission.[10]

The Social Democrats were arguing for a different type of colonialism, not for alternatives to colonialism.

---

[9] Both quotes from Horst Gründer, *Geschichte der deutschen Kolonien*, Paderborn (Schöningh) 2000 (4th edition), 74.

[10] Quoted from Henning Melber, '"... dass die Kultur der Neger gehoben werde!" – Kolonialdebatten im deutschen Reichstag', in: Ulrich van der Heyden and Joachim Zeller (eds.), *Kolonialmetropole Berlin: Eine Spurensuche*, Berlin (Berlin Edition) 2002, 67–72, quote on p. 68.

CHAPTER 4

The German colonial empire

Between 1884 and 1919, Germany amassed one of the largest colonial empires of the epoch. Most territories were ceded during the first months of the First World War, and Germany was officially dispossessed of her colonies at the Paris Peace Conference in 1919, when her former territories were handed over to the mandate powers. In geographical terms, the German colonial empire was focused on Africa, where it acquired its first territories in 1884 and 1885. Germany's expansion was an integral part of the larger 'scramble for Africa' that substituted the 'informal imperialism' of control through military influence and economic dominance by that of direct rule. It was initiated with France's move into Tunisia in 1881 and with the British take-over in Egypt in 1882, and formalized in 1884 with the 'Congo Conference', called by Bismarck and held in Berlin to settle competing claims over the Congo and West Africa. At the conference, in the absence of representatives from Africa, the European powers (including the Ottoman empire) laid down rules for the continent such as free access to the Congo and Niger rivers and the freedom of missionary activity in all of Africa. The most momentous of the provisions was the definition of colonial territories by the criterion of 'effective occupation', which triggered a rush to take possession of lands not yet annexed by European powers.

The smaller areas in north-eastern China and in the Pacific were added only in 1897 and 1899. German expansion into east and south-east Asia, too, was an element in a larger European (and Japanese) contest over commercial privileges, strategic military bases, and spheres of influence in the region. Also in the following years, colonial lobbyists continued to disseminate plans, and more often fantasies, to further enlarge the colonial empire. Among the places preferred

36

by colonial lobbyists were Morocco (which forced Germany into deep foreign policy crises in 1905 and 1911), the Belgian Congo (as an ingredient in plans to create a German Central Africa), the Portuguese possessions (parts of Angola and Mozambique), Brazil, Chile, and the Middle East. But these projects added more to the diplomatic difficulties of the *Kaiserreich* than to its empire. With the annexation of Kiaochow, Samoa and New Guinea, German expansion had come to an end.

Compared to the older colonial powers France, Britain, and the Netherlands and their established modes of taking into account local structures of political negotiation that had emerged over centuries, German colonial policy aimed at a more rigid penetration of the colonized territories and population. While in the older empires pre-modern structures of governance survived well into the twentieth century, colonial newcomers such as imperial Germany and Japan, in particular in the closing years before the First World War, were driven by the idea of achieving more 'modern' and efficient forms of rule based on investment in infrastructure and human capital. In social practice, however, the ideal of 'scientific colonialism' – systematic and efficient, based on knowledge and not on repression, aiming at development and not exploitation – was barely carried out.

The colonies' legal status was contradictory. In general, it was assumed by Germans that 'New Germany' was part of Germany for the purposes of international law; on the other hand, laws governing the German state did not apply there. Thus the executive, represented both by the central colonial administration in Berlin and by the governor and the local branches, could enact legislation in the colonies irrespective of the metropole's law code. This led to discriminatory regimes, particularly in the fields of migration control, recruitment and administration of labour, and segregation of populations according to the category of race.

The regions that Germany had claimed differed widely in geography, geology, and climate. More importantly, the local populations and societies varied greatly, and their interaction with, and resistance to, the new rulers led to different dynamics. As a result, the effects of the German presence in the colonies were also far from homogeneous. Before moving into the more analytical chapters, the following sections will first give a brief overview of developments in the six colonial territories under German rule.

GERMAN SOUTH-WEST AFRICA

In 1884, South-West Africa, present-day Namibia, became the first German 'protectorate' (Map A). South-West Africa was large and, with only 200,000 inhabitants, sparsely populated. The colony was initiated by a Bremen-based tobacco merchant, Adolf Lüderitz (1834–86), who was involved in illegal trading of arms on the coast of south-western Africa. As his enterprise and forays into the hinterland in the search for gold and diamonds ran into difficulties, he was forced to sell his possessions and soon obliged the German government to step in, not least to avoid a serious loss of prestige. In the following years, tensions between the two major local ethnic groups, the Herero and Nama, made it easier for the Germans to establish power; both groups' leaders, Samuel Maharero and Hendrik Witbooi, attempted to make use of the German presence for their own purposes.

A systematic colonial policy with viable strategies for its long-term development began only in 1894, when Theodor Leutwein became governor; he remained in this position for ten years. Public declarations of peaceful conquest notwithstanding, the process of securing power continued to involve a large number of military expeditions. One crucial aim of Leutwein's politics was to turn South-West Africa into Germany's only settler colony. In the following years, the German state very actively promoted white, and in particular German, settlement in the area. In order to render the colony economically self-sufficient from the motherland and profitable for settlers and merchants, Leutwein began expanding the colonial bureaucracy, as a means of ensuring the rule of law and facilitating a methodical economic exploitation of the territory. At the same time, he strengthened the positions of the local power-holders, deploying a strategy of divide and rule that became known in Germany as the 'Leutwein System'.

The policies were essentially contradictory, as the influx of settlers led to the expulsion of African land and livestock and thus threatened the living conditions of the local population. The colonial government confiscated 70 per cent of the country's land and gave it to

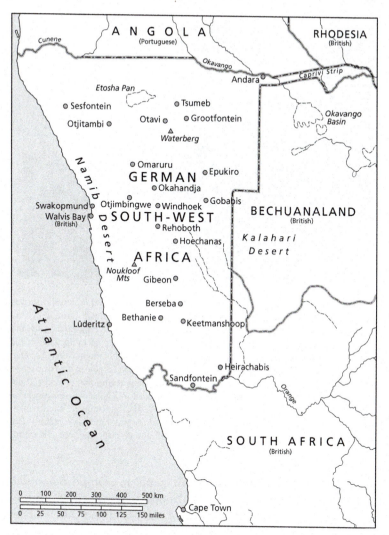

Map A German South-West Africa

German farmers (see Illustration 7). By the First World War, there were about 14,000 European settlers living in South-West Africa, 12,000 of them German. (Namibia is the only former German colony where there is still a German-speaking minority today.) Only few

Illustration 7 The seizure of large tracts of land by German authorities and settlers changed the traditional land order largely based on communal possession, and transformed and threatened the life of African communities. The expropriation of land accelerated after the cattle epidemic of 1897 and was further sped up in the wake of the Herero war. Only in the north of the country, in the Ovambo kingdoms, where German governmental control hardly reached, were large groups of peasants able to hold on to their land. Following independence in 1990, debates about the redistribution of land and the dispossession of white settlers have not abated. Compared to Zimbabwe, this process is much less characterized by violence, because the SWAPO government has its main constituency in the north where colonial expropriation was much less radical. The picture shows a German settler, together with his African staff, posing in front of his farm.

restraints existed to prevent an almost complete expropriation of the Nama and Herero peoples. Regulations were issued to control Africans, and to enable the seizure of their land and cattle. These new rules, backed by the dual legal system, destroyed African economic independence and forced local peasants into dependency on European employers. Their economic situation was further worsened by the outbreak, in 1897, of an epidemic of rinderpest, a disease of cattle that robbed large numbers of Herero of their means of existence and made them dependent on German settlers. The rebellion of the Herero, and the brutal war fought by the Germans against the Herero

Illustration 8 Windhoek was founded by the Germans in 1890 as the first city in sparsely populated South-West Africa. It grew slowly and had a population of about 10,000 when German colonial rule ended in 1915. Life in Windhoek was rigidly segregated along ethnic lines, with specific quarters allotted to the African population. The picture shows General Lothar von Trotha and Governor Theodor Leutwein in front of the 'Hotel Stadt' in Windhoek.

and the Nama between 1904 and 1907, was triggered by economic hardship brought about by the policies settlement.

In the years after the war, as opposition and resistance had become even more difficult, African cultivators were forced into small and unprofitable plots. Political arrangements with local groups, as in the decade before 1904, were no longer deemed necessary. The majority of adult men were subjected to forced labour, rigid working regulations and identity controls in an attempt to create a racially segregated exploitative state that in some of its measures bordered on the totalitarian. Fantasies of social disciplining and total control were frustrated, however, in daily practice as Africans found ways to evade, sabotage, and undermine the rigid rules.

Commercially, the colony was of almost no importance to the German economy. As the land was infertile and unsuitable for tillage, the only profitable activity for the settlers was cattle-raising. The only lucrative enterprises were copper mining (from 1907 onward) and diamond production. The discovery of diamond deposits in 1908 meant that from then onwards, German South-West Africa produced the highest private-sector profits of any of the German colonies; but for the German government, the high levels of expenditure incurred for railway construction and military activities meant it was the biggest loss-maker (see Illustration 8).

In July 1915, the small garrison of German colonial troops surrendered to South Africa. After the war, South-West Africa became a mandate and remained under South African control until gaining its independence in 1990 as Namibia.

CAMEROON

Formal German presence in Cameroon was established in July 1884 through a treaty signed by the chiefs of the coastal port of Douala and Gustav Nachtigal, a well-known explorer with many years of experience in Africa. Nachtigal acted on behalf of Chancellor Bismarck, but the real driving force of the territorial acquisition were private trade interests as represented by the Woermann family.

German rule in Cameroon, which had approximately 3.85 million inhabitants at the time, was concentrated on the coastal region, in particular Douala, and the inland administrative centres of Yaoundé and Edea (Map B). Communication and economic exploitation were facilitated by the short railway routes that connected Douala with the nearby regions. However, control over the vast areas in the north-east such as the kingdom of Bornu and Adamawa, a region famed for its allegedly inexhaustible supply of ivory, was sparse (see Illustration 9).

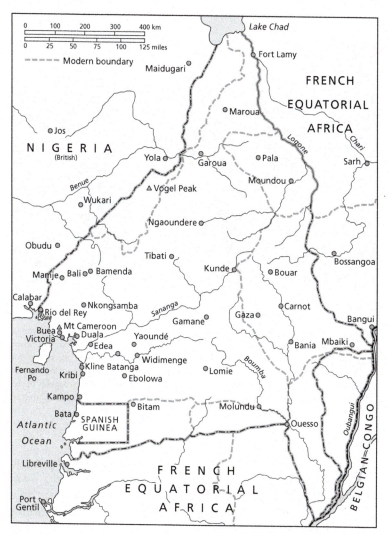

Map B Cameroon

In the 1890s, large parts of the north-east were brought under control as the result of several small-scale if bloody wars and military expeditions, but *de facto* power remained with local potentates. Adamawa in particular remained largely autonomous. It formed part of the Sokoto

Illustration 9 In the early years of colonial rule, ivory was one of the few products that promised high returns for German traders in Cameroon. In the local economy, ivory was a high-prestige good, and its exchange was limited to the social elites. In colonial times, elephants were mostly hunted by Hausa traders in northern Cameroon who then transported the ivory to the coast and exchanged it via the European merchants for industrial products, tobacco, and alcohol. Rumours about rich deposits of ivory were among the driving forces that lured German expeditions into the northern regions of the colony. In 1908, the government issued a decree that sought to control elephant hunting and prohibited the shooting of female and young elephants.

caliphate, a large pre-colonial state formation resulting from the advance of Islam in western Africa. It was initiated by the *jihad* of Usman Dan Fodio in 1809 and exerted tributary rule over large stretches of northern Cameroon and what was to become British Nigeria. Formally under German and British rule, the different emirates of the Sokoto caliphate used the support of the colonial powers to further extend their rule.

Because the climate in the region was felt to be unsuitable for Europeans, with malaria taking huge tolls among the missionary and merchant communities, Cameroon was never considered as a potential German settlement colony. In 1913, only 1,871 whites lived there. In Germany, Cameroon was notorious for an endless series of scandals that involved abuses of power and outright brutality, much of it tolerated during the long reign of Governor Jesco von Puttkamer (1895–1907).

In part, these infringements were related to the system of economic exploitation put in place in the 1890s. Cameroon developed, under German rule, into the largest plantation colony in western Africa. The cultivation of cocoa proved especially profitable; experiments with coffee and tobacco were less successful. The creation of plantations relied frequently on forced labour and on an uncompromising land policy under Governor von Puttkamer, who confiscated land that was supposedly 'ownerless' and sold it to large corporations. This process of violent dispossession resulted in massive resistance by the Duala that culminated in a letter to the *Reichstag* in 1905. In the letter, published by the Social Democratic press, King Akwa and twenty-seven other potentates denounced German misrule and called for the removal of Puttkamer and his staff. Puttkamer was finally replaced in 1907, pressured out of office not least by a coalition of missionaries and large trading companies who both opposed his policies of grant-ing land concessions to the plantations. This was not the end of the struggles over land, however. One month before the end of German rule, the Germans publicly executed the ex-Paramount Chief Rudolph Duala Manga Bell on trumped-up charges of treason, as the last episode in a lengthy dispute over racial segregation and land expropriation in the city of Douala.

Economically, Cameroon was Germany's most important colony. Most of its exports, however, were created by the domestic economy and despite all the investment, the contribution made by the planta-tions remained small. Rubber (which was in high demand for use in the electrical and automotive industries; see Illustration 10) as well as ivory, palm oil, and palm kernels, among other products, were trans-ported by long caravans of bearers from the hinterland to the coast. Frequently, they passed through the hands of Hausa traders, who had established themselves as successful mediators between the hinterland and the world market. For Germany, Cameroon's overall trade bal-ance remained negative, as exports never exceeded imports. After the First World War, Cameroon was partitioned and became a British and French mandate.

Illustration 10 Rubber had been known in Latin America for centuries, but the discovery of vulcanization by Charles Goodyear in 1839 led to a global demand in rubber and a boom in the Amazon region. Thanks to its multiple applications, particularly in the expanding automobile industry, rubber produced from latex tapped from rubber-trees became a product in demand worldwide. In the late nineteenth century, natural rubber resources were detected in Africa; they had not traditionally been exploited by Africans. The Congo, the colony privately owned and ruthlessly exploited by Belgian King Leopold II, soon emerged as the infamous centre of rubber production. In Cameroon too, rubber was the most profitable export good. Well into the twentieth century, rubber trees were felled, and latex extracted, before the German government attempted to take preventive measures against this form of forest destruction. Forty-nine companies employing close to a quarter of all Europeans in Cameroon had invested in the trade, and about 25,000 African caravan carriers were involved in transporting the 'white gold' to the coast. With expansion of rubber production to East Asia (based on seeds smuggled out of Brazil) and the beginning of synthetic rubber production in the early years of the twentieth century, the rubber trade decreased in importance.

TOGO

With its free-trade policy and tiny European population, Togo was a typical trading colony. By 1884, when German emissary Gustav Nachtigal signed a treaty with the local chief Mlapa III, the coast of Togo had been integrated into the Atlantic trade for centuries. Partly, this integration was driven by the slave trade. During the fifteenth and sixteenth centuries, Portuguese explorers and traders visited the coast. For the next 200 years, the coastal region was a major raiding centre for Europeans (including the Dutch, English, French, and Danish) in search of slaves. Much of the trade in Ewe slaves operated through ports just outside present-day Togo, such as Ouidah to the east, but some of the trade flowed through Petit Popo (present-day Aneho) – the only significant port on the Togolese coast until the colonial period (Map C).

While German missionaries had been active in the region as early as 1847, the acquisition of Togo was primarily driven by commercial interests. The Europeans, never more than 350, lived along the coastal strip of this long, narrow colony (the coastline was only 50 kilometres wide). There were no major uprisings among the Ewe in southern Togo, but colonial rule was at times brutal and based on notions of racial superiority that were enforced much more rigidly than in neighbouring British (Gold Coast, present-day Ghana) and French (Dahomey) possessions. Local elites protested against infringements on their political and trade rights, but also against chain gangs and flogging.

Administrative control of the colony barely reached beyond the roads and the two railway lines into central Togo. Even after considerable use of force, the northern parts of the country remained almost inaccessible to Germans; for security reasons the northern territories could be accessed by Europeans only with special governmental permission. In the north, inhabited largely by Muslim populations, the power of local potentates remained almost unchanged.

In Togo, too, there were attempts, primarily by the Togo Company, to acquire large amounts of land for plantations. However, in contrast to Cameroon, and because of the pressure of traders and missionaries who each pursued their own and sometimes contradictory interests (see Illustration 11), the large corporations played a very minor role.

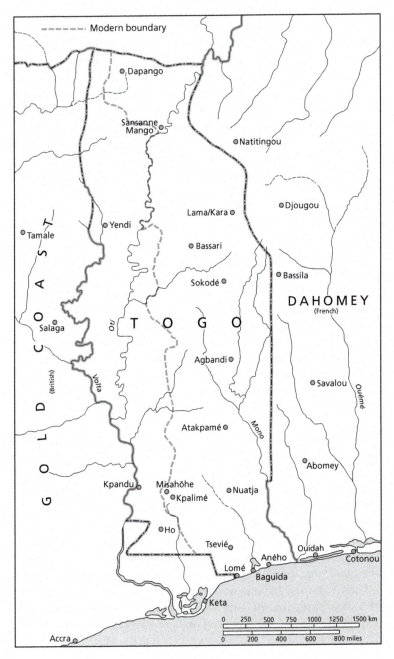

Map C Togo

Illustration 11 In the German colonial empire, schools were predominantly (up to 95 per cent) founded and run by the missionary societies. They were most numerous in Togo, where close to 1.5 per cent of all children received some kind of education in mission schools. Schools were a representative institution of the colonial project as they embodied the philanthropic ideology underlying the civilizing mission, and at the same time limited the education of Africans to basic instruction. Most members of the national elites in post-colonial societies, however, looked back to an experience in a mission school. This image shows a mission school in the city of Ho in south-western Togo.

Exports were dominated by palm oil and palm kernels, produced by the existing native industry. The local Ewe producers and merchants remained influential.

Particularly powerful were the cosmopolitan Afro-Brazilian elites, who soon took charge of the trade in the coastal areas. One example was Francisco Olympio, son of a father of Portuguese origins and a mother of African and Amerindian extraction who moved from Brazil to Togo in the 1850s. Olympio was a product of the Black Atlantic: he worked as a slave trader and later founded his own plantations in Togo. His son Octaviano (died 1940) was sent to Nigeria and London to study, worked for a British trade company, helped found a Catholic mission school in Lomé, expanded into coconut planting and cattle-raising, and emerged as a key figure in the anticolonial protest movement against the Germans. His nephew Sylvanus (1902–63) would become the first president of independent Togo in 1961.[1]

For the Germans, Togo, with its population of approximately one million, was not an important colony in economic terms; however, there were no major colonial scandals and only minor military conflicts and it was thus the only German colony, apart from Samoa, that did not require financial assistance from Germany. The German administrators had to leave Togo in August 1914, and France and Britain split the territory lengthwise. Whereas in the British mandate territory the majority voted for a connection with Ghana in 1956 (becoming independent in 1957), French Togo became independent as a national state in 1960.

GERMAN EAST AFRICA

As with the other African colonies, German rule in East Africa began with an imperial charter for a private corporation. This was largely the work of Carl Peters. Trained as an historian, in late 1883 he explored the region as a private citizen and concluded 'contracts' with local potentates in his quest for a German 'India in Africa'. The German government decided to treat these documents as official German contracts of protection (*Schutzverträge*) and granted territorial powers to Peters' German East Africa Society. After a few years, however, constant conflict and wars led the imperial government to intervene and, in 1891, to take over the administration of the region.

The coastline of East Africa had been firmly integrated into transregional trade routes, migratory regimes, and cultural interactions for many centuries. The influence of Islam was profound, and the region was part of the larger system of networks that stretched across the Indian ocean. Before the arrival of Vasco da Gama and the Portuguese in 1498, the port city of Kilwa had been the most important nodal point of the trade routes. Under Portuguese rule, the island of Zanzibar emerged as a powerful hub, taken over in the eighteenth century by the Arab sultanate of Oman. Trade routes extended to Lake Tanganyika and brought gold and iron as well as slaves into the

---

[1] Alcione M. Amos, 'Afro-Brazilians in Togo. The Case of the Olympio Family, 1882–1945', *Cahiers d'Études Africaines* 162 (2001), 293–314.

Indian ocean region, and textiles, porcelain, and spices from Asia to East Africa.

German East Africa, which was made up of the present-day states of Tanzania, Burundi, and Rwanda, was by far the most populous of the German colonies, with 7.75 million inhabitants (Map D). For a long time, colonial administration and settlement were limited to the coastline. From the 1890s German military expeditions were sent inland with the aim of conquering the hinterland, meeting fierce resistance from Africans and Arabs. Despite massive military deployment, the use of violence, and thousands of mostly African victims, real colonial power remained limited. In Rwanda and Burundi, in particular, the colonial state reached accords that left local potentates in power.

A crucial event in the history of the colony was the Maji-Maji War between 1905 and 1908, a major uprising against foreign rule that killed, together with the subsequent famine, about 300,000 Africans. After the war, the new governor, Albrecht von Rechenberg (1906–12) initiated a radical change in policy. He attempted to curb the power of the large plantations with their insatiable demand for local labour; their harsh recruitment methods had been among the prime causes of the war. Instead, Rechenberg envisioned East Africa as a trading colony, open also to African, Indian, and Arabic merchants. Within certain limits, he also foresaw a gradual participation of Africans in the administration of the colony. His ambitious reform plans earned him the fierce opposition of the German settler population, and in the end were not successful.

In economic terms, German East Africa was Germany's most valuable colony. But it was still a drain on the *Reich*'s finances. Total imports – consisting of consumer goods for the German and local populations and material for infrastructural development – were consistently almost twice as high as exports. The large German cotton and sisal plantations produced important export goods with the help of Africans who frequently worked under conditions close to slavery. African producers supplied most of the goods consumed locally and in the region. Moreover, they held a share of about 50 per cent of exports, too, in particular of cotton, copra (the dried flesh of coconuts, used to make coconut oil), and groundnuts.

During the First World War, East Africa was the scene of protracted fighting by retreating German troops. A large force of African

Map D German East Africa

soldiers (*askari*), under the leadership of General Paul von Lettow-
Vorbeck (1870–1964), conducted – against the explicit orders of
Heinrich Schnee, last governor of the colony (Illustration 12) – a
guerrilla war that ended only in November 1918 with surrender to

Illustration 12 After spending time in New Guinea and Samoa, Heinrich Schnee (1871–1949) served as the last governor of German East Africa (1912–19). He is mostly remembered as the most vociferous and relentless campaigner for recovery of the German colonies during the Weimar Republic. With his books *Die koloniale Schuldlüge* and *Deutsches Kolonial-Lexikon* translated into English, French, Italian, and Spanish, he was an influential voice in the revisionist camp. Schnee was the colonial spokesperson of the right-liberal German People's Party (*Deutsche Volkspartei*), and he publicly demanded the return of the colonies as 'a requirement for German honour' and as a 'vital necessity for the German people'. As an internationally renowned colonial expert, Schnee was nominated to the committee of the League of Nations that wrote the Lytton report on Japan's role in Manchuria in 1932. In Germany, his influence waned after the enforced *Gleichschaltung* (co-ordination of institutions as part of the Nazi system of totalitarian control) of all colonial associations in 1936. This image shows him with parading African troops (the so-called *askari*) in 1912.

British forces. East Africa came under the protection of the League of Nations and was turned into a British mandate, until its final declaration of independence as the state of Tanzania in 1964. Burundi and Rwanda were placed under the mandate of Belgium and gained independence in 1962. More than the other colonial possessions,

East Africa – symbolized by Carl Peters, and the figure of Lettow-Vorbeck and his 'loyal' *askari* – remained an important site of post-colonial memory in Weimar and Nazi Germany.

Ever since the travels of James Cook and the German Georg Foster, who accompanied Cook on his second voyage from 1772 to 1775 and wrote a report on his experiences, the South Pacific had held an important place in the German imagination. The acquisition of New Guinea and Samoa in 1899, which were objects of prestige without any military or economic significance, was partly a result of these pre-colonial projections, which imagined the inhabitants of the Pacific, especially those of Samoa, to be 'noble savages'.

From about the mid nineteenth century, the islands of the South Pacific also came into the purview of German trade interests. In the 1880s, the German New Guinea Company, founded by banker Adolph von Hansemann and other German financial magnates, pressed for the acquisition of the north-eastern part of New Guinea; Australia had occupied the southern part, and the west belonged to Dutch India. As in the case of other German colonies, this New Guinea colonial society was at first granted sovereign rights until, following its financial collapse, the German state took over rule in 1898–9. The German-occupied part of New Guinea (Map E), together with the Caroline, Marianas, and Marshall islands (acquired from Spain after defeat against the USA in 1898), had a total population of about 600,000, of whom fewer than 1,000 were Germans.

Governor Albert Hahl, who was in charge of the colony from 1902 to 1914, aimed to achieve cautious modernization, while leaving indigenous customs as little changed as possible (see Illustration 13). He integrated local officials into the colonial administration, such as the *luluai*, local officials who mediated between the colonial administration and the native population. This was different from indirect rule in most African colonies, where it must be understood as acceptance of the failure of direct control, as the *luluai* were formally integrated into the German administrative hierarchy and were charged with collecting taxes and executing infrastructural work. Hahl also sought to limit the influence of the German planters and

Map E German New Guinea

promoted the native cultivation of land. Eventually, more than half of the export of copra derived from local production.

The islands of Western Samoa were regarded as the German 'pearl of the South Seas' and had no more than 40,000 inhabitants (and never more than 300 German citizens). It was acquired in 1899 as part of an international agreement that ceded Western Samoa to the USA (today it remains one of the Insular Areas of the United States) and the eastern islands, mainly Savai'i and Upolu, to the German empire.

The long-time governor of Samoa, Wilhelm Solf (1900–11), was even more than Hahl committed to a paternalistic form of colonial rule that aimed to achieve gradual cultural 'elevation'. He pursued policies of minimum coercion and – apart from the abolition of the

Illustration 13 Governor Albert Hahl (1868–1945) served as governor of German New Guinea for twelve years. A trained jurist, Hahl made his career in the colonial bureaucracy. As a middle-class professional, neither a member of the military nor a Prussian citizen, Hahl was an exception in the higher echelons of the colonial service. His combination of modernization policies and ideals of preservation of local traditions contrasted sharply with the prevalent approach taken in colonial Africa. This picture shows Hahl with members of the native population on the Micronesian island of Pohnpei. In the 1920s and 1930s, Hahl was one of the most active lobbyists for the colonial movement.

local monarchy – only careful modification of existing power structures. More than in any other colony, existing judicial authorities were integrated into the German administrative system. There were no German soldiers or police in Samoa and Solf energetically rejected the suggestion by the few German settlers that land should be confiscated from the indigenous population. This was frequently accompanied by a belief that it was the Germans' responsibility to protect the Samoans from the 'excesses' of the modern age. One effect of this attitude was the decision to rely not on Samoans but largely on imported Chinese workers for plantation labour.

In contrast to Germany's African colonies, there were no serious violent clashes in New Guinea or Samoa. This was due not least to the

Illustration 14 Wilhelm Solf (1862–1936) was a trained philologist and Sanskrit scholar with some additional training in law. He espoused what he called 'humane colonialism', a form of paternalistic and highly regulated traditionalism. 'Colonizing is to do missionary work, and I mean missionary work in the full sense of cultural education. But this does not imply education in European culture, but in a culture that can grow roots in the soil and the *Heimat* (homeland) of the natives and is adapted to their intellectual and spiritual characteristics.' After retiring from colonial service, Solf served as the last foreign minister of the German *Kaiserreich* in 1918 and as Germany's ambassador to Japan 1920–8. After his death, his wife Hanna became the centre of the so-called *Solf-Kreis*, a loose group of members of the elite who met clandestinely to exchange views in opposition to the Nazi regime.

circumspect approach to colonial rule adopted by Governors Hahl and Solf (see Illustration 14), both well-educated representatives of the bourgeoisie and not part of the military hierarchy. However, the Pacific colonies were not the idyllic places portrayed by German colonial propaganda, or the ethnological museums that historians sometimes make them out to be. The colonial authorities did employ force if power interests were threatened. And the practices of labour recruitment as well as the often brutal treatment of plantation workers, most of them Chinese, are among the most violent chapters of German history in the South Seas.

In economic terms, the two trading colonies were not significant. Even their main export, copra, contributed only 8 per cent of German copra imports. In total, trade with the Pacific colonies made up less than 0.15% of total German foreign trade (1909 figures). In the early months of the First World War, Samoa was occupied by New Zealand troops, New Guinea by Australian and the South Sea islands by Japanese troops; after the Versailles Treaty, the Pacific colonies were placed under the mandate of these countries by the League of Nations and the United Nations until eventual independence.

KIAOCHOW

In 1897, the murder of two German missionaries provided the German empire with an excuse to occupy the bay of Kiaochow (modern spelling Jiaozhou), in the province of Shandong in northern China. Formally, the region was leased from China for ninety-nine years, but Germany treated the zone, 50 kilometres wide with a population of 190,000, like a colony (Map F). The lease agreement also allowed the Germans to construct a railway line from Kiaochow to the provincial capital of Jinan, and to exploit the coal deposits in the province (see Illustration 15). The imperial government increasingly saw the whole province as a German 'sphere of influence' and as the starting-point for plans to move further into China.

In contrast to the other German colonies, which were initially administered by a section of the Foreign Office and then, from 1907 onwards, by the *Reich* Colonial Office, Kiaochow was under the control of the Naval Ministry. While the Foreign Office was still dominated by the German aristocracy, the Navy saw itself as a modern, bourgeois institution and, in line with German naval expansion, expected Germany to play a more prominent role in world affairs. The Navy saw Kiaochow as a model for colonial development and hoped to use it to show, in Alfred von Tirpitz's words, 'what Germany could be capable of'.[2] Kiaochow was to be a showcase for the cultural, scientific, and technological achievements of the German

---

[2] Quoted from Gründer, *Geschichte der deutschen Kolonien*, 188.

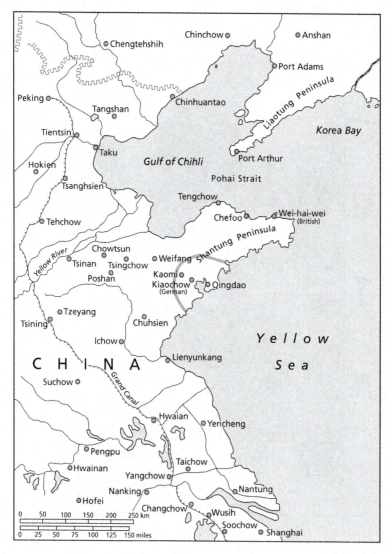

Map F Kiaochow

Illustration 15 In this Chinese representation, the imperialist threat around the turn of the century, after China's defeat at the hands of Japan in 1895, becomes apparent: Russia, Japan, the United States, Great Britain, Germany, and France attack the Qing Empire from without, while alcohol and opium exert their corroding influence from within. The German colonization of Kiaochow was not typical in this scramble for China, as most powers followed the 'open door' rhetoric of the United States and aimed for spheres of influence and privileged access to Chinese goods and markets. The representative institution was thus not a colonial government, but China's Imperial Maritime Custom Service run, in the name of the western powers, by Sir Robert Hart. To retain a central Chinese government was in the interest of this finance-driven imperialism, which aimed to export capital more than goods.

Illustration 16 In 1905, in the wake of the Boxer war and the Russo-Japanese war, the late Qing government abolished the centuries-old imperial examination system with its focus on the Confucian classics. A modern school system was established with primary, secondary, and college levels reflective of western models, and 'modern' subject matters including natural sciences were introduced. Schools were also created by the western powers and in particular the missionary societies. In comparison with the more than 5,000 French and 2,000 American schools, the thirty education institutions in the German colony of Kiaochow – basing their instruction on translations of French- and English-language textbooks – made up a tiny minority. The German Chinese College in Qingdao shown in this photo, with about 400 Chinese students in 1914, was the only institution of higher learning in the German empire.

empire. The modernization programme included the creation of new urban structures in Qingdao, the main city of the region. In addition, the Germans invested in a railway line, a modern port, a programme of afforestation, medical and hygiene facilities, a modern sewerage system and a telegraph system. In 1909, they founded the German Chinese College (*Hochschule*), the only tertiary educational institution in the German empire (Illustration 16). This made Kiaochow the most expensive of Germany's colonial projects.

Interventions were not limited to infrastructure and the economy, but also extended to the organization of society. Kiaochow was intended, by high Navy officials, as a site to establish a model social order under conditions of colonialism and military rule. Different from the British crown colony of Hong Kong, Kiaochow was subjected to a rigid regime of segregation and control. Interaction between Chinese and Germans, but also between military and civilians, was severely limited, and different parts of the town of Qingdao were designated for the different ethnic groups, with the centre of town off-limits for Chinese residence.

Like Hong Kong, Kiaochow was designed purely as a trading colony. But the hopes that many (not only in Germany) placed in the 'immense' Chinese market were not fulfilled. The coal excavated in Kiaochow was not of the quality required, and was expensive, and attempts to set up a modern silk manufacturing industry also failed. Qingdao did develop into a thriving marketplace, but Germany profited very little from this. Just before the First World War, the German share in trade through Qingdao was only 8 per cent. The vast majority of imports came from Japan.

The Chinese population reacted to the Germans' rule with scepticism and resistance. During the first few years, in particular, conflict and repression were frequent. The constant conflicts between the Catholic missions and the local authorities increased tensions further. These tensions culminated in the Boxer war of 1900. Fighting in the province of Shandong was violently suppressed by its governor Yuan Shikai, but the brutal actions of the German troops commanded by General Waldersee (his rank of *Feldmarschall* was ridiculed, in the contemporary press, as *Weltmarschall* ('World Marshall')) left a trail of destruction and death behind them that remained a focus of collective memory in China for many years afterwards. The period of German rule came to an end in November 1914, when, after a brief battle, Kiaochow was handed over to Japanese troops.

PERIODIZATION

This short overview makes it clear that the German colonial empire was a highly heterogeneous entity. The geographical and natural conditions – tropical rainforest in Cameroon, humid and dry savannahs in East Africa, a moderate climate in Kiaochow, deserts in Namibia – had nothing in common. And the existing societies and local groups differed greatly; these differences were then reinforced by the colonial policy of divide and rule. Moreover, the specific relationship in each location between locals and Germans meant that the dynamics and chronology of colonial experiences were completely different from one colony to the next.

If we attempt to generalize and divide the years of German colonialism into different periods, we must keep these differences in mind. But, glossing over some of the complexities, we can identify three different phases. After a pre-history in which missionaries, geographers, and a few merchant houses dominated, the colonial era proper began in 1884, with the issue of imperial charters and the founding of colonial companies. Some of these were based on the model of the British East India Company. The imperial charters guaranteed territorial power, which frequently led to violent attempts to enforce this power. Generally, 'agreements' were made with local potentates, often under the threat of violence. Particularly notorious are the ruthless activities of Carl Peters and his German Colonization Company in East Africa. Peters demanded 'the uncompromising and decisive enrichment of one's own people at the cost of other, weaker peoples'.[3] Explicit as these words were, in many cases the situation of conquest was not as clear-cut. Differing interests, and also different interpretations of the contracts and agreements – for example the fact that abstract ideas about ownership and sovereignty were of lesser importance in African societies – created room for manoeuvre that both sides attempted to make use of. On the part of the Africans, this included refusal to cooperate with the colonial powers, and resistance. Revolts and violent conflict, including the 'Arab rebellion' in East Africa 1888–89, and internal mismanagement meant that from the late 1880s onwards, the German empire felt it had no option but to convert the 'protectorates' into formal colonies.

This marked the start of the second phase, during which the powers of the 'men on the ground', often acting on their own initiative, were reduced and a more bureaucratic form of rule introduced. As in other European empires, German colonial policy was still shaped by the principles of the pre-imperial era. It was founded on a belief in cultural dominance and aimed to achieve the gradual cultural 'elevation' of the

---

[3] Quoted from Wehler, *Bismarck und der Imperialismus*, 333.

colonized peoples, officially with the goal of eventual assimilation. Economic policy combined a form of mercantilist skimming-off of trade products with the promotion of European settlement, and the resulting creation of extensive plantations. The planters were supported by the state through various kinds of land seizure, through taxation policy and through an obligation on the native population to take up paid work. This essentially repressive and exploitative policy was one of the causes for the large-scale revolts in German South-West Africa (1904–7) and East Africa (1905–8), which put a serious question mark over German colonial rule.

In reaction to the difficulties that these two wars had caused for German colonial rule, the administration of the colonies was reorganized. This was the third phase of German colonial rule. In 1907, a *Reich* Colonial Office was set up and put in charge of all Germany's overseas possessions except for Kiaochow. The new Colonial Office was led by a banker and left-liberal politician, Bernhard Dernburg. Dernburg was from a Jewish background and was neither a member of the aristocracy nor a career civil servant. He had made a name for himself by restructuring troubled companies and represented a belief that utilitarian principles and management skills were needed in colonial policy. 'In earlier days, colonization was carried out with methods of destruction', he wrote, 'but today colonization can be done with methods of preservation, and these include both the missionary and the doctor, both the railway and the machine; in other words, advanced theoretical and applied science in every area'.[4]

As with the earlier phases, Germany was by no means alone in moving towards a policy aimed at 'developing' the colonies. Its new direction picked up on a debate on reforms that had been taking place across Europe since the late 1890s, focusing on achieving a modern, scientific colonial policy. Exploitation was to be replaced with investment and 'the utilization (*Nutzbarmachung*) of the earth, its treasures . . . and especially the people'.[5] Investment in both infrastructure and human capital was required, and often involved the development of local economic structures and a movement away from the use of forced labour on the

---

[4] Bernhard Dernburg, *Zielpunkte des deutschen Kolonialwesens: Zwei Vorträge*, Berlin (Mittler) 1907, 9.

[5] Ibid, 5.

plantations. This form of colonial modernization could certainly benefit those colonized. But it was aimed mainly at achieving effects that would 'benefit the economy of the colonizing nation', as Dernburg did not fail to emphasize.[6] In any case, Dernburg's reforms had repercussions only in those colonies where they were supported by the local governor. Where that was not the case, for example in German South-West Africa, they had a negligible effect on the actual practice of colonial rule. The more recent research has focused on the realities of rule on the ground, the less the appointment of Dernburg appears as a watershed in Germany's colonial history.

A very different question is whether the few short decades of German rule marked a turning-point or change for the regions involved. From the standpoint of local societies, one can justifiably ask to what extent the short life of the German empire had any major effects. In the 1960s, the Nigerian historian J. F. Ade Ajayi suggested that the colonial era as a whole had only an ephemeral character. In the context of centuries of African history, the colonial intermezzo was just a minor and short-lived episode, he argued.[7] Given the trauma caused by foreign rule, one that is still reflected in present-day memory, this viewpoint is certainly an exaggeration. And in terms of social history, we cannot ignore the transformative nature of the nineteenth and twentieth centuries, during which the agrarian societies of Africa underwent fundamental social change. But this change was partly the result of structural conditions – such as the integration of the world market, industrialization, and the communications revolution – on the one hand, and indigenous initiatives and regional dynamics on the other; it cannot be seen as caused solely by colonial intervention. This applies even more strongly to the German colonial empire, which existed only until the First World War and thus during a period when, although the balance of power was clearly with the colonists, real and far-reaching colonial control of the kind achieved after, say, 1930, had not yet become established.

---

[6] Ibid.
[7] J. F. A. Ajayi, 'Colonialism: An Episode in African History', in: Louis H. Gann and Peter Duignan (eds.), *Colonialism in Africa, 1870–1960, vol. 1: The History and Politics of Colonialism, 1870–1914*, Cambridge (Cambridge University Press) 1969, 497–509.

CHAPTER 5

The colonial state

Although the era of colonial power, and especially that of German colonialism, was a short one, it had one long-lasting effect: it led to the creation under international law of territorial states that aspired to a state monopoly on power and to fixed external borders. This took place in regions where boundaries had previously been imprecise and constantly changing, and where there had been a wide variety of different types of political order with very different degrees of centralization. Especially in Africa, German colonization introduced a completely new principle of political organization, which was reinforced under British and French rule after the First World War.

The colonial states controlled by the German empire were set up in a belief that the model of European state systems could simply be applied to the colonies. But in fact the practice on the ground turned out to be very different from the theory. The colonial state was not simply an extension of the western European model, but, as Jürgen Osterhammel suggests, 'a political form in itself'.[1] And colonial states themselves were organized in a variety of very different ways. Even the laws and regulations that were applied differed greatly from one colony to the next. The structures of colonial power varied according to regional differences and different types of colony, and they followed different chronologies. But they were also affected by local geography and by the dynamics of local societies. The level of control desired by the colonial state also depended on the objectives being pursued for each colony. In trading colonies like Togo, the state's presence was limited to a small number of administrators whose task was primarily to secure the economic exploitation of the region. By contrast, in

[1] Jürgen Osterhammel, *Kolonialismus: Geschichte, Formen, Folgen*, Munich (C. H. Beck) 1995, 62.

settlement colonies such as German South-West Africa and plantation colonies such as Cameroon, the presence of German settlers and
the demands for labour by German landowners led to the state
taking more control over local territories. In addition, any analysis
of colonial power needs to differentiate between different time
periods, because the structures of colonial state power changed –
drastically in some cases – during even the short period of German
domination.

Nevertheless, we can discern some general patterns of colonial
power, although these principles were in many cases overridden by
specific local processes. The following account examines, concentrat-
ing mainly on the African colonies, the difference between the modern state, defined by Max Weber[2] in terms of territoriality, monopoly
on the use of physical force and bureaucracy, and the colonial state. It
focuses on four main themes. Firstly, the European empires often
built on pre-existing forms of rule. This was particularly true of the
early colonial period. Secondly, the colonial state was generally weak
in terms of the extent and depth of its control. This was partly related
to its lack of legitimacy and of ideological hegemony, the third issue
I will examine. In this context it was, fourthly, no coincidence that
violence and warfare were a central feature of colonial rule; in fact they
were inherent in the colonial system.

CONTINUITIES OF RULE

One of the unspoken assumptions of colonial rulers was that before
their arrival the state in Africa had hardly existed, and that the
structures of rule were temporary, flexible, and hardly consistent.
Europeans believed that the colonial state would allow power and
administration to be rationalized and would lead to a modernization
of the institutions of rule, of control, and of legitimation. Historians
of colonialism have often adopted this viewpoint, even when they
were actually taking a perspective critical of colonialism. But the fact
that the European concept of a state cannot be applied directly to
African societies should not lead us to believe that no states of any
kind existed before the colonial era.

[2] Max Weber, *Wirtschaft und Gesellschaft*, Tübingen (Mohr) 1922.

The forms of rule and power in what later became the German colonies differed greatly and it is almost impossible to describe them using a unified set of categories; in addition, they underwent constant change. But as a broad generalization, it can be said that in contrast to the territorial states that had been developing in Europe from the early modern period onwards, political power in many regions of central and southern Africa during the early nineteenth century was not based (primarily) on control over land. Land was, in general, abundant, and in many regions only sparsely inhabited. For that reason there was little competition for land, and because the soils were not ploughed, the inhabitants' investment in a particular location was minimal. In the event of danger, it often made more sense simply to move on than to fight for control of a particular area of land. Power was generally based on personal relationships. Typically, ownership rights over land were of little importance, but ownership of people was regulated in a wide variety of ways. The status accorded to land frequently meant that control over a territory, and control over the people living in it, were two separate legal issues.

As a result, there were usually no mechanisms for securing borders; there were typically no state limits on human mobility. Often, relationships with other power groups were not seen as a separate issue from the internal exercise of power. Instead, they were the result of complex relationships of sovereignty that allowed potentates to make agreements both with their own subjects and with subjects in neighbouring regions. Wars, too, were fought not over land, but for booty. Often, what was at stake was the most valuable asset of a territory, its slaves, rather than control of the territory itself. This logic continued to hold sway well into the period of German rule, in particular in regions in which German control was limited. The Islamic Fulbe states in Ademawa, in northern Cameroon, for example, proclaimed a 'holy war' every year during which slave raids were launched into neighbouring regions. The purpose of these campaigns was less to add to the Fulbe's sphere of power than to reinforce their economic position; their economy was based principally on slave labour.

The area of land actually controlled by political units was usually relatively small, its extent depending primarily on the infrastructure available. The power of a ruler, and his control over the population, generally extended to approximately the distance that a messenger could travel within one month. The biggest empires thus developed in the savannah belt of western Africa, where camels and horses could be used to transport soldiers. In some areas of Africa, there was no form of centralized political organization beyond that of the village. Because power meant, essentially, power over people, the form, extent, and duration of power depended to a large extent on the personality of the individual ruler. In addition, societies that did not use writing had no bureaucracy and thus none of bureaucracy's institutionalizing effects.

It would be wrong to assume that this means that states did not exist in Africa before the advent of colonialism. Instead of applying the rigid definition of a European territorial state, it seems to be more useful to establish the particular form that political rule took in each particular place. Generally speaking, African empires were non-territorial in nature, with power conceived as links between and control over people. African empires were often very dynamic. During the early part of the nineteenth century, in particular, some African states began to expand. Historians of Africa have even described this process as a pre-colonial 'African partition of Africa'. The process was reinforced by the cross-border effects of trade and weapons smuggling. But this expansion did not usually mean the end of the non-territorial exercise of state rule. To an extent, the same can be said for the colonial states of the late nineteenth century. In some ways, they followed the patterns of the African exercise of power, and this hybridization was one of the factors that made colonial states unique. This partial adaptation to local circumstances can be observed at two levels.

Firstly, German rule, especially during the early years, made use of the infrastructure of the research expeditions. In East Africa, in particular, both the people involved in these expeditions, and the knowledge they had gathered, were adopted by the new administrative regimes of the protectorates. And the research expeditions had themselves operated within the structures created by inter-regional trade caravans. The knowledge of indigenous traders was often appropriated by German colonial rulers. 'These local roots', Michael Pesek has recently argued, 'contributed just as much to the formation of colonial power and statehood as did the decrees

Illustration 17 Particularly in the early years of colonial rule, the patterns of exploration and control owed much to pre-colonial structures. In this image in 1885, a German is travelling in a hammock with an awning, carried by Togolese porters. In later years, three railway lines were built in Togo connecting Lomé with Palime and Atakpame in the hinterland, and with Anecho along the coast (along the so-called 'coconut line'). In the hinterland, however, transportation continued to depend on porters and caravans, given that draught animals were hardly used as a result of livestock disease in southern Togo.

and programmes of the colonial politicians in Berlin and Dar es Salaam'.[3] (See Illustration 17.)

Secondly, the colonial state, like the African states, focused on people rather than on territory. Because there were so few administrators, a bureaucratic institutional state did not really develop. This was particularly true of the more peripheral regions away from the colonial centres. Power for the most part meant personal power. For this reason, German administrators usually made extensive use of ceremonies and of ceremonial meetings with African chiefs. A typical example was their adoption of the East African tradition of *shauri*, a

[3] Michael Pesek, *Koloniale Herrschaft in Deutsch-Ostafrika: Expeditionen, Militär und Verwaltung seit 1880*, Frankfurt am Main (Campus) 2005, 26.

form of negotiation with local potentates that could take on the functions both of a court case and of issuing instructions. This use of power opened up scope for negotiation and action that could be exploited by the chiefs.

The colonial state, then, was not set up on a *tabula rasa*. Local continuities combined with new forms and institutions in different ways. Frequently, these new links were the result of negotiation (although such negotiations took place under conditions of considerable inequality). Indigenous influence did play a role. Africans were able to exploit asymmetries in knowledge in their own ways, as interpreters and intermediaries, as guides and as local experts. But this understanding that the colonial state did, in some ways, make use of existing structures must not blind us to the fact that local societies often experienced the establishment of the colonial state as a deep transformation, and as a major turning-point.

ISLANDS OF POWER

The second characteristic feature of the colonial state was that it reached into local societies only to a limited extent. There was a vast difference between the colonial powers' aspiration to total control of the colonies, and social practice; the presence of the state was often very limited. In theory, colonial states were territorial states, which aspired to achieve a monopoly of power over the entire territory to which they laid claim. In the Congo Conference in Berlin in 1884/5, Germany's suggestion that effective control over an area would determine colonial rights was defeated, in favour of Great Britain's insistence that the responsibility of the occupying power should be limited. However, Germany's (unachievable) level of power remained the official ambition of the colonial bureaucracy. The annual reports sent home by the governor of German South-West Africa, Theodor Leutwein, are strongly evocative of a desire to prove that South-West Africa was becoming a 'modern' state based on the European model. In these texts, the aspiration to establish a bureaucratic, well-organized colonial administration is clearly evident.

However, these visions remained largely unfulfilled; theory and social reality did not coincide. For the most part, the German colonial states in Africa did not have full control over their territories. The colonial states were weak states, even though the office of governor was equipped with a wide range of powers. As in the other European colonial states, these included both executive and legislative powers, and, because governors could issue ordinances, they could add regulations to the legal system almost at will. The governor was the head of the colonial administration and commander-in-chief of the colonial military. The German Foreign Office, and, from 1907, the *Reich* Colonial Office, had very little control over the governors' actions – the letters that were the main form of communication between Berlin and the colonies took two months to arrive. In addition, this concentration of powers in the office of the governor made continuity in colonial policies less likely. Each governor stayed in his post for only a few years; every change of governor could result in a change in focus or even a complete change of policy.

Below the governor, the local administrative units were led by the district officers (*Bezirksamtmänner*) and station heads. They were the most important representatives of colonial power and, like the British district commissioners and the French *commandants de cercle*, they had a range of competencies over which the governor, in his turn, had little control. They were the real creators of empire. Their local powers were such that in Togo, for example, one *Bezirksamtmann* dismissed every single one of the 544 chiefs in his district over the course of his twenty-year rule, appointing more favoured candidates in their stead. Like their superiors, the *Bezirksamtmänner* attempted an aristocratic style of power enforcement and insisted on their autonomy from the seat of government; they justified this with their superior knowledge of the situation on the ground. For this reason, we can describe the situation outside the main colonial cities as a form of sub-imperialism over which the governor had little actual control.

Because of this, the bureaucracies within the colonies were extremely heterogeneous. This was reinforced by the fact that a large number of other representatives were involved at a local level, for example the members of expeditions sent out by anti-slavery committees, and missionaries. They were independent of the colonial administration and did not feel bound to respect the latters' wishes. In fact, the colonial administration needed the cooperation of these individuals who were not, formally speaking, representatives of the state. Because of the costs involved, a large number of regions had no colonial presence at all.

But here, too, we must differentiate. The administration's ability to control its territory generally increased over time, and especially after the Colonial Office was set up in 1907. It also varied from one colony to the next; a greater degree of control was possible in Kiaochow than, for example, in northern Cameroon. In towns and coastal regions, colonial rule was more thoroughly institutionalized than in the hinterlands. Dar es Salaam was completely transformed, becoming a modern colonial metropolis. But outside these colonial centres, the creation of a full system of colonial rule remained incomplete. In 1900, 415 German officers and colonial administrators in East Africa were (supposedly) in charge of between eight and ten million African and immigrant inhabitants. At this level, the administrative presence was actually slightly higher than in the British colonies, but some sixty times lower than in Japanese-occupied Korea. Over large areas of the colonies, then, real implementation of the supposed colonial monopoly on the use of force was impossible. Colonial administrators undertook travel outside the area of real control at their own risk. If an officer went on leave or was absent for any other reason, administrative activities often ceased for a considerable period. The few administrative stations within the country were 'islands of power' (in Michael Pesek's words) that struggled to maintain a semblance of authority (see Illustration 18).

In 1903, for example, there were only thirty German stations and military posts in German East Africa, and in many cases they were almost helpless to direct events in their surrounding regions. In most cases, the infrastructure available meant power could really be exerted only at isolated points. After the *Reich* Colonial Office was set up in 1907 and Rechenberg installed as governor (in 1906), and with the changing focus on rational, 'scientific' colonial policy, this began to change. Life in the colonial stations became strictly regulated, and the separation between officers and troops, and Germans and Africans, was implemented much more forcefully. Police regulations were imposed on local societies, natives were obliged to greet every German they encountered, and a curfew was introduced. All inhabitants were required to register their address, to make administration easier; they were also banned from changing their names. In practice, however, these policies were almost impossible

Illustration 18 Because of a lack of German troops, the conquest of the African colonies was to a large extent the work of African soldiers. Beginning with the Abushiri war of 1889–90 waged by coastal elites, German colonial rule and its military strength in East Africa rested on the conscription of Africans. They formed the core of the *Schutztruppe für Deutsch-Ostafrika* (armed forces for German East Africa) and were referred to by the Germans as *askari*, a term of Arabic origin meaning 'police'. Initially recruited among disbanded Egyptian and Somali soldiers of the Anglo-Egyptian army, they soon comprised people from various regions in East Africa. Their reputation as a fierce, sometimes brutal, but always loyal military force was reaffirmed in 1905–7 when their efforts were crucial in subduing the Maji-Maji war. Their drawn-out resistance to the Allied forces during the First World War, under the leadership of General von Lettow-Vorbeck, established the myth of the undefeatable and loyal *askari* that proved to be a powerful image for revisionist circles after 1918. The employment of African soldiers, however, was not limited to the *askari*. This picture shows recruitment among native 'volunteers' for the protection force in the German colony of Togo in 1890.

to enforce. The African population was able to make use of their superior knowledge of the local situation for their own purposes. Mobility, in particular, continued to be used strategically by the rural population and the administration found this very difficult to control. In addition, the stations in the colonial hinterlands were often dependent on the cooperation of local traders and power-holders.

This dependence on local actors found its administrative expression in the classic imperial institution of intermediarity, i.e. the delegation of power to local and regional power-holders and elites. The new power-holders had no option but to enter into alliances with locals, who were themselves pursuing their own goals. The colonial state in many ways depended on indigenous authorities and was thus a 'consumer' of local power.[4] The strategy of divide and rule was, of course, not unique to Germany. This form of indirect rule was common practice in the British colonial states, most famously in Nigeria under Lord Lugard. The objective was to achieve careful modernization while maintaining traditional structures; and to benefit from local hierarchies and loyalties. The other end of the colonial spectrum – at least in theory, because in practice these differences tended to become blurred – was represented by France and Portugal, who aimed to achieve complete control over their colonies, with little scope for local agency. German policies were located somewhere in the middle. During the early phase of German colonialism, power was based on close cooperation with chiefs like Samuel Maharero in South-West Africa (although he was later to lead the armed resistance to German rule; see Illustration 19). Later, the Germans tended more to involve selected local individuals in the colonial administration. Examples were the *akida*, used as local administrators in the coastal regions of German East Africa, or their counterparts in New Guinea, the *luluai*. This was not indirect rule as such, because the power of the colonized was not derived from their own power resources and traditional structures of authority; rather, they were taking on a role within the colonial administration.

In some regions, however, even the concept of indirect rule was a mere fiction. In northern Cameroon, for example, German rule should really be described as coexistence with local rule. The Islamic Fulbe rulers were formally subjugated through a series of military expeditions but the Germans had little real economic or political control. In fact, the Fulbe aristocracy themselves made use of the colonial power and were able, with the military support of the Germans, to expand their own area of domination. Similar structures persisted in the hinterland of Togo and German East Africa.

---

[4] Karen E. Fields, *Revival and Rebellion in Colonial Central Africa*, Princeton (Princeton University Press) 1985, 31.

Illustration 19 Samuel Maharero (1856–1923) is one of the icons of public memory among the Herero today, celebrated as the hero of the anti-German resistance. In his early career, however, he greatly benefited from cooperation with the German colonial state. Educated in a missionary school, Samuel Maharero was able to assume leadership over the Herero not least because of backing by the German colonial government against internal competitors. He supported Governor Leutwein and in some instances offered military assistance to the Germans; in return, he was able to convince Leutwein to adopt more restrictive measures that slowed down the process of dispossession of Herero land. When conditions for the Herero continued to worsen, however, Maharero initiated the armed revolt of the Herero against German rule.

LEGITIMACY

As we have seen, the institutions of the colonial state had only a sparse presence across the colonial territories. The power of the state was further reduced by its lack of 'grass-roots' legitimacy – the fact that the colonized did not believe that colonial rule was legitimate. Colonial regimes always attempted to create the impression that their interventions were done for the benefit of those ruled. They counted on the promises and allure of the 'civilizing mission', and on the appeal of their project of modernizing. The colonizers firmly believed that the state's organizational achievements would meet with the approval of the colonized populations.

The *mission civilisatrice* promised to gradually modernize the colonized societies and to improve individual standards of living. It was closely linked to a world-view that thought in terms of development and of progress. It was founded on a strong belief in the superiority of western civilization and the backwardness of African societies, and a conviction that the achievements of the colonial state would be such that those colonized would willingly go along with colonial rule. Roads, railways, buildings, the teaching of reading and writing, medical care, the creation of a western system of education, military superiority, and a (compulsory) work ethic enforced by a regime of physical punishment – all these were, in part or in whole, the result of political or economic interests, but it was also hoped that they would help to demonstrate to the native population the organizational powers of the colonial state, and the emancipatory potential of modern societies. In practice, however, these interventions, though propounded in terms of the cultural mission, often triggered resistance and as such actually helped to undermine colonial rule.

Another limit to the on-the-ground legitimacy of the colonial state was the fact that colonial rule always meant foreign rule. Even where cultural and technological change met with the approval of the population, this deficit could never be completely overcome. Anti-colonial national movements always picked up on this issue, even when they themselves were fundamentally interested in pursuing modernizing policies of the type that the colonial government had previously been engaged in. In structural terms, colonial rule was a form of 'dominance without hegemony', as Ranajit Guha has described the rule of the British empire in India. Following Antonio Gramsci, Guha uses 'hegemony' to mean the broad acceptance of a particular cultural or ideological belief in a society not through force (i.e. dominance) but through the 'agreement' of its members. In contrast, the colonial state had little chance of relying on shared beliefs and had to make use of force on a regular basis.[5]

This applied even when colonial government attempted to embrace local traditions. The British empire in India was a model in this respect, too: the East India Company adopted the institutions of the defunct Mogul empire in order to profit from the latter's prestigious status. Similarly, German colonies made use of indigenous customs and habits, typically in the context of institutions of indirect rule. This strategy was most successful in Samoa, where Governor Solf assured one group of Samoans in 1901: 'I have often told natives that the German government wishes them to be ruled, not according to white mans ideas [sic], but according to the Faa Samoa [Samoan custom] . . . For this reason I do not wish to interfere in your Samoan titles and such things.'[6] Also in Africa, German officials increasingly attempted to reconstruct local traditions and to ensure that German rule would make reference to them, and thus appear less disrupting to local ways of life. The recovery and codification of what was called 'native law', developed by legal experts such as Rudolf Asmis in Togo, was the most important element of these attempts to share in local structures of legitimacy.[7]

Nevertheless, full rights of participation in modern societies remained inaccessible to the colonized population – and thus the legitimacy of rule, by necessity, remained limited. This was one fundamental difference between colonial societies and European nation-states. Describing British-occupied Bengal, Partha Chatterjee has spoken of a 'bi-furcated public sphere'. Under the conditions of colonial rule, it was impossible for an independent civil society to

---

[5] Ranajit Guha, *Dominance without Hegemony: History and Power in Colonial India*, Cambridge, Mass. (Harvard University Press) 1998.

[6] Cited in George Steinmetz, *The Devil's Handwriting: Precoloniality and the German Colonial State in Qingdao, Samoa, and Southwest-Africa*, Chicago (University of Chicago Press) 2007, 319.

[7] Arthur J. Knoll, 'An Indigenous Law Code for the Togolese: The Work of Dr. Rudolf Asmis', in: Rüdiger Voigt and Peter Sack (eds.), *Kolonialisierung des Rechts: Zur kolonialen Rechts- und Verwaltungsordnung*, Baden-Baden (Nomos) 2001, 271–92.

emerge. Instead, the colonial state claimed and controlled large areas of the public sphere, not least by limiting education, freedom of expression, and opportunities for co-determination.[8] Similarly, the German colonial authorities did not envisage any form of popular democratic representation.

VIOLENCE AND WARS

The fourth way in which the colonial state differed from its European counterpart has to do with the extent to which its rule involved violence. This violence reflected a high degree of asymmetry in military technologies. Neither local warlords nor rulers of centralized African states had much in the way of military resources with which they could counter the occupying forces. One symbol of this military superiority was the machine gun: 'Whatever happens, we have got/ The Maxim Gun, and they have not', as the British writer Hilaire Belloc cynically remarked.[9]

On the other hand, the ubiquity of violence also reflected the weaknesses of the colonial state. Its administrative presence was limited and it was not accepted as a legitimate government by the colonized. This resulted in their refusing to cooperate, a refusal that was expressed in a variety of forms of resistance. The colonial state then saw no other means to enforce its authority but to threaten, and use, violence. I wish to differentiate between two different dimensions of this violence: the everyday violence employed in the colonial exercise of power, on the one hand, and, on the other, the escalation of violence into colonial wars that claimed many lives.

It should be emphasized that violence was an ongoing component of colonial rule. Even during the so-called 'quiet phase' in German East Africa, that is after the so-called Arab rebellion and before the Maji-Maji war, a total of sixty-one major 'penal expeditions' were carried out between 1891 and 1897. These military campaigns, often launched by independently minded officers without formal approval

---

[8] Partha Chatterjee, 'The Disciplines in Colonial Bengal', in: Partha Chatterjee (ed.), *Texts of Power: Emerging Disciplines in Colonial Bengal*, Minneapolis (University of Minnesota Press) 1995, 1–29.
[9] Hilaire Belloc and Basil Temple Blackwood, *The Modern Traveller*, London (Edward Arnold) 1898, 41.

from the colonial capital, took place mainly in the interior of the colony.

These military expeditions took place in an environment in which more low-key violence was an everyday occurrence. Because the colonizers could control the vast interior of the country only at isolated points, it often did not take very much to trigger such violence. Often, punishment was enacted in a symbolic manner to make the intervention more visible and to ensure that its effect was more pronounced. Michel Foucault has famously shown that measures to discipline and punish in western Europe were increasingly hidden from public view in the nineteenth century, and that contemporaries saw this as a process of rationalization and civilization.[10] In the colonies, by way of contrast, the exhibition of violence and the staging of symbolic acts of brutality remained standard practice. Prisoners in chains, public executions, and public displays of the bodies of 'rebels' and 'criminals' were all part of the enactment of colonial rule. Criminal justice made extensive use of beatings, other forms of corporal punishment, and chaining of prisoners. Corporal punishment did not decline even after Dernburg's 'rationalizing' reforms of colonial policy. In Cameroon, for example, the number of instances actually rose from 315 in 1900 to 4,800 in 1913, and we can assume that behind these official statistics, the actual rates were considerably higher. On plantations and farms, and in the private households where Africans were often employed, there was little chance of legal recourse or even of any official awareness. Thus, there was a constant threat that conflicts would be resolved through the use of violence.

Beyond this constant threat of escalation, violence was unleashed in the most forceful manner in the three major wars that the German empire fought in its colonies. The first of these, the 'Boxer war' in northern China in 1900, was not a colonial war in the classical sense. It was fought within the Chinese empire and, in part, against the imperial Chinese government. Although Chinese power had declined markedly during the latter years of the Qing dynasty, China remained, for the most part, an independent state. The activities of

[10] Michel Foucault, *Discipline and Punish: The Birth of the Prison*, New York (Random House) 1975.

the Boxers (*yihetuan*) – the name originated in traditional boxing schools – were directed not against any particular form of foreign rule but in general against the imperialist infiltration of the country; the activities of the Christian missions and their interventions in local conflicts on behalf of Chinese Christians caused particular anger. But this very heterogeneous movement, which made use of elements of regional popular culture such as mass trances and invulnerability rituals, must also be viewed in the context of political conflict about the modernization of China. This conflict intensified after the defeat of China by Japan in 1895 and the failure of reforms in 1898.

When, after some initial hesitation, the Chinese emperor intervened in the war on the side of the Boxers, the other imperialist powers, including the United States and Japan, launched a joint, coordinated campaign (see Illustration 20). This was unique in the history of colonialism. In reaction to the murder of the German envoy to Peking, Clemens von Ketteler, command of this campaign was given to Germany. Emperor Wilhelm saw off the German troops in Bremerhaven in July 1900, and gave his infamous speech that both expressed the fears of a 'yellow peril' held by the nationalist right, and helped prepare the ideological ground for later atrocities (see Illustration 21):

Should you encounter the enemy, he will be defeated! No quarter will be given! Prisoners will not be taken! Whoever falls into your hands is forfeited. Just as Attila's Huns of a thousand years ago made a name for themselves, one that even today makes them seem mighty in history and legend, may the name German be affirmed by you in such a way in China that no Chinese will ever again dare to look askance at a German.[11]

By the time the German contingents under Alfred von Waldersee actually arrived in China the international forces had already taken Peking. In the spring of 1901, the German forces fought rearguard actions across northern China with the aim of the 'pacification' of 'rebel' provinces. Their campaign included many brutal attacks and massacres. These were heavily criticized both by the German public, which was able to follow the events in China through extensive press

---

[11] The full version of the speech, including the parts that were delivered but originally unpublished, can be found in Bernd Soesemann, 'Die sog. Hunnenrede Wilhelms II.', *Historische Zeitschrift* 222, 342–58.

Illustration 20 In Germany, the Boxer war was represented as an element of European policing on a world stage. As this postcard on 'The War in China' illustrates, different European powers cooperated in their effort to subdue the revolt. The caption 'We will strongly and truly bowl him down, hooray' also betrays the xenophobic rhetoric of the time, moored in the larger discourse of the 'yellow peril'. It merged notions of cultural and racial superiority with the perception of a demographic and economic threat posed to Europe and the 'white race' in general. There were, however, also other voices, critical of the violent engagement in China. Social Democrat papers such as *Vorwärts* collected and published soldiers' letters home with first-hand accounts of atrocities committed by German soldiers in China.

reporting, and in the *Reichstag*, where the Social Democrats and the *Freisinnige* (German Free-Minded Party, a liberal party founded in 1884) condemned the imperialist war. But such protests did little to change the draconian measures used to end the war, which included huge compensatory payments and a Chinese 'mission of atonement' to Germany and Japan. In China, this defeat was a major turning-point. Nationalism established itself as the hegemonic ideology and, in the years that followed, the imperial court introduced extensive reforms in the form of the 'New Policy' (see Illustration 22).

The war in German South-West Africa (1904–7) was fundamentally a war about land ownership and foreign rule. The Herero, the largest population group in the colony, had been particularly badly

Illustration 21 On 27 July 1900, Emperor Wilhelm II delivered a speech to the departing troops in front of the Lloyd depot in Bremerhaven. The most outrageous parts of his speech were censored by the German Chancellor Bernhard von Bülow but soon leaked into the press. The call to administer violence and to repress brutally any form of resistance met with criticism in the *Reichstag*, but fell on fertile ground with General Field Marshal Alfred von Waldersee (1832–1904), who directed the troops in China. In a letter addressed to the emperor in December 1900, Waldersee reported: 'There has been no lack of harsh handling (*schärfstem Anfassen*), and this will no doubt remain in the memories here for a long time. As a result, the number of Chinese killed is quite substantial. There is a fresh spirit visible in all parts of the troops.'

affected by the German governor's plans for land seizure. Three-quarters of the country's territory was to be handed over to German settlers, with the rest remaining as reservations for the African population. In addition, the rinderpest epidemic of 1897 had seriously weakened the Herero's cattle stocks, the material basis of their nomadic existence. In this difficult situation, the Herero launched attacks on German farmers that took both the settlers and the German colonial government completely by surprise. German troops, led by Governor Leutwein, attempted to stop the conflict escalating and opened negotiations with the Herero leader Samuel Maharero. But

Illustration 22 The German troops – this photograph shows the entry of the cavalry into the Forbidden City – arrived in China one full month after Allied forces, led by the Japanese, had defeated the uprising and occupied Peking. The Chinese capital was subject to destruction and looting. The Forbidden City remained the headquarters of the Allied forces for more than a year, before the Dowager Empress Cixi was able to return to the capital. In the following years, she initiated a policy of cautious reform, including the promise of a constitution along Western lines, and most spectacularly the abrogation of the Imperial Civil Service Examinations that also paved the way for the establishment of a modern school system. The Boxer war, however, had fundamentally weakened the position of the dynasty, and efforts at reform came too late. In 1911, the Qing dynasty was toppled, and long decades of dramatic transformation and turmoil began.

the German imperial government, which, not least because of the symbolic character of this challenge to German colonial rule, insisted that the conflict could end only in the unconditional surrender of the Herero, reacted by transferring command to General Lieutenant von

Illustration 23 General Lothar von Trotha (1848–1920), shown here with his staff in Keetmanshoop (Southern South-West Africa) in 1904, was responsible for the brutality and atrocities committed in the Herero war. The official account of the General Staff reported: 'This bold undertaking demonstrates brilliantly the relentless energy of the German leadership in pursuing the beaten enemy. No efforts, no sacrifices were avoided in order to dispossess the enemy of the last remainders of his power to resist; he was chased from one watering hole to the next like hounded game, until he finally became deprived of his will and a victim of the force of nature in his own country. The waterless Omaheke was to execute what the German arms had begun: the annihilation of the Herero people.'

Trotha. Lothar von Trotha had already gained extensive experience in colonial wars in East Africa and during the Boxer War. He declared open war on the Herero and, after initial failures, developed a strategy that interpreted the war as a racial war, which would necessarily lead to 'rivers of blood' and which would 'be concluded only with the annihilation or complete subjugation of one side'[12] (see Illustration 23).

His infamous order to shoot any Herero on German territory, even women and children, the introduction of prisoner camps, and the forcing back of the Herero into the Omaheke desert have led many

[12] Quoted from Horst Drechsler, *Südwestafrika unter deutscher Kolonialherrschaft: Der Kampf der Herero und Nama gegen den deutschen Imperialismus (1884–1915)*, Berlin (Akademie-Verlag) 1966, 156.

modern historians to view Trotha's war as a war of annihilation. After public criticism erupted Trotha was recalled, but this did not prevent him being awarded the Imperial medal 'Pour le Mérite'.

In late 1904, the Nama, who lived in the southern part of the colony, led by Hendrik Witbooi, also declared war, although they had initially supported the German troops against the Herero. In contrast to the Herero, they engaged in a small-scale guerrilla war that lasted for two more years. Together, these two wars resulted in large numbers of casualties, decimating the two African peoples. None of the figures available is completely reliable, but the census of 1911 reports a total of only 15,000 Herero, against about 80,000 before the war. The Nama population, totalling about 20,000 people, was roughly halved in the course of the war. Of the 14,000 German soldiers involved, about 1500 died, in battle or through disease.

In contrast to the events in South-West Africa, the German public was almost unaware of the Maji-Maji war in German East Africa (1905–8). It, too, was a reaction to foreign rule in general and land policy in particular. The specific events that provoked the outbreak of violence were the government initiatives to increase the colony's profitability through taxation, pressing the Africans to pay in cash and no longer in kind, and forcing many into unpaid public labour; an obligation to plant cotton; and the introduction of village administrators, often non-local Arabs, which placed the autonomy of the villages in question.

But in contrast to the situation in South-West Africa this revolt was not led by one large political community; it took place in a region inhabited by a large number of different groups. The war received transregional support only because of a religious movement. This developed after a religious awakening by the prophet Kinjikitele Ngwale in late 1904 and was partly based on the cult worship of water (in Swahili, *maji*), which was ascribed a miraculous power, even against the weapons of the colonists. This movement was able to unite the mainly peasant population across linguistic, social, and cultural boundaries, and ensured that a 'locally limited rebellion by a few half-savage tribes', as Governor von Götzen described it, developed 'into a kind of national struggle against foreign rule'.[13]

---

[13] Gustav Adolf von Götzen, *Deutsch-Ostafrika im Aufstand 1905/06*, Berlin (Reimer) 1909, 63.

Initially, the colonial government underestimated the rebellion. For a long time it was not even clear which regions were actually involved. After initial massacres through German use of the machine-gun, the Africans soon adopted guerrilla tactics that broke fighting up into small episodes, prolonged the war and also allowed the colonial power to play individual groups off against each other. The war was not, like that in South-West Africa, commanded from Berlin, but remained within the colony. And the Germans did not see this conflict as a 'racial' war or war of annihilation but rather as an attempt to 'pacify' rebellious regions that was to be carried out mainly through the use of African troops. This qualitative difference notwithstanding, the number of victims was huge. Despite only small losses on the German side, at least 80,000 Africans died in the fighting – and almost 300,000, when we include the victims of the famine that resulted from the destruction of fields and villages in the war.

CHAPTER 6

Economy and work

One of the main motivations for Germany's acquisition of colonies was the promise of rich financial rewards. But these hopes remained largely unfulfilled; in economic terms, Germany profited very little from its colonies. However, the economies and societies of the colonies themselves were deeply transformed by imperialism. Characteristic features of colonial economies included a monopoly (by the colonial state) on taxation, control over currencies, and controls over imports and exports. Of even greater significance for the societies affected were changes to market structures, to production, and to ownership, in particular of land. At the same time, it is important to remember that colonial economies were not created out of nothing; there were many continuities, both in agricultural production and in terms of links to export markets. Large parts of Africa were already engaged in trade links with other parts of the world in pre-colonial times; trade connections across the Indian ocean, for example, linked the eastern coast of Africa with the Arabian peninsula and with south Asia. In many instances, for example in western Africa, the colonizers continued to use the export infrastructure and links that had been there before they arrived. The persistence of pre-colonial trade links was even more pronounced in the case of Kiaochow; even after the takeover by the Germans, Japan remained its most important foreign trading partner.

COLONIAL ECONOMIC POLICY: PLANTATIONS, FARMS, OR TRADE?

Most of the colonial conflicts – within the colonial administration, between different colonial interest groups, between Germans living in the colonies, and finally between Germans and the colonized populations – had to do with economic policy. There were three main competing visions of economic development propagated by different colonial interest groups in Germany (although in practice these often overlapped). The first was a plantation economy, made up of large areas of monoculture worked by native labourers, focusing on the export trade. This model required high levels of capital investment and large amounts of labour (in 1912, almost 12,000 people were employed on plantations in Cameroon), often recruited only with the use of force. Brutal treatment and inadequate conditions caused many deaths among plantation workers. While the colonial governments, for example that in East Africa, claimed that the abolition of slavery was one of the main objectives of German colonialism, the plantation owners established new forms of bonded labour that had high mortality rates too.

Setting up plantations also required the seizure of fertile land, which had major impacts on local land ownership patterns. This was particularly true of Cameroon, where the largest system of plantations in the whole of Africa was created. Under Governor Puttkamer, fertile lands around Mount Cameroon were seized and the local Duala population was forced to move to less fertile regions. The beneficiaries were large corporations, which used the plantations mainly to grow cocoa and coffee and, later, cotton and rubber for the electrical and automotive industries. Plantations were also created in German East Africa and in the Pacific (where mainly coconut palms were grown); by contrast, there were only a few in Togo.

The second model for the colonial economy was based around the idea of individual farms run by German farmers. This model was closely linked with socio-political objectives. It was most common in German South-West Africa; under Governor Theodor Leutwein, the region was to be turned into Germany's only settlement colony, involving large-scale land seizure that dispossessed and impoverished large groups of African farmers. Leutwein's policy of land re-allocation was complemented by an active immigration policy supported by the German Colonial Society. This was based not only on political and demographic reasoning, but also on the idea, popular in *völkisch* and nationalist circles, that in these peripheral lands Germany could experience a 'renewal', a rebirth. These German settlers farmed their own plots, mostly employing only a few African workers. Because the soils in most parts of German South-West Africa were not very fertile, agriculture was possible only at a subsistence level and the new farmers, like the indigenous groups, focused on raising cattle. In German East Africa, the number of farmers increased after 1906, to approximately 600 by 1914. This was a result of railway construction, of infrastructural improvements, and of the rubber boom on world markets, whose effects countered the end of government subsidies to settlers as a result of the Maji-Maji war. Despite their small number (compared with the 14,000 settlers in South-West Africa), they were a powerful lobby and demanded that the government seize extensive areas of land and purportedly 'unoccupied' territories.

However, the governors were often interested in promoting a third model of economic development. This relied neither on plantations nor on small farmers but on trade in goods produced by the local population. This approach created a conflict of interest between the colonial governments and the farmers, in German East Africa, for example, and most particularly in Togo, in the Pacific colonies and in Kiaochow. This conflict had three main dimensions. One issue was land. Land seizures led to conflict with the local population, as in German East Africa, where the government regarded the activities of farmers as one of the main causes of the Maji-Maji war. The second aspect was labour, as German farms and plantations demanded a work force that could be secured only through (technically) legal coercion and outright force. These forms of unfree labour were among the major causes of social unrest and colonial uprisings. The third dimension concerned the question of the most efficient economic policy for the colonies. Those in the colonial governments, and in Germany itself, who supported liberal trade interests felt that settling Germans in the colonies was inefficient; they believed that promoting indigenous agriculture would be the most profitable course of action. In this, they were frequently supported by the Christian missions, although the latter's reasons for supporting indigenous agriculture were different. The missions argued that a free, native system of small-scale farmers should be encouraged, so as not to destroy local societies (in both economic and cultural terms). Ideas about promoting small-scale farming communities were put forward as an explicit counter-model to the proletarianization that plantations involved.

Illustration 24 All claims to modernization and infrastructural development notwithstanding, large parts of the colonial economy in Africa rested on traditional means of transportation. Most products were carried by long caravans of porters to the commercial nodal points and ports along the coast. On the eve of the First World War, it is estimated that on the route between the inland administrative centre of Yaoundé and the port city of Kribi in Cameroon alone, about 80,000 porters were employed. In the eyes of the German plantation owners, porter caravans drew an excessive part of the labour force away from the plantations. As they were also the preferred conveyance of African traders and thus of market competitors, the caravan owners were criticized for their use of slaves and for breach of the regulations governing caravans issued by the colonial state.

The economic policies favoured by the governors were also welcomed by the colonial reformers in Dernburg's circle, who believed that native producers would be the most effective drivers of colonial development. And trade in goods produced within the African economies themselves actually made up the majority of exports. Even in Cameroon, with its huge monocultures, the share of foreign trade contributed by the plantations was small compared to that contributed by indigenous production. In other words, colonial exports (not to mention local consumption) were made up mainly of products from local hunting-and-gathering economies and cultivation by African farmers. These products were brought in long caravans to the market towns on the coasts (see Illustration 24).

'EDUCATING TO WORK'

As in the other European empires, the 'labour question' was regarded as the most important issue for colonial policies. As slavery had been officially abolished, and as putting an end to slavery had been one of the legitimating strategies of European colonial intervention, access to local labour, in particular in Africa, became a thorny issue for European plantations. Drawing on the then prevalent views of medical doctors and scientists, those involved in colonial policy believed that Europeans were not suited to physical work in the tropics, and discussions thus focused on African labour. Initially, and despite their anti-slavery rhetoric, the German colonial authorities allowed slavery to continue in a number of places, for example in East Africa. The authorities were concerned that the local pre-colonial economies should not be destroyed. In 1900, there were still some 400,000 slaves in German East Africa. They were owned by African and Arab elites and made up about 10 per cent of the total population. But German-owned plantations were unable to make use of slave labour, not least for legal reasons. The development of a market for labour, therefore, depended on the gradual decline of slavery. After 1900, this set in quickly. The transition from slavery to waged work, however, was not a linear process, as recent research has shown. The use of seasonal and temporary migrant labour was characteristic of the development of the capitalist system in Africa.

Because local economies were subsistence economies, and because of the continued existence of slavery, there was no native labour market to which the plantation owners had access. Ostensibly, the problem was that the natives were regarded as lazy. The Africans' 'notorious indolence and laziness' was frequently cited, and opinions were given on how to deal with the 'limitless idling and lazy existence' of the new subjects and how to 'target loafers'.[1] The pervasive nature of this stereotype indicates that, even at the height of colonial conquest, European colonial power was less than absolute. Continual complaints about 'laziness' reveal the limits of the availability of native subjects.

---

[1] Gerhard von Byern, *Deutsch-Ostafrika und seine weißen und schwarzen Bewohner*, Berlin (Süsserott) 1913, 13; H. Bohner, 'Die Einführung geregelter Arbeit in Kamerun', *Die deutschen Kolonien* 1 (1902), 67–72, quote on pp. 70–1.

As a result, four main recruitment strategies were generally discussed as to how best to secure local labour (though there were some differences between the colonies). The first was the use of compulsion – the introduction of an obligation (for Africans) to take up work. This was demanded by business owners and self-styled adventurers such as Carl Peters: 'The Negro was created by God for rough work', he declaimed. 'It would not exactly harm the Negro to have to serve the state for a number of years as German, French, and Russian citizens have to do . . . Prove to me that it is inhuman to force a lazybones to work.'[2] However, no statutory period of compulsory labour service was ever introduced (see Illustration 25). The second strategy was to introduce forms of periodic taxation such as hut taxes or poll taxes. The need for money to pay these taxes would, it was hoped, force Africans to take up paid employment in German plantations. In German East Africa, for example, such measures were taken in 1897. The regulation stipulated that taxpayers in arrears could be assigned to the administrative authorities or to private plantations in order to work off the taxes they owed. However, this taxation was rejected by the colonized, who reacted with a variety of evasive strategies. In fact, the introduction of the tax on huts must be seen as one of the causes of the 1905 Maji-Maji war in German East Africa. Not much tax revenue was raised, in the end, partly because many district heads were afraid of social unrest and thus did not make any concerted attempts to collect the taxes.

The third potential solution was to recruit cheap labour from Asia. This was done in German East Africa and, especially, in the German Pacific colonies. Chinese contract workers, known as 'coolies', were hired (often under coercion). Their numbers totalled 4,000 in Samoa and New Guinea and 1,000 in German East Africa. Because of brutal treatment by their German masters, recruitment became increasingly difficult and was finally discontinued. The fourth strategy drew upon the racially loaded discourse of 'educating to work', which was linked with the concept of the cultural mission. 'Educating to work' was an ubiquitous element of German colonial policies. It was supported by a flimsy coalition made up of the colonial government, business owners, and the missions. The economic reasoning was accompanied by

[2] Carl Peters, *Zur Weltpolitik*, Berlin (Karl Siegismund Verlag) 1912, 129.

Illustration 25 Even if no formal system of compulsory labour was ever introduced in the colonies, forced labour was an everyday reality. Beyond the official rhetoric of free trade and free labour markets, various forms of coercion were regularly employed. In many regions, the plantation managers looked after their own recruitment and forced the chiefs in the region at gunpoint to provide young men as labourers. Until the turn of the century, at least, the colonial government rarely questioned the legitimacy of such methods of recruitment. In fact, work under colonial conditions – especially during the early years of colonial power in Africa – could often scarcely be differentiated from indentured labour or forced labour. There was often no clear-cut dividing line between slavery and compulsory labour, or between these and paid labour. The picture shows a chain gang of convicts in Dar es Salaam in German East Africa.

a belief in the civilizing task in which the Christian missions saw themselves engaged. Its aim was to form the characters of the local population, and engaging in regular, physical labour was believed to be an essential element in this process. Although the missions were always at pains to emphasize to German farmers and plantation owners that this labour should be of a humanitarian, non-exploitative character, and mission staff frequently protested against the ruthless methods used on the plantations, hard labour was performed on the mission stations and the mission plantations as well. Tellingly, *ora et labora* ('pray and work') emerged as the main slogan of the colonial missions.

In many regions, labour policies such as these represented a major social change. By 1910, 90 per cent of men in German South-West Africa were working for the Europeans. And the victory of European ideas about 'work' was not limited to the actual activity involved, but had much larger repercussions; it affected individuals, economies, and societies as a whole. The many and diverse effects also included, to give an important example, changes in the social and gender division of labour. Across Africa, women had traditionally done a large part of the work in maintaining food supplies. While cattle-herding (where it was practised at all) was reserved for men, agricultural cultivation, which was integrated in native cosmologies and often had religious implications, was usually the responsibility of women. Complicated and regionally diverse domestic divisions of labour were often seen by German administrators and missionaries as economically and socially backward in comparison to a system of patriarchal monogamy; African polygamous traditions were interpreted as absolving the men from the responsibility to perform manual labour. In colonial discourse, preventing women from carrying out agricultural work, even forcibly, was regarded as a contribution towards emancipating and 'civilizing' them (see Illustration 26).

In many ways, 'educating to work' was not just an instrument of economic policy and of social discipline but corresponded to the contemporary European belief about the link between work, the development of the subject, and modernization. Those involved in the missions and the colonial administration did not think this necessarily involved deprivation or repression. In many cases, the emancipatory rhetoric used was genuinely meant. This viewpoint was sometimes shared by Africans. In retrospect, especially, members of the elite often expressed their esteem for the education provided by the missionary centres. Reactions to the measures taken by the colonial powers thus sometimes differed and also depended on different interests, social status, gender, and origins. More often, however, the reaction to these colonial ambitions was complete incomprehension and resistance in a variety of forms.

TAKING STOCK

The creation of colonial economies and the integration of some areas of cultivation into world trade had drastic effects on local societies.

Illustration 26 Most of the products offered in the market in Notsé, Togo (1906) were grown, in all likelihood, by women. The German colonial government as well as the mission societies were keen to transform the gendered division of labour found in many African societies. In their view, the combination of women's work in the fields and polygyny released men from the one type of activity that was of importance from a European point of view. To deal with this situation, the missionary Alexander Merensky called for the introduction of a marriage tax because 'the easier the women make the African's life the less inclined he is to look for work'. At least, that is, for the kind of work missionaries had in mind: physical, male work, not in the private sphere of the home but in the public sphere, in the fields. The social, economic, and political contexts of local societies were completely ignored by the project of educating-to-work.

One particular characteristic of work in colonial societies was that conflicts between business owners and workers were perceived as part of the foreign rule. One of the main reasons for this was that the official ban on slavery did not lead to the establishment of a system of voluntary waged labour (even though wage labour, as one form of labour relations, did exist, particularly in the port cities); a multiplicity of non-economic forces worked together, so that in many cases the boundaries between free and bonded labour remained indistinct and mostly fictitious. The labour mobility with which many Africans reacted to the new situation also had long-lasting consequences, often leading to the dissolution of village-based family structures. But it is also important to note that the vast majority of the African population in Germany's African colonies continued to live their lives in an agrarian world and many remained almost unengaged in the colonial market economy.

Some groups were also able to use the situation to their advantage. This applied especially to trade. The Hausa in western Africa, for example, profited from colonial structures and were able to extend their activities to the south of Cameroon. They sold small quantities of a wide range of goods, usually for lower prices than their European competitors, and this allowed them to secure their own markets. Despite protests by local German traders, the colonial administration in Cameroon reinforced the Hausa's position because they felt that the services provided by the Hausa – for example the supplies of livestock and meat that they acquired from the Islamic Fulbe states further north – were indispensable.

Some German businesses made substantial profits in the colonies. The German Trading and Plantations Company (*Deutsche Handels- und Plantagen-Gesellschaft*), for example, which dominated the copra trade in New Guinea and also traded in cocoa and rubber, paid out high dividends to its shareholders. But in terms of the German economy as a whole, trade with the colonies was of little importance. Only 2 per cent of German capital investment went to the colonies; imports from the colonies made up less than 0.5 per cent of the country's total imports, and most of these were agricultural products such as cotton, rubber, and coffee. Mining was negligible, with the exception of diamonds, mined in South-West Africa from 1908 onwards. Nor did the colonies develop as export markets for domestic German products to the extent hoped. While consumer goods for German settlers – alcohol, textiles, and weapons, and materials for infrastructural development – were all exported, by 1913 exports to the German colonies still made up less than 1 per cent of total German exports. And the reverse also applied: by 1914, trade with Germany made up only 8 per cent of Kiaochow's trade figures, for example. In fact, even within Africa, other regions – South Africa, Egypt, and Morocco – were more important as trading partners for Germany than the German colonies.

Illustration 27 The railway was one of the most powerful icons of imperialist takeover. In imperialist rhetoric, it was associated with progress and development, and symbolized the modernizing impulse that colonial rule promised to bring. Railways were also preferred targets of anti-colonial resistance movements, most conspicuously in China during the Boxer war. Beyond their discursive appropriation, railways helped stabilize colonial rule and, most importantly, guaranteed the incorporation of colonial territories into global markets. This photograph shows African workers on the railway line linking Dar es Salaam and Morogoro in German East Africa (1907).

For the German state, the colonial empire was actually a loss-maker. Almost none of the colonies was self-financing. Only the smallest and economically least important colonies, Samoa and Togo, reached the stage, towards the end of Germany's colonial era, of not being a drain on imperial finances. Although some private businesses did make profits, the German state did not benefit much. Because the costs of administration and of the wars, especially those in South-West Africa and China, were so high, Germany ended up spending colossal sums on its colonial empire over a thirty-year period.

After they became independent, some of the former colonies were still able to make use of the infrastructure created during the period of German rule. Of primary importance were the railways, which had been financed using German government loans (see Illustration 27).

Roads and harbours had also been constructed. These investments were portrayed by the Germans as contributions to the development of the colonies. But the transport links created were designed with the short- and medium-term needs of European markets in mind. The railway lines that were constructed linked areas of agricultural cultivation with the harbours on the coast. There was a deliberate absence of industrial development; all the materials for building the railways, for example, were imported from Europe. The objective of these investments was to establish markets for sales of German exports and to extract raw materials for European industry, not to introduce modernization for the benefit of local communities.

CHAPTER 7

Colonial society

It is impossible to speak of a single 'colonial society'. In fact, the colonies were made up of a number of different societies. A large local population, itself often extremely heterogeneous, can be contrasted with a small minority of European (or American, or Japanese) inhabitants. These two groups were clearly delineated and separated, in theory and often in practice. Colonial policy was devised largely to produce and maintain this difference, although this does not necessarily mean that colonialism excluded the possibility of any kind of integration. In fact, the French policy of assimilation, practised most commonly in northern Africa, aimed to achieve cultural homogenization. (The policy was by no means egalitarian, however: Algerians who wanted to obtain French citizenship had to abandon Islam.) Integration went even further in the Japanese empire, where, according to the policy of assimilation (*dôka*), colonial subjects in Taiwan and Korea were, in principle, treated like Japanese citizens, though with some discriminatory limitations. This policy was based on ideological beliefs about ethnic affinity and the cultural closeness of eastern Asian countries with a shared history of Confucianism; and it was based on repression, as the forced name changes of Koreans testify. These examples show that colonialism could cover a wide range of different degrees of distinction and assimilation. These could range from integration, sometimes forcible, to apartheid. A tension existed between these different forms of colonial policy. But at a more fundamental level, this tension was an inherent part of the colonial project. Strategies of difference and of convergence, in complex and ambivalent ways, went hand in hand. The differentiation between the colonial masters and the colonized, a differentiation that was increasingly expressed in terms of 'race', stood in opposition to the concept of 'elevation' preached by the proponents of the cultural mission that was one of the main ideologies driving the colonial project. At the same time, the colonizers always felt that those at home suspected them of adapting too much to local conditions – of going native. This double tension – colonial difference *vis-à-vis* the civilizing mission on the one hand, and going native on the other – formed the deep ideological structure of colonialism.

SOCIETIES, IN PLURAL

In the German colonies, Germans encountered a wide variety of different societies. While Kiaochow was an intrinsic part of the Chinese empire and had a relatively homogeneous population, Germany's colonies in Africa were inhabited by a variety of different groups with heterogeneous political, cultural, and linguistic characteristics. The vast majority of the inhabitants were engaged in agriculture, and this did not change substantially. However, during the course of the nineteenth century, mobility increased, and was promoted further during the colonial period. One influence was the introduction of plantations, which attracted migrant workers, as did the copper mines of south-western Africa. Urbanization, still in its infancy, was also strongly driven by colonialism. In most regions, there had been only a few isolated urban settlements before Europeans arrived in force; in what became German South-West Africa, there were none at all. From the late nineteenth century onwards some of these centres were expanded, especially those close to the coast or located at strategic positions along trade routes.

By far the biggest city in the German colonial empire was Qingdao (Illustration 28). What had originally been a small fishing village grew rapidly into a centre of trade and administration, equipped with a modern harbour that also acted as a naval base. In 1914, after a period of extremely rapid growth, its population totalled 55,000, of which 95 per cent were Chinese. The vast majority (over 40,000) of the city's population were male. Most were not descendants of the local peasant population, but had come to the region temporarily, as workers or, in a few cases, as merchants. The situation in Dar es Salaam, in German East Africa, was similar. Here, the majority native population numbered about 19,000, while the European population was not quite

Illustration 28 Founded in 1898, Qingdao was intended as a showcase for the modernity of the German empire and a 'particularly pleasant residence' for Europeans in Asia. To avoid overpopulation and the driving out of Europeans as a result of an anticipated massive Chinese influx, the city was divided into Chinese and European quarters. The segregation was rhetorically motivated by sanitary considerations and fear of 'the Chinese with their inevitable dirt and stench'. As this panorama shows, the European part of the city was dominated by an idyllic cottage style reminiscent of German small towns, and avoided incorporation of elements of Chinese architecture. Shortly after the outbreak of the First World War, Qingdao was ceded to Japan before being returned to China in 1922.

1,000. Most of the Africans were labourers and workers, but the city was also a locus for a number of groups that mediated between the native and the imperial societies: translators and interpreters, various kinds of merchants and wholesalers, African members of the *Schutztruppe* (armed forces), and missionaries.

In German East Africa, the intermediaries also included Arab and Indian groups. Arab village administrators (*akida*) often took on a number of local administrative functions, and Arab merchants and caravan traders also played an important role. The Indian population was engaged for the most part in trade. In 1914, the Indian population of the colony was about 9,000. These traders dominated large areas of internal trade, earning the dislike of German settlers, who felt that the Indians were strengthening the position of small-scale local producers to the settlers' disadvantage. Under Governor Rechenberg, who was opposed to limits on immigration to the colony, government policy would in effect (according to the *Usambara Post*) make 'German East Africa into a colony of civil servants, Negroes and Indians'.[1] The Indian population was also heterogeneous in itself (although, until 1914, it was predominantly Muslim) and its position, caught between the protests of the settlers and the prejudices of the African majority population, remained insecure.

In all the German colonies, the inhabitants of the European enclaves made up a tiny minority of the population as a whole. These enclaves were highly male-dominated societies, composed of civil servants and administrators, soldiers and officers, merchants, plantation owners, settlers and missionaries. In German East Africa and German South-West Africa, tension developed between the urban population and the farmers (a quarter of whom originated from other European countries); the farmers saw the town-dwellers as symbols of bureaucratization and, in German East Africa, of an overly lenient land policy. The German inhabitants of the cities were themselves by no means homogeneous, but their small numbers meant that they became a close-knit community (see Illustration 29).

The settlers' relationship with their homeland was ambivalent. In cultural terms, they generally pursued a bourgeois lifestyle, character-ized by *Kaffee und Kuchen*, literary circles and societies, musical get-togethers, and beloved folk songs. These activities were intended to document the colonists' proximity to their homeplace even in a strange and far-away land. At the same time, some of the settlers and, especially, some of their representatives in Germany, saw the colonists as the avant-garde of a renewal of the German nation, one that would be far removed from the social, regional, and religious conflicts of the *Kaiserreich*. The idea was to found a new Germany that was not riven by internal conflicts and thus to go beyond the political unification of the *Kaiserreich* in 1871 that nationalist and *völkisch* milieus considered incomplete.

These ideas were often linked to utopias of a pre-industrial world where manual work predominated. German South-West Africa, in particular, was envisioned becoming a settler colony, and the first governor, Theodor Leutwein, initiated a series of measures to

---

[1] Cited in Gründer, *Geschichte der deutschen Kolonien*, 164.

Illustration 29 In colonial clubs and associations, German communities fostered their cohesion and celebrated forms of overseas Germanness that turned these communities, in the eyes of participants and even more in the nationalist press in Germany, into strongholds of true national virtue. In large cities such as Qingdao, leisure activities included horse races, concerts, and balls. In smaller communities elsewhere, singing groups (named 'Harmony' or 'Happiness') and 'German Societies', bowling groups and masked balls, gymnastic groups, shooting, rowing, and excursion societies, fraternities, and charitable groups helped to create a community and forms of organized sociability, but were also seen as outposts of the national defensive struggle. They were joined by the churches, which played a major role in defining Germans. This image shows a shooting club in Cameroon.

establish large plantation owner and settler communities there. Large colonialist associations like the German Colonial Society (*Deutsche Kolonialgesellschaft*) supported these projects that were fuelled not only by considerations of power politics and international competition, but also by visions of a reconstruction of Germanness. Long debates ensued in governmental and colonialist circles in the quest for the ideal settler, who was not only to be manly and productive but was to assume the role of bearer of German culture. As recruitment of migrants proved difficult, a number of different schemes was employed that even included attempts to establish tuberculosis sanatoriums in the colony.

In the end, however, the politics of colonial settlement proved frustrating. Before 1914, there never lived more than 24,000 Germans in all the overseas possessions combined – small even in comparison to the tiny German principality of Schwarzburg-Sondershausen. Nevertheless, as a result of these debates and initiatives, the beginnings of a colonial identity began to emerge. And this identity lived on even after the end of the colonial empire: after 1919, about half of the 14,000 settlers stayed on in German South-West Africa even though it had lost its links to Germany.

POLICIES OF DIFFERENTIATION

Colonial power during the nineteenth century was founded on a politics of difference. Colonial encounters had always required that explicit hierarchies be established. Yet in comparison with earlier phases of colonialism, when cultural interactions and sexual relationships between groups were frequent, from the late eighteenth century onward the distance between the colonizers and the colonized, generally speaking, grew ever wider. Examining the British empire in South Asia, Partha Chatterjee has coined the influential term 'rule of colonial difference'. By this he means the ideological, and practical, importance for the reality of colonial power of the idea that there was a fundamental dichotomy between the colonial masters and the (supposedly inferior) colonized population. This concept was central even where the government and administration believed that their colonial subjects would at some point in the future be capable of becoming citizens with equal rights to those of citizens at home.[2] Strategies to uphold, and guarantee, the line between colonizers and colonized were thus crucial ingredients of colonial rule.

The policy of differentiation was ideologically supported by the contemporary discourse of race. It is important to acknowledge that this discourse was never a single monolithic concept. Even around the turn of the century, there were many different, and competing, understandings of race in Europe. And the complex relationship between culture and biology was interpreted in a number of different

[2] Partha Chatterjee, *The Nation and its Fragments: Colonial and Postcolonial Histories*, Princeton (Princeton University Press) 1993.

ways. To generalize somewhat, it is possible to identify two main strands of thought. The first was a concept based on older traditions of cultural philosophy that assumed that 'races' could change. A paternalistic emphasis on education was coupled with the promise that in the long term the inferior peoples could become emancipated. The second main view of race drew more strongly on a biologistic understanding of the term, based on the notion of unchanging biological traits. It formed the basis for repressive demographic measures and 'biopolitical' interventions. However, this differentiation is a theoretical one. In social practice, a variety of eclectic views developed. What is more, references to racial categories were also frequently used to legitimize other forms of exclusion, for example on the basis of class or religious affiliation.

In everyday life, the politics of difference in the colonies manifested itself in the separation of living spheres. This was most obvious in towns and cities, where the townscape, even the architecture reflected the basic dichotomy between 'whites' and 'natives'. Qingdao in Kiaochow, which the German Navy intended to develop as a model of a decidedly modern form of colonial policy, is a particularly good example. Outside the main town, nine small settlements were completely flattened. New residential areas were then constructed on the basis of detailed plans. The architecture and urban structure that resulted reflected the social order that the colonial power wished to impose. The zones designated as residential areas for the Chinese population were on the periphery, with the European city as the core. While the German authorities interfered only little in the rural areas and left most of the administration of the countryside to Chinese institutions, Qingdao became a model for a completely segregated society.

The rigid separation of Germans and Chinese that this spatial structure prescribed was reinforced by the legal situation of the two groups. A separate set of laws, known as 'native law', was enacted for the Chinese population. A number of basic human rights (such as *nulla poena sine lege*, 'no punishment without a law') applied only to the Europeans in the colony. The 'Chinese regulations' included many about hygiene and sanitation; for example, every Chinese inhabitant over the age of ten had a right to accommodation providing 'empty space of 8 cubic metres and a floor area of 2.5 square metres'. These 'Chinese regulations' regulated physical space. They also detailed a precise regime of time and visibility. 'Between 9 pm and sunrise, no Chinese person may set foot on the roads without carrying a lighted lantern or having one carried before them.'[3] The Chinese population reacted to these repressive measures with adaptation, avoidance, and resistance, but also, in some cases, with unveiled admiration. Sun Yat-Sen, for example, the later revolutionary and, after 1911, the first provisional president of the republic of China, saw Kiaochow as a model for his vision of modernization in China.

As in the British, French, and Dutch empires, this kind of dual legal system was a characteristic feature of colonial rule (Illustration 30). 'Nothing facilitates a fruitful and peaceful colonization more than the upholding of traditions and legal customs of the population', the legal scholar Otto Köbner (1869–1934) underlined.[4] A separate legal system applied to 'natives' – a legal category that, in New Guinea, included Chinese workers but not Japanese citizens, as the latter were seen as members of a 'civilized' nation and defined, in 1900, as 'non-coloured'. The laws of the *Kaiserreich* applied only to Europeans, while the colonized were dealt with on the basis of separate legal principles. Often, 'natives' had no way of appealing decisions, and there was no separation between the powers of the judiciary and the executive. Judgments were made by the district governor – although he did sometimes consult local legal experts – and were seen as an extension of his administrative activities. Reference was frequently made, especially in civil disputes, to what was termed 'traditional law', although there was often debate about whether certain practices that Germans found unacceptable, for example polygamy, should be banned. In those regions that were ruled by Germany indirectly, through local powerholders – such as in Burundi, Rwanda and northern Cameroon – the Germans had no alternative but to 'delegate' judicial decision-making to local potentates. For the local 'chiefs', as they were called in contemporary parlance, the legal authority had

[3] Quoted from Klaus Mühlhahn, *Herrschaft und Widerstand in der 'Musterkolonie' Kiautschou: Interaktionen zwischen China und Deutschland, 1897–1914*, Munich (Oldenbourg) 2000, 230.

[4] Otto Köbner, 'Die Organisation der Rechtspflege in den Kolonien', *Verhandlungen des Deutschen Kolonialkongresses 1902*, Berlin (D. Reimer) 1903, 336.

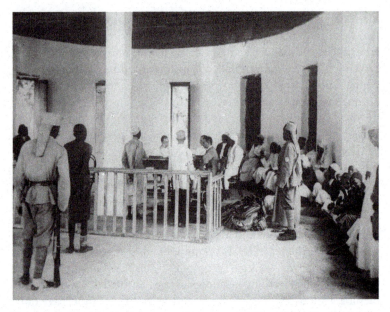

Illustration 30 The dual legal system was devised to enlist the support of local potentates, and at the same time was based on the fiction of separate legal spheres. The courts presided over by local chiefs were complemented by higher-ranking European courts (as in this image taken in German East Africa) where German administrators judged conflicts among the African population. They were heavily dependent on local intermediaries, in particular the interpreters, who carved out positions of power and influence for themselves.

ambivalent effects. On the one hand, it added to their power and helped secure their position in a changing environment. In fact, the fusion of legal and political power enabled them to extend their influence into spheres hitherto inaccessible to them, such as family conflicts and domestic issues. At the same time, their close collaboration with the colonial administration – in particular when they needed to supply workers or were asked to deliver delinquents to the German bureaucracy – also infringed on their legitimacy among the African population.

In any case, legal practice was just one aspect of a policy whose objective, in general, was to perpetuate hierarchical differences, supporting colonial power by essentializing alterity and thus treating differences between peoples and cultures as unchanging. 'Native policy' was intended to produce a situation of unambiguousness, of clear-cut cultural differences, although the reality was much more complicated. For this reason, heterogeneous indigenous population groups were divided up into ethnic groups and 'tribes'. These were then granted their own powers on the basis of the traditions and customs ascribed to them. The codification of local law, to return briefly to that example, involved the written formalization of regulations that in social practice were changeable, in some cases negotiable, but that were now formalized and fixed as abstract principles. In this way, traditions were 'invented', to use the ingenious term coined by Eric Hobsbawm and Terence Ranger.[5] They helped to separate ethnic groups and to differentiate them for the purposes of colonial 'divide and rule'.

One example of how this mechanism worked was the differentiation between Hutu and Tutsi in Rwanda, then part of German East Africa. In this region, ethnic groups were differentiated with a degree of exactitude that had never previously been applied in everyday practice. The differentiation was carried out by colonial officers who based their work on ethnological and legal knowledge, some of which they had actually created themselves, with the help of the 'Instructions for Ethnographic Observation and Collections in German East Africa' provided to them by Felix von Luschan, director of the Museum of Ethnography in Berlin. This differentiation between Hutu and Tutsi, carried out for administrative reasons and continued by the Belgian authorities after 1919, promoted a kind of ethnogenesis that set aside political and social differences and existing patterns of interaction in favour of a differentiation based on ethnic differences. In recent years, there has been considerable debate about whether this assignment of ethnicities during the period of German rule, perpetuated under later Belgian control, was one of the pre-conditions for the genocidal massacres in the region in 1994.[6]

---

[5] Eric Hobsbawm and Terence Ranger (eds.), *The Invention of Tradition*, Cambridge (Cambridge University Press) 1983.

[6] See Hans-Walter Schmuhl, 'Deutsche Kolonialherrschaft und Ethnogenese in Ruanda, 1897–1916', *Geschichte und Gesellschaft* 26 (2000), 307–34. For the mechanism of ethnic essentialization and the fixation of ethnic differences through legal categories, see also Mahmood Mamdani, *Citizen and Subject: Contemporary Africa and the Legacy of Late Colonialism*, Princeton (Princeton University Press) 1996.

While the nation-state devoted itself to homogenizing its populations, then, the colonial state reproduced cultural and ethnic differences, or even, in some cases, created them. To do so, it needed
control – very far-reaching control. In German South-West Africa,
the colonial authorities attempted to record the details of every one of
their subjects. All Africans above the age of seven were to receive a
numbered badge to 'attach to their clothes or their loincloth'[7]
(see Illustration 31). After the Herero war of 1904, identity cards
were introduced. Their aim was to monitor, and where possible to
prevent, all movements by individuals outside their 'tribal areas'. By
1914, three separate 'Native Regulations' had been introduced in an
attempt to achieve strict separation.

In practice, of course, separating population groups in this way was
almost impossible. And the differentiation between separate legal
systems was not always absolute either. Officially, there were two
separate legal systems, but those involved still lived in the same world
and could make use of one or other of the legal systems strategically.
The further we move away from the abstractions of the colonial
bureaucrats, the clearer it becomes that colonial subjects had considerable scope for action even in legal terms. In particular, different
forms of movement and mobility often undermined the supposed
order. The frequent impossibility of reliably identifying individual
subjects was a regular cause for administrative concern. The government's helplessness is reflected in an instruction by Governor Seitz,
who required his officials in German South-West Africa 'to do whatever is needed to ensure that the native, having once adopted a name,
retains it from then on'.[8] These fluctuations and uncertainties of
colonial reality put paid to attempts to create a model colonial state,
although many of the interventions did, of course, have a drastic effect
on the lives of the indigenous inhabitants. In practice, the politics of
difference were never implemented to the extent that those who
drafted them had hoped.

[7] Quoted from Jürgen Zimmerer, 'Der totale Überwachungsstaat? Recht und Verwaltung in
Deutsch-Südwestafrika', in: Rüdiger Voigt and Peter Sack (eds.), *Kolonialisierung des Rechts:
Zur kolonialen Rechts- und Verwaltungsordnung*, Baden-Baden (Nomos) 2001, 183–207, quote
p. 185.
[8] Quoted from ibid., 202.

Illustration 31 After the Herero and Nama wars, the German South-West African native laws of 1907 put into law rigid control of the African population. All Africans above the age of seven were required to register with the local authorities and to carry an identification mark as shown above. The metal mark carried an identification number and was intended to identify all Africans unambiguously. For any movement outside of the home district a travel document was obligatory. Further regulations stipulated that no more than ten families were allowed to live together in one compound, thus securing a well-proportioned dispersion of Africans across the land. The German government intended these measures not only as repressive interventions, but also as the basis for rational rule and effective exploitation. In social practice, the modernist vision of permanent monitoring and total control was never realized.

CIVILIZING MISSION

Apart from these obstacles on the ground and the complexities of social practice, it is important to recognize that the politics of difference were also consistently challenged on a theoretical level as they opposed the principle of the colonial ideology of 'elevating' the 'natives'. This 'civilizing mission' was the ideological core of the colonial project. Even critics of German policy, for example the Social Democrats, generally supported the ideas on which it was based, which helped to win large segments of the German population over to the colonial projects. The 'civilizing mission' was based on a belief that Germans (and Europeans more generally) were at the very top of a universal process of development. Thus, it was a product of the Enlightenment idea that civilization was a secular, inner-worldly process. This belief was supported by evolutionary theories and the assumption that a 'ladder' of development existed. The civilizing mission aimed to promote comprehensive social 'development': to facilitate technical progress, end despotic rule, create a social order that was based on emancipation (for example for women) and participation, and introduce 'modern' cultural dispositions. At the same time, it involved rejecting superstition and other 'damaging' practices, which were to be replaced by Christianity and secular education. One important feature of the civilizing mission was that it was not limited to the colonial world; it was also concerned with society at home, targeting peasants and urban underclasses in Germany itself.

The impulse for a cultural mission was based on a world-view that was not necessarily linked to religion. The cultural mission worked as a background assumption, a generalized discourse that helped motivate and justify actions and interventions undertaken by administrators, settlers, plantation owners, and the military. The goal of 'elevation' covered a wide range of different measures, many of which were imposed despite local resistance. They included the teaching of reading and writing and of German culture in the newly founded schools, the creation of westernized medical services and the introduction and maintenance of a regime of hygiene; the ongoing efforts to 'educate the natives to work' (which often legitimized exploitation); and the introduction of western legal standards. But they also included references to a range of secondary virtues – 'honour' and 'respect', 'diligence' (*Tüchtigkeit*), 'honesty', and 'discipline' – that seemed necessary if the 'lazy natives' were to become individuals who could take responsibility for their own lives. This discourse of 'elevation' was more than just strategic. It often corresponded to the self-view and the well-meaning intentions of those involved. It was also appropriated by parts of the colonized elites. The anti-colonial and national movements in Africa often perpetuated the values, aims, and corresponding mentality of the civilizing mission discourse.

In many ways, then, the 'civilizing mission' was a secular project based on ideas about the modernization of the colonies. But it was also influenced by Christianity and its values. Conversely, the Christian missions were also engaged in activities that were not directly related to saving souls or conversions. The Christian missionaries were among the most important agents of the cultural mission during German colonial rule: the cultural mission and the Christianizing project were, in fact, complementary.

The Christian missions provide a good example of these overlaps. Protestant missionary societies had grown up from the early nineteenth century onwards, a part of the religious awakening movement spreading from England to many European societies. The Catholic missions were born in France; once the German *Kulturkampf* had ended, German Catholic missions were also permitted to become active in the German colonies. In the scholarly literature, historians have mainly concentrated on the question of whether the missions were an instrument of colonialism. Certainly, the infiltration of Africa by these missionaries formed part of the colonial conquest; they were part of the colonial project and rarely criticized colonialism in itself. Not only did they profit from the state's opening up of the colonies; they also provided the ideological fuel for doing so. The indigenous population often saw the Christian missions and the colonial state as one and the same. 'First the missionary, then the Consul, and at last the invading army', was how the well-known British critic of imperialism, J. A. Hobson, summarized a view he encountered among Chinese elites.[9] At the same time, the missions occasionally proclaimed themselves to be the advocates of the 'natives', and missionaries helped expose a number of major colonial scandals. The missions also became heavily involved in the struggle against the spread of alcoholic drink and opium and against slavery. In many cases, the real conflict was not between the missions and the colonial state, but between those two institutions and the European settlers and plantation owners.

---

[9] J. A. Hobson, *Imperialism: A Study* [first published 1902], (Koebel Press) 2009, 215.

The missions were important in other ways, too. They played a vital economic role. Each mission station had its own farm, and the churches had large plantations. In German East Africa, for example, almost a quarter of all private plantation lands were held by the missions. Of course, their main objective was to Christianize the population, with Catholic and Protestant missions competing to convert the 'heathens'. By the First World War, the Protestant societies claimed – whatever this means in practice – to have converted 64,000 people in the German colonies, while the Catholic missions claimed some 142,000 souls. Soon, especially in the Protestant mission societies, African (and Chinese) missionaries were entrusted with the work of conversion. As a result, Christianity itself became modified and altered in many ways. In many cases, it would be more accurate to describe the result as a hybrid, a fusion of Christian beliefs with local religions. The best-known example of the adoption of elements of Christianity in this way was that of the Taiping in China, who suffered huge losses in their fight for a Christian state in China during the 1850s. Their leader, Hong Xiuquan, claimed to be a brother of Jesus and propounded a variation on Old Testament-based Protestant Christianity in which, for example, any contravention of the Ten Commandments would be punished. Within the German colonial empire, too, Christian ideas were appropriated locally, for example in the Maji-Maji movement or among the Chinese 'Boxers'.

But of even greater importance than these religious activities were the more wide-ranging attempts to culturally 'elevate' the population. 'It is the missions which are spiritually conquering our colonies and assimilating them', Joseph Schmidlin, the Catholic missions theoretician, claimed.[10] This cultural conversion was usually based on a conservative view of society, influenced partly by the petit-bourgeois background of most of those involved in the missions. Family, village structures, and a pre-industrial society were the keys. Friedrich von Bodelschwingh, for example, who became involved in the Protestant Mission Community, saw German East Africa as a possible sphere of influence that, he believed, was 'as far as possible untouched by the

---

[10] Joseph Schmidlin, *Die katholischen Missionen in den deutschen Schutzgebieten*, Münster (Aschendorff) 1913, 278.

depraved culture of Europe'. Hard work, an ordered daily routine, and a strong work ethic were important features. It was even suggested that 'conversion to Christianity should be given up, at least temporarily, as the main objective of the missions, and replaced with educating to work'.[11]

In addition, the missions were the most important group involved in organizing the colonial school system. The new educational system aimed to replace the existing local ways of passing on knowledge, much of which consisted of oral tradition. However, Islamic Koran schools continued in existence, especially those in German East Africa. Schooling remained overwhelmingly in the hands of the missions (up to 95 per cent). For many Africans, their encounters with the missionaries were not related to Christianity, therefore, but to the education provided by the mission-stations.

There was considerable variety in the actual infrastructure of schools. School types ranged from small rural assemblies to well-organized urban facilities that were frequented mainly by the local middle classes. The education provided was almost always limited to practical farming skills, rudimentary Bible readings and an elementary introduction to aspects of European culture. Little attention was paid to local cultures, although vernacular languages were sometimes taught: in Togo, for example, the school system was relatively well developed and the Ewe language was taught. There was no form of higher schooling and certainly no local universities, with the single exception of the one that was established in Qingdao in 1908. But the conditions in Kiaochow differed hugely from those in Germany's African colonies. In Kiaochow, a formal system of education had already existed, and the German schools had to agree their curricula with the requirements of the Chinese state, to ensure that they would be compatible with the Chinese examination system. In addition, the idea of a hierarchy of civilizations, which was supported by the discourse of race, meant that the idea of a tertiary educational institution in China, with its long-standing cultural traditions, was conceivable to Germans, while such an idea in any of Germany's African colonies was never even considered.

---

[11] Eduard Pechuel-Lösche, quoted from Gustav Warneck, *Evangelische Missionslehre: Ein missionstheoretischer Versuch, vol. III.1: Der Betrieb der Sendung*, Gotha (Perthes) 1897, 67.

Illustration 32 Colonial schools were the emblematic institution of the civilizing mission. This image shows a mission school in Ovamboland in the northern part of German South-West Africa. While some of the other colonial powers – especially France in west Africa and Algeria, and Japan in Korea and Taiwan – institutionalized a public school system in principle modelled on the secular public system in the metropolis, in the German colonial empire schooling was predominantly in the hands of the mission societies. The few exceptional government schools were intended to train a native elite to be recruited to the lower rungs of the colonial administration.

The school system (see Illustration 32) is a good example of the tension between assimilation and difference, between 'elevation' and the maintenance of fundamental differences that characterized the colonial project as a whole. Western education was supposed to make its recipients familiar with the principles of European/Christian civilization, but at the same time, teaching was limited to a very basic level. This is not to say that it did not provide resources that colonized inhabitants could access. It allowed the children of slaves and other dependent groups (who were often the first to attend at mission schools) access to education and, thus, the prospect of improving their social position. Many members of the national elites who would later lead their countries into independence also attended the mission schools. Emancipation was indeed a goal of these schools, but it was certainly not intended that those attending would become equal citizens. 'The Whites draw firm boundaries around the realm of knowledge that they bring to us', a school boy in the Basel mission school in Douala, Cameroon, remarked, 'because they do not want that we know as much as they do'.[12] The schools were to create perfect 'natives', not black Europeans.

Another example of this ambivalence was the suggestion that a specific form of 'colonial German language' should be developed for the overseas colonies. These ideas were of little importance in practice, but they reflect the mechanisms of cultural interaction. The starting-point was a desire to allow communication with the inhabitants of all the colonies, across linguistic boundaries. The language to be developed would have a small basic vocabulary, ensuring that a colonial subject would be able 'in the shortest possible time to fulfil his obligations as a useful worker, carrier or servant etcetera'.[13] The basic vocabulary would be made up of only 150 words, which would include terms such as work, money, God, *Kaiser*, and the numbers from one to twelve. No abstract concepts were included. A little European language and culture was a good thing, but too much, as the Leipzig mission director D. von Schwartz declared, could 'easily have terrible consequences'.[14] This fear of *too much* assimilation was reflected in contemporary caricatures of 'trouser-wearing Negroes' (*Hosenneger*), which made fun of the very idea of an educated, bourgeois African. Colonial policy was constantly concerned that the boundary between the colonizers and the colonized should remain clearly visible.

GOING NATIVE

Fears that the colonized might assimilate went parallel to concerns about the 'kaffirization' of whites, worries that they would adapt local habits and customs. In her work on Dutch rule in south-east Asia,

[12] Quoted from Ulrike Schaper, *Recht und koloniale Ordnung unter deutscher Herrschaft in Kamerun 1884–1916*, PhD thesis Free University of Berlin 2010, 273.
[13] Emil Schwörer, *Kolonial-Deutsch: Vorschläge einer künftigen deutschen Kolonialsprache in systematisch-grammatikalischer Darstellung und Begründung*, Diessen vor München (Huber) 1916, 48.
[14] D. von Schwartz, *Mission und Kolonisation in ihrem gegenseitigen Verhältnis*, Leipzig (Verlag der Evangelisch-Lutherischen Mission) 1912 (2nd edition), 29.

Ann Laura Stoler has described these fears as concerns about being unable to identify who was who, about the absence of clear boundaries, and has shown that they were typical of colonial societies.[15] Similar fears arose in the German colonial empire. 'The German character is itself receptive to foreign elements; this tendency develops quickly and widely in the protectorate. In more than a few cases Germans have actually become "kaffirized" in the protectorates', according to a 1908 edition of the *Hamburger Nachrichten*. 'And', it continued, 'while some Germans, protected by a good education, maintain their pure Germanness in their inmost being, in terms of outer form and behaviour every one of them sins'.[16]

In this context, three main issues of concern were discussed. The most important area of debate was that of 'mixed marriages'. In 1905, an administrative decree was issued in German South-West Africa forbidding marriage between German men and African women (the reverse never occurred) and even annulling any such marriages already in existence. Over the next few years, the German colonies in East Africa and Samoa followed suit. Also in other colonial empires, sexual relationships between the colonizers and indigenous women were disapproved of. In Samoa, Governor Solf explicitly referred to the British model of strict separation, contrasted with the putatively 'Dutch' policy of *laissez-faire*, as a source of inspiration.[17] But, in this era of high imperialism, an actual legal ban on such relationships was unique to the German empire.

The motivations, and implications, of the prohibition of 'mixed marriages' were very different. In Samoa, the decree was observed much less strictly than in South-West Africa, and it also did not have retroactive effects. Upon request, children of German men and Samoan women could be recognized as 'cultural Germans' provided they were able to prove language proficiency and some level of education. In the Pacific territories, living with native women was widely accepted; Governor Albert Hahl was one of many who had a

---

[15] Ann Laura Stoler, 'Rethinking Colonial Categories: European Communities and the Boundaries of Rule', *Comparative Studies in Society and History* 31 (1989), 134–61.
[16] Quoted from Birthe Kundrus, *Moderne Imperialisten: Das Kaiserreich im Spiegel seiner Kolonien*, Cologne (Böhlau) 2003, 199.
[17] For Solf's view on race mixing, see Lora Wildenthal, *German Women for Empire 1884–1945*, Durham (Duke University Press) 2001, 121–9; Steinmetz, *The Devil's Handwriting*, 341–50.

child with his New Guinean wife (Illustration 33). In South-West Africa, by contrast, the colour line was drawn much more rigorously. Apart from discrediting German–African couples, the regulation had important legal consequences. The women involved and the children of the marriage no longer had the right to German citizenship, and the men were stripped of their right to vote and some of their other civil rights. The settlers affected were furious. One Carl Becker, a farmer, appealed against the ruling by pointing out that his wife '[was] almost white . . . and in moral and intellectual terms can easily measure herself against every completely white woman in the protectorate'.[18] As this quote illustrates, the discourse of racial difference was so pervasive that even criticism of these bans was framed within the categories that were used to justify them.

Fears about the development of a 'mixed race' actually reflected fears of a situation in which there was a lack of certainty. These were reinforced by the nightmarish vision of a creole population who would, it was believed, be disloyal to the colonial power. Contemporary observers warned that in colonial history, creole populations frequently emerged as leaders of anti-colonial uprisings. These fears received some scientific underpinning from the theories of Lamarck, the botanist and early evolutionary biologist, who believed that acquired characteristics could be passed on and become hereditary. On the basis of this theory, 'going native' would, eventually, mean the end of the German people. Lamarckian aspects of eugenic thought were a central element of colonial discourse and linked the trope of the degeneration of the race with concerns about the sexual transmission of cultural faults and malformations. The prohibitory measures were accompanied by a programme designed to bring large numbers of German women to Africa. Some of these women attended new 'women's colonial schools' where they were prepared for their future tasks and deliberately acquainted with the values of Germanness and feminine domesticity. 'With true femininity, they will place the stamp of their natures on the new, overseas Germany', argued the head of the colonial school in Witzenhausen, Countess Zech. 'Filled with the spirit of true Christianity, they will be the high priestesses of German customs, the bearers of German culture and a

[18] Quoted from Gründer (ed.), *Rassismus, Kolonien und kolonialer Gedanke*, 286.

Illustration 33 In the Pacific possessions of the *Kaiserreich*, sexual and marital relations between German men and local women were more common and less disapproved of than in Africa. A good example is Governor Albert Hahl of New Guinea, who lived among the Tolai, a people on the Gazelle peninsula who had been strongly influenced by Christian missions from the 1870s. Hahl learned the Tolai language and had a child with a Tolai woman (shown in the picture).

blessing to these faraway lands.'[19] Over 2,000 women eventually travelled to German South-West Africa, accompanied by the hopes of some nationalistically minded groups that they could prevent the male-dominated German colonial society from going native.

[19] Quoted from Katharina Walgenbach, *'Die weiße Frau als Trägerin deutscher Kultur': Koloniale Diskurse über Geschlecht, 'Rasse' und Klasse im Kaiserreich*, Frankfurt am Main (Campus) 2005, 131.

Undoubtedly, sexuality was the most important area in which issues of belonging and exclusion were negotiated in the colonies. But other phenomena also drew the criticism of *völkisch* commentators. A second field of concern included the strategy of making use of the insignia of local power-holders to increase the legitimacy of the colonial power. A number of German governors were known to employ this strategy, most extensively Wilhelm Solf in Samoa. Solf was an offspring of the German bourgeoisie, had studied law and written a dissertation on sanskrit. His view on Samoan society was influenced by the ethnographic writings of the time. He argued that colonial power in Samoa should be *fa'a Samoa*, based on Samoan traditions, and in selected situations acted like a native king. Every meeting with local elites was opened and closed with the traditional ritual of kava-drinking. He used Samoan words and gave his children Samoan names. These symbolic acts took different forms and were directed not only at local dignitaries. Solf took pride in his hermeneutic approach towards the local population that differed from the blatant racism of the settlers who had 'too little education to find their way in the complicated mental processes of a Samoan brain' and therefore relied, according to Solf, on stereotypes such as 'bloody Kanaka, this damned nigger'.[20] People like Solf also used their intimate knowledge of local society to distinguish themselves from other German groups, primarily from the settlers and the aristocratic elites in the German Foreign Office.

Similar methods were used by the emphatically nationalist missionary Johann Baptist Anzer, who often presented himself to the public as a hybrid of a Chinese mandarin and a Catholic bishop. In many cases, this kind of cross-dressing was only partly strategic; it was also driven by a desire to identify at an imaginative level with a different culture. The best-known example of this was, of course, the Englishman Richard Burton, who in 1853 took part in a pilgrimage to Mecca dressed as a Muslim, but there are a number of German examples too. They include the pioneering geographer Gerhard Rohlfs, who travelled to Morocco during the 1860s as a Muslim using the name Mustafa Nemsi. The best-known example was perhaps the medical doctor Edward Schnitzer, alias Emin Pasha, who

---

[20] Solf cited in Steinmetz, *The Devil's Handwriting*, 351.

changed his name and converted to Islam while working for the
Ottoman empire. From 1876 onwards he worked in Sudan, where
he was later awarded the Ottoman title of Pasha. In 1888, he was taken
prisoner by the Sudanese 'Mahdi' and spectacularly freed by Henry
Morton Stanley.

The third perceived threat to the binary order was the presence of
underprivileged Europeans in the colonies. These threatened to
undermine the model of European superiority and native backwardness or inferiority. These 'white subalterns' included the unemployed
and 'vagabonds', beggars, criminals and tramps, sailors who had been
dismissed from service, and European prostitutes. They were not
many in number – many fewer than in the British empire – but the
excited debates they provoked and the reactions of the administration
towards them showed the extent to which their mere existence was
seen as a threat to the 'situation coloniale' (Georges Balandier).[21] A
wide variety of different approaches to deal with them were adopted,
ranging from financial support to imprisonment and deportation. In
German East Africa, the government relocated impoverished settlers
back to Germany, sometimes upon their explicit demand, but also
without their consent, since poor whites posed an unacceptable threat
to the colonial racial order. The goal was to mitigate a situation which
'would demean the image of the Europeans in the eyes of the coloureds'. Eduard von Liebert, the governor of German East Africa, felt it
to be 'simply unthinkable that we could here allow a European to be
seen by the coloured population to be begging or slowly starving.'[22]

The insertion of the word 'here' indicates that the conditions that
applied in the colonies were perceived as different from those at home.
Colonial policy was constantly concerned with demarcating difference and maintaining otherness, because ultimately, it was on this
difference that its claims to sovereignty were based. The results were
regulations of language-use, bans on marriage, divisions of labour,
limits on immigration, and segregation. At the same time, those
involved were constantly aware of the instability of their position, a

---

[21] Georges Balandier, 'La Situation Coloniale: Approche Théorique', *Cahiers Internationaux de Sociologie* 11 (1951), 44–79.
[22] Quoted from Minu Haschemi Yekani, *Prekäre Deutsche: Armut, Rassismus und koloniale Ordnung in Deutsch-Ostafrika*, MA Thesis Free University of Berlin 2007, 63.

position that was weakened further by the fact that they were in a minority. Social relationships in the colonial context were always ambivalent. Social differences, gender-specific assumptions, and even religious allegiances intersected with the binary opposition of black and white that was thought to be unalterable but that, in everyday life, was more precarious and more insecure than colonial discourse allowed.

CHAPTER 8

Knowledge and colonialism

In recent years, prompted by the rise of postcolonial studies and the interrogation of the cultural roots of colonialism, an intense debate has taken place about the relationships between power, knowledge, and the scholarly disciplines in the colonial context. Edward Said's critique of Orientalism and of the western 'order of knowledge' as an epistemological precondition for imperialism was central to the development of this debate.[1] From the late eighteenth century onwards, European expansion went hand in hand with an explosion of interest in the world outside Europe and in exploring that world. Initially this took the form of travel reports, but it soon moved into academic disciplines as well.

That knowledge and power are closely linked has been a paradigmatic assumption of historians building on the work of Michel Foucault. This insight also applies to colonial history.[2] Generating knowledge about the countries outside Europe was a necessary precondition for colonial conquest; but the colonial experience, conversely, also left its traces in the different forms of western knowledge. Knowledge and scholarly research were not instruments of neutral, 'objective' description. Rather, they could not and cannot be separated from hierarchies of power and mechanisms of rule. At its most self-evident, this means that academic research made an indispensable contribution to the European conquest of the world. Engineering, land surveying, weapons technology, vaccination and

---

[1] Said, *Orientalism*.
[2] Foucault, *Power/Knowledge*. For an attempt to transfer Foucault's categories to colonial settings, see Ann Laura Stoler, *Race and the Education of Desire: Foucault's* History of Sexuality *and the Colonial Order of Things*, Durham (Duke University Press) 1995.

medical research, legal theories, Oriental studies, ethnology, linguistics – the entire arsenal of academic disciplines was pressed into service for the territorial conquest of the planet.

But the link between knowledge and power went beyond this functional level, beyond the conscious objectives and goals of the colonial rulers. Modern forms of knowledge were not just an instrument and a weapon but, at a more fundamental level, themselves the product of a context that had been shaped by the colonial order. The cultural and social constellations of the colonial era were reflected in the European order of knowledge. In particular, knowledge about non-western societies was linked to colonial ambitions in a number of complex ways. The creation of knowledge cannot be completely separated from colonial power structures even in seemingly apolitical disciplines such as botany or biology.

As a result, central categories of the social sciences bore traces of the colonial encounter. Seemingly neutral terms, in other words, were the product of the asymmetries of the colonial world, and some of them continue to structure our thinking about social formations, history, and development even today. One example is the disciplinary separation of sociology and anthropology that essentially reproduces the power differential between Europe and its 'other' in the nineteenth century. This dichotomy opposes the developed and 'modern' societies of the West (as objects of sociological analysis) to the backward and primitive peoples and 'tribes' that can be approached only through anthropological research: social change on the one hand, and stagnation and cultural particularity on the other.

Likewise, consolidation of university disciplines from the first half of the nineteenth century had led to the virtual disappearance of non-European pasts from European historiography. Whilst Asian civilizations had been an integral component of the great universal histories of the Enlightenment period, they disappeared for the most part over the course of the nineteenth century, during which historiography specialized in the writing of national histories. This development – the expulsion of 'people without history' from European historiography – remains unintelligible outside the larger colonial context.

This differentiation between a history of Europe and traditions and customs unworthy of history was closely connected to two central concepts of European historiography: linearity and progress. The concept of a linear, continuous development, which conceived of the past as qualitatively different from the present and thereby made history a story of progress, was characteristic of European historiography of the nineteenth century. In the wake of colonial expansion, this perspective was spread throughout the whole world. In many societies, a new vocabulary was required to render the concept of progress terminologically possible. As a result, the national histories of India, China, Argentina, and elsewhere were written within this paradigm.

Scholars have argued that the global hegemony of European historical consciousness has helped to marginalize, if not efface, alternative cosmologies. A multiplicity of different pasts, in other words, was transformed into the formatted genre of history. As Prasenjit Duara explains, the spread of European historicity helped to 'occlude, repress, appropriate and, sometimes, negotiate with other modes of depicting the past and, thus, the present and future'. He continues: 'The closures of modernity and History have not enabled a language that can recognize and negotiate with that which has been dispersed and repressed.'[3]

At the same time, it is important to recognize that notions of linear development and progress were innovations in Europe as well, and that this innovation itself needs to be understood in the context of the increasing asymmetry in the relationships between Europe and the non-European world. Johannes Fabian has demonstrated that since the nineteenth century, travel to remote regions came to be understood as travels in time: foreign cultures appeared to European observers to represent earlier stages of human history. In Europe's appetite for the 'foreign' and 'primordial', a longing for its own origin manifested itself as well. Europe and its others appeared as two worlds of different times. This 'denial of coevalness', as Fabian calls it, was at the same time the foundation for the construction of a progress from the 'primitive' societies to the height of European civilization. The expansive new ordering of space in the nineteenth century was dependent on a fundamental reorganization of time. The colonialization of the

---

[3] Prasenjit Duara, *Rescuing History from the Nation: Questioning Narratives of Modern China*, Chicago (Chicago University Press) 1995, 5, 50.

world and the transformation of the past into histories of progress were closely linked.[4]

Following the Darwinian revolution – and its mirror image, Social Darwinism – these links were rendered invisible and transformed into social theory. But there were moments when the connection between colonial encounters and the evolutionary notion of time came to the surface. When the doctor Rudolf Virchow (1821–1902) was faced with criticisms of the practice of presenting people from the colonies to the German public in the context of animal parks and *Völkerschauen*, he insisted that this exhibition of the exotic would be to the 'greatest benefit of anthropological science'. 'Yes, in fact, these images of humanity' – representations of asynchrony that Fabian had described – 'are very interesting for everyone who wants to know about how humans survive in nature and about the development that humanity has achieved'.[5]

KNOWLEDGE AND POWER IN THE GERMAN EMPIRE

As in the other empires of the time, German expansion was closely linked to scientific research and exploration. This is true in a very concrete way of the early geographical societies, which were among those who campaigned most vigorously for the German empire to acquire colonies. The research expeditions that had been carried out from the 1860s onward into the 'unexplored interior' of the African continent were of particular importance in this regard. Before the German empire could consider any political or economic expansion, it needed geographical information about the most important regions and about possible sources of raw materials and markets for German goods. In 1873, the founding document of the German Society for the Exploration of Equatorial Africa pointed out that the territories being explored by the geographers would 'sooner or later become trade markets' and that scholarly research was thus a precondition for the expansion of production and trade. 'World trade', the

[4] Johannes Fabian, *Time and the Other: How Anthropology Makes Its Object*, New York (Columbia University Press) 1983.
[5] R. Virchow, 'Eskimos von Labrador,' *Zeitschrift für Ethnologie* 12 (1880), 253–84, quote on p. 270.

document continued, could develop only from the 'utilization of the aids supplied by the geographical sciences'.[6] Geographers thus self-fashioned themselves as pioneers of the world economy.

One example of such a geographer was Ferdinand von Richthofen, who travelled around the Chinese empire between 1868 and 1872. Richthofen, 'the single best-travelled European in China after Marco Polo', sent regular (and unsolicited) memoranda to Bismarck about the opportunities that would be offered by establishing a German colony in China.[7] Richthofen's main focus was on China as a market for German goods. He became one of the most influential proponents of German expansion into eastern Asia and saw the acquisition of Kiaochow as a possible starting-point for the development of a 'German India' in China. Richthofen was not a populistic colonial enthusiast like Friedrich Fabri but rather sided with rational, development-minded administrators such as Bernhard Dernburg.

During the late nineteenth century, geographical study meant mainly geography of conquest and exploitation. It was a discipline that described plateaux and mountain ranges, river courses and impassable regions, climatic conditions and the presence of raw materials. One famous example was the report on the 'first ascent' of Kilimanjaro (in German East Africa) in 1899 by the geographer and publisher Hans Meyer. Meyer was filled with a conviction that he was carrying out a national mission. The 'highest mountain in Germany', as contemporary German schoolbooks described it, was a source of great fascination in Germany. The ways in which scientific exploration and territorial acquisition overlapped manifested themselves symbolically at the moment when Meyer seized the topmost stone of the mountain peak and stowed it into his rucksack, presenting it, on his return to Germany, to *Kaiser* Wilhelm himself. 'His Majesty', the geographer later reminisced, 'graciously accepted the dedication of the Kaiser Wilhelm Peak', which Meyer had 'physically brought home. The very peak of the highest mountain in Germany is

---

[6] *Correspondenzblatt der Afrikanischen Gesellschaft* No. 1, 1873, 2, quoted from Franz-Josef Schulte-Althoff, *Studien zur politischen Wissenschaftsgeschichte der deutschen Geographie im Zeitalter des Imperialismus*, Paderborn (Schöningh) 1971, 60.

[7] Jürgen Osterhammel, 'Forschungsreise und Kolonialprogramm. Ferdinand von Richthofen und die Erschließung Chinas im 19. Jahrhundert', *Archiv für Kulturgeschichte* 69 (1987), 150–95, quote on p. 151.

now resting on the desk of the man who himself is at the very highest point in Germany.'[8]

Geography was in many respects a national and colonial discipline. In 1892, 'Geography of the German Colonies' was introduced as a subject in schools, and it remained in the curriculum well into the Weimar Republic. The first university chair in Colonial Geography was founded in Berlin in 1911. What is striking, however, is the extent to which geographers' contribution to nationalism, in particular in the early years leading up to 1884, was produced within transnational settings. These included, on the one hand, the help and agency of African mediators. On the other, famous geographers like Heinrich Barth began their careers as part of international scientific expeditions, frequently under British leadership. The feats of the German geographers in Africa were represented and celebrated as national German accomplishments, even though they were possible only within transnational contexts.

Geography was by no means the only discipline to become caught up in the colonial project. The foundation in 1887 of the Berlin Seminar for Oriental Languages, which was dedicated to linguistic and cultural training that would allow the administration of the German colonies to become more efficient, was a reaction to administrative needs, as was the setting up of the Hamburg Colonial Institute in 1908. The discipline of tropical and colonial medicine also had close links to power and rule. The colonies were occasionally regarded by these disciplines as a location in which social or medical experiments could be carried out. During the Herero war, for example, prisoners were used for medical experimentation. The progress of their illnesses or recoveries served as teaching material and was used to collect statistics. The well-known bacteriologist and Nobel prize winner Robert Koch, who spent eighteen months in German East Africa in 1906 attempting to find a cure for sleeping sickness, also made use of the colonial situation for interventions that would not have been possible in Germany. At home, medical experiments on

---

[8] Hans Meyer, *Ostafrikanische Gletscherfahrten: Forschungsreisen im Kilimandscharo-Gebiet*, Leipzig (Duncker und Humblot) 1890, 255–6. See also Alexander Honold, 'Kaiser-Wilhelm-Spitze. 6. Oktober 1889: Hans Meyer erobert den Kilimandscharo', in: Alexander Honold and Klaus R. Scherpe (eds.), *Mit Deutschland um die Welt: Eine Kulturgeschichte des Fremden in der Kolonialzeit*, Stuttgart (Metzler) 2004, 136–44.

Illustration 34 Robert Koch (1843–1910), director of the Prussian Institute for Infectious Diseases, is known as one of the founding figures of the field of microbiology. He was awarded the Nobel Prize in 1905 for his research into tuberculosis. On the Sese islands in Lake Victoria in (British) East Africa, where more than 20,000 people had died of sleeping sickness over a few years, Koch experimented with heavy doses of toxic medicines administered to African patients. This image shows Koch (on the right) on one of his research trips to Africa.

humans had been banned since 1900. But in East Africa he injected a thousand patients a day with arsenic preparations, at dangerously increasing dosages and with high mortality rates (see Illustration 34).

Links and interactions between scientific developments and colonial actions can thus be identified, although with different dynamics, for most academic disciplines. Linguists and legal scholars were also active in the colonies in their quest to find the *Ursprache* (the 'original' language) and the *Urrecht* (the law of man in the state of nature). The colonial discipline *par excellence* was anthropology. In contrast to the British approach to anthropology, which was based on an evolutionist view of human history, German anthropologists assumed a fundamental distinction between 'civilized' and 'primitive' peoples (*Kultur-* and *Naturvölker*). This dichotomy suggested that only certain peoples were capable of developing a 'civilization'. The others, including the African 'primitive peoples', were investigated using anthropometric analysis and a study of their tools and utensils. It was assumed that both methodologies represented their direct, supposedly ahistoric reactions to their environment. Over the course of German rule, thousands of objects, including innumerable skulls, were seized and sent to anthropological collections in Germany (Illustration 35), where many are still held today. Clear links to the colonial project are also manifest in eugenics and racial theory. One of the most important proponents of these theories was Eugen Fischer, who carried out a study into the 'half-caste [*Mischling*] population' of German South-West Africa. Fischer was one of the scientists who later had a major influence on the Nazis' population policies.[9]

Emphasizing the link between knowledge and power does not necessarily mean equating knowledge with oppression. From the perspective of historical actors, in particular, the embeddedness of knowledge in power structures did not automatically imply suppression and exploitation. Following Foucault, 'power' should, rather, be understood as a 'positive', regulating force that did not only issue from the colonial state (although the asymmetries of colonial rule were always important). Local actors, both Europeans and colonized, were not simply passive receivers of this power-structured knowledge; they did not just make use of it but were themselves shaped by the hegemonic discourses at work. Colonial knowledge was thus also appropriated by colonized subjects, especially if access to knowledge promised an increase in social status.

So the link between knowledge and power did not automatically imply a link between knowledge and the power of the state. For this reason, the intentions of the scholars involved could also vary. Some academics were explicitly critical of colonialism, such as the geographer and ethnologist Leo Frobenius, who regarded the Africans as living documents of a lost human past. His discovery of the ancient Yoruba culture can be read as a powerful polemic against Eurocentrism. While he remained within the dominant discourse that saw Africa as the 'childhood' of humanity, he viewed this in a positive light. For him, 'childhood' meant spontaneity, intuition and creativity, all traits that Europe had lost during the development of

---

[9] See Pascal Grosse, *Kolonialismus, Eugenik und bürgerliche Gesellschaft in Deutschland 1850–1918*, Frankfurt am Main (Campus) 2000, 184–92.

Eine Kiste mit Hereroschädeln
wurbe kürzlich von den Truppen in Deutsch-Süd-West-Afrika verpackt
und an das Pathologische Institut zu Berlin gesandt, wo sie zu wissen=
schaftlichen Messungen verwandt werden sollen. Die Schädel, die von
Hererofrauen mittels Glasscherben vom Fleisch befreit und versandfähig
gemacht wurden, stammen von gehängten oder gefallenen Hereros.

Illustration 35 One of the most bizarre stipulations of the peace treaty of Versailles in 1919 was article 246, which obliged Germany to restitute the skull of Sultan Mkwawa, chief of the Wahehe in East Africa, who mounted a seven-year war of resistance against the German empire in the 1890s. After the defeat of the Wahehe, the head of the murdered chief was severed and transported to Germany, ending up in the skull collection of renowned medical doctor and anthropologist Rudolf Virchow. The measurement of skulls was a standard technique in craniology and anthropology in the late nineteenth century. In particular in the wake of the great colonial wars, large numbers of skulls were sent to Germany. Scientists supplied detailed guidelines for colonial officers about how to treat and preserve captured skulls and bones. The image shows German officers, presumably in Swapokmund in 1905/6, with boxes of skulls from Herero who were killed during the war. The skulls were cleaned with shards of glass by Herero women before being sent on to the Anthropological Institute, Berlin.

civilization. He was a sort of anti-Hegelian, then, and his writings had a considerable influence on the poet, post-colonial intellectual and later president of Senegal Léopold Senghor and the latter's concept of *négritude.* Senghor believed that 'no one better than Frobenius revealed Africa to the world *and Africans to themselves*'.[10]

COLONIZATION OF THE IMAGINATION

In recent years, some authors, especially in the field of post-colonial studies, have suggested that it was in the area of culture and knowledge that colonialism has had particularly long-lasting effects. In this reading, the conquest of foreign territories was followed by an even more fundamental cultural imperialism, by the internalization of the imperial gaze and the promise of progress that was linked to it. On both sides, a colonial self-image became naturalized in the form of the 'colonization of the imagination'. The colonizers' interventions established a world-view that even the colonized societies were unable to escape and whose cultural hegemony (Gramsci) outlived formal independence and decolonization.[11] It was in this sense Mahatma Gandhi famously warned that independent India was in danger of simply continuing the modernizing projects of the colonial era: 'English rule without the Englishmen'.[12]

In this context, a large number of post-colonial intellectuals, starting with Frantz Fanon and Aimé Césaire in the 1950s, called for a 'decolonization of the mind'.[13] Central concepts of social and political thought were investigated to establish their complicity with the colonial knowledge order: 'progress', 'modernization', and 'history'

---

[10] Léopold Sédar Senghor, 'Les Leçons de Leo Frobenius', in: Eike Haberland (ed.), *Leo Frobenius: Une Anthologie*, Wiesbaden (Steiner) 1973, vii; original emphasis. See also Suzanne Marchand, 'Leo Frobenius and the Revolt against the West', *Journal of Contemporary History* 32 (1997), 153–70.

[11] See Antonio Gramsci, *Selections from the Prison Notebooks of Antonio Gramsci*, ed. and trans. Quintin Hoare and Geoffrey Nowell Smith, London (Lawrence and Wishart) 1971.

[12] Mohandas K. Gandhi, 'Hind Swaraj [1909]', in: *The Collected Works of Mahatma Gandhi, vol. X (Nov. 1909 – March 1911)*, New Delhi (Publications Division, Ministry of Information and Broadcasting, Government of India) 1963, 15.

[13] See Frantz Fanon, *Black Skin, White Masks* [1952], trans. Charles Lam Markmann, London (Pluto) 1986; Aimé Césaire, *Discourse on Colonialism* [1955], trans. Joan Pinkham, New York (Monthly Review Press) 1972. See also Robert J. C. Young, *Postcolonialism: An Historical Introduction*, Oxford (Blackwell) 2001.

were revealed to be part of the colonial project. For Partha Chatterjee, even the references or appeals to the nation's own dignity and sovereignty that formed the basis of anti-colonial movements were simply a 'derivative discourse' founded in western thought.[14] Following Foucault, Gayatri Spivak has even spoken of 'epistemic violence' in order to make it clear that the strict categories of the dominant (western) discourse allowed those involved only limited ways of expressing themselves, and marginalized alternative forms of knowledge.[15]

These criticisms have helped to reveal the multi-layered nature of the colonial encounter, which was not limited to military superiority, territorial rule, and economic exploitation. Expressed in such absolute terms, however, such ideas are in danger of suggesting the existence of completely incompatible regimes of knowledge, of civilizational orders, between which no dialogue is possible. This kind of cultural essentialism, treating cultures as fixed and unchanging entities with clear-cut boundaries, can overlook the extent to which both indigenous traditions (themselves often 'invented' in the context of cultural exchange) and the seemingly universal forms of knowledge of the modern western world were the result of complex processes of interaction and influence. In many cases, the encounter with cultural resources from Europe did not entirely deprive existing cosmologies of their value. Rather, a multitude of new practices and discourses developed. The Africanization of Christianity – or rather the grafting of Christian elements on to African religious practice – is a good example.

This example also reveals the ability of social agents to adapt hegemonial knowledge in a creative fashion and to make use of it for their own ends. Colonial knowledge, too, could be used for anti-colonial purposes. The linguistic studies of the German missionary Diedrich Westermann in Togo, for example, were foundational texts for an emerging European discipline.[16] Westermann became the first

---

[14] Partha Chatterjee, *Nationalist Thought and the Colonial World: A Derivative Discourse?*, Tokyo (Zed Books) 1986.
[15] Gayatri Spivak, 'Can the Subaltern Speak?', in: Cary Nelson and Lawrence Grossberg (eds.), *Marxism and the Interpretation of Culture*, Chicago (University of Illinois Press) 1988, 271–313.
[16] Diedrich Westermann, *Wörterbuch der Ewe-Sprache*, 2 vols., Berlin (Dietrich Reimer) 1905–6.

European to speak the Ewe language; he wrote a number of books about it and compiled a grammar. These studies were extremely useful to the missions and instrumental to the needs of the colonial administration. But they also became a point of reference for Ewe nationalism and for demands for the unification of the Ewe peoples (in Togo and Ghana). Colonial knowledge could be adopted for use in very different strategies. It was, as Homi Bhabha has argued, ambivalent: both an instrument of rule and a resource with which claims to rule could be questioned and undermined.[17]

[17] Homi K. Bhabha, *The Location of Culture*, London (Routledge) 1994.

CHAPTER 9

The colonial metropole

One of the most innovative ideas to come out of the field of post-colonial studies and more recent studies on empire has been the suggestion that the histories of the colonizers and the colonized should be examined within one coherent analytic field. For a long time, historiography was dominated by a perspective that interpreted colonial contacts in terms of influence and diffusion. In this view, European expansion led to irreversible changes in indigenous societies, changes that could be interpreted as being either positive (cultural mission and modernization) or negative (oppression and exploitation). Thus Europe, it was believed, had radically changed the world without itself being greatly affected by those changes. This one-sided view has recently been replaced by a perspective that no longer views European history and colonial history as separate entities, but accepts that the numerous links and processes of exchange that existed between them were constitutive for both.

This approach has brought interesting results for British history in particular; it has revealed the extent to which colonial links shaped the dynamics of British society and economy, everyday life in the metropole, and British nationalism.[1] Such a change in perspective can also be useful for understanding German society. Because the German colonial empire lasted for a much shorter period, it is not surprising that the

[1] For a first overview, see Catherine Hall (ed.), *Cultures of Empire: A Reader: Colonizers in Britain and the Empire in the Nineteenth and Twentieth Centuries*, Manchester (Manchester University Press) 2000; Catherine Hall and Sonya O. Rose (eds.), *At Home with the Empire: Metropolitan Culture and the Imperial World*, Cambridge (Cambridge University Press) 2006; John Marriott, *The Other Empire: Metropolis, India and Progress in the Colonial Imagination*, Manchester (Manchester University Press) 2004; John MacKenzie (ed.), *Imperialism and Popular Culture*, Manchester (Manchester University Press) 1987.

effects are less obvious, can be found primarily in the areas of representation and popular culture, and were themselves shorter-lived. Yet here, too, we can identify cases of 'double inscription', as Stuart Hall has termed the complex interactions between metropole and colony.[2] Wilhelmine Germany, in diverse and not always obvious ways, was shaped and influenced by the effects of the colonial encounter.

Here we should once again remember that Germany's colonial experience was not limited to processes of exchange with its own official 'protectorates'. Quite the contrary: German emigration to Brazil, the Boer war (and earlier the famous 'Krüger telegram' of congratulation from Wilhelm II to Paulus Krüger, president of the Transvaal Republic, after the defeat of the Jameson raid) and the Moroccan crisis in 1911 were all events that captured the public and political imagination. Contemporary colonial visions and political activities reached outside the boundaries of the German colonial empire. Furthermore, the colonial project was in many ways a European (and American and Japanese) project and it would be pointless to attempt to separate out the colonial repercussions in each society focusing solely on each country's own colonial empire. German colonial imagination was inspired not just by thoughts of Togo and Samoa, but also by the empires of its neighbours. Robert Koch, for example, did not limit his activities to the German empire, but carried out experiments in Egypt, India, and southern Africa (Illustration 36). Wilhelm II was known to dress up as an Ottoman pasha, implicitly accepting the pasha's international status; it would never have occurred to him to take on the role of an African potentate. The global circulation of images and representations was supported by capitalist market structures that allowed Germany to import wheat from Argentina and guano from Chile, with which it had no formal colonial ties, not just palm oil from Togo.

COLONIAL IMAGINATION

While imperial rule had far-reaching effects on the colonies themselves, within Germany the overseas territories were initially the subject only of

---

[2] Stuart Hall, 'When Was "the Post-colonial"? Thinking at the Limit', in: Iain Chambers and Lidia Curti (eds.), *The Post-colonial Question: Common Skies, Divided Horizons*, London (Routledge) 1996, 242–60, quote on p. 247.

Illustration 36 In the realm of the imagination, German colonial expansion was represented as beneficial to the colonized populations and to humanity at large. One of the symbols of the myth of peaceful and civilizing conquest was Robert Koch, whose experiments in Africa were touted as contributions to universal progress. Even though the medicine against sleeping sickness was developed only in the 1920s and thus after his death, it was associated with Koch. Its name *Germanin* reflects the colonial revisionist atmosphere of the times. In 1943, it emerged as the subject of a Nazi propaganda film that demonstrated, as the Nazi newspaper *Völkischer Beobachter* wrote, 'the colonizing mission of German culture'. Koch was also the protagonist of another propaganda movie entitled 'Robert Koch, the fighter against death', in 1939.

images, desires, and the imagination. The power of colonial representations was expressed mainly in popular culture, colonial board games, the popular collectable pictures that accompanied Liebig's meat extract, travel literature, and works of popular science fiction. Here, colonialism had a considerable effect. Literary texts with colonial references were widely read. They include the writings of now-forgotten authors such as Gustav Frenssen and Frieda von Bülow, who travelled around the German colonies and set their novels there. Even the more popular works of Karl May, for example his *Orient* cycle, created in the context of the Balkan crisis and German political and economic interest in the territories of the Ottoman empire, were to some extent colonialist, and shaped the mentalities of entire generations. The lure of the exotic was also translated into architecture and design. The Yenidze cigarette factory in Dresden, built in 1909 and modelled on an Islamic mosque, was among the best-known examples of Orientalizing architecture in the *Kaiserreich*.

Another important forum for the colonial imagination was the series of ethnographic spectacles and dioramas that seemed to spring up everywhere during the second half of the nineteenth century (see Illustration 37). They transferred the imperial situation into the

Die von dem Afrikareisenden Dr. Stuhlmann mitgebrachten beiden Akkazwerginnen im Museum für Völkerkunde zu Berlin. Nach dem Leben gezeichnet von E. Hosang.

Illustration 37 Colonial populations were exhibited not only in *Völkerschauen* (ethnographic shows), but also in academic contexts. This contemporary drawing shows Aka people from central Africa, brought to the Anthropological Museum in Berlin by Franz Stuhlmann. In colonial times, the Aka were classified as one of the nomadic African pygmy people, and they aroused the interest of anthropologists and a larger public. Stuhlmann (1863–1928) spent twenty years in East Africa as a cartographer, natural scientist, and ethnographer. He also fought in the so-called Arab rebellion in 1888 and later served as the acting governor of German East Africa.

metropoles, often carrying on after the end of formal colonialism. The ethnographic shows were closely linked to the history of the zoological garden in Europe and became established during the 1870s, when the Hamburg animal dealer Carl Hagenbeck introduced spectacles featuring exotic-seeming people to make up for the falling profit margins in his animal-import business. These ethnographic shows presented the Germans as masters of the world, and as benevolent civilizers in the colonies. They also brought home the message to the German audience that there were natural hierarchies of races and peoples, and suggested that the social order in Germany, with its class and gender differences, be regarded as natural (Illustration 38).

One of the representations of the colonial world that had the widest impact was the huge Berlin Colonial Exhibition held in south-eastern

Illustration 38 Colonial exhibitions aimed to represent the native populations in their 'traditional' garb and 'natural' environment and thus conveyed the image of timeless and unchanging societies. They were taken to represent the pre-history of modern civilization and thus to make plausible the notion of a natural hierarchy of peoples. This picture, taken from an exhibition of New Guinea in the Colonial Museum in Bremen in the 1930s, is evidence of the ongoing attraction and resonance of the German empire well into the post-colonial period.

Berlin in 1896 to accompany the Trade Fair. It was visited by over seven million people and was opened by *Kaiser* Wilhelm II, in whose honour a 'war dance' was 'performed by our black compatriots'.[3] For a small fee, 'we enter our colonies, picturesquely located by the carp pond between the bushes', as Julius Stinde's novel described the event, 'and can get an impression of our acquisitions in Africa'.[4] The exhibiting of over a hundred Africans from the German colonies – different from those shown at the usual ethnographic fairs, they were mostly skilled artisans and educated – was widely received and was one of the most popular parts of the colonial fair. At the same time, however, it was also criticized by some colonial enthusiasts, who paradoxically were afraid both of the impression that this overseas 'New Germany' would make on the Berlin public, and of the 'bad civilizing influence that whites have on natives', implying that liberal European customs such as relationships between genders would have detrimental effects on an alleged native innocence.[5] In fact, the recruitment of 'exhibits' from almost all the German colonial regions was banned five years later, in 1901.

Along with people, dances, and folklore, the Berlin exhibition also included consumer goods produced in the colonial economies. Coffee, chocolate, and bananas were regarded as luxuries and it was hoped that the show would introduce them to a wider public. Much of the attractiveness of these colonial goods lay in their exotic flair, and pictorial advertising made extensive use of images of the colonies and stereotypical representations of foreignness. These images conveyed seemingly static landscapes and people, but over the course of the colonial era they changed as well; after 1900, the insignia of German rule increasingly found their way into representations and advertising

---

[3] *Vossische Zeitung* 25 (1896), quoted from Alexander Honold, 'Ausstellung des Fremden – Menschen- und Völkerschau um 1900: Zwischen Anpassung und Verfremdung: Der Exot und sein Publikum', in: Sebastian Conrad and Jürgen Osterhammel (eds.), *Das Kaiserreich transnational: Deutschland in der Welt 1871–1914*, Göttingen (Vandenhoeck & Ruprecht) 2004, 170–90, quote on p. 186.

[4] Julius Stinde, *Hotel Buchholz: Ausstellungs-Erlebnisse der Frau Wilhelmine Buchholz*, Berlin (Freund & Jeckel) 1897, 200.

[5] Quoted from Harald Sippel, 'Rassismus, Protektionismus oder Humanität? Die gesetzlichen Verbote der Anwerbung von "Eingeborenen" zu Schaustellungszwecken in den deutschen Kolonien', in: Robert Debusmann and Janos Riesz (eds.), *Kolonialausstellungen – Begegnungen mit Afrika?*, Frankfurt am Main (IKO) 1995, 43–64, quote on p. 61.

images, and African people were gradually racialized and depicted as fundamentally different.

There can be no doubt that the German image of the colonies was 'Orientalist' in Edward Said's sense[6] and contributed to the construction – and the colonial domination – of its subject. These representations of the colonial 'other' were embedded in unequal power relationships and were closely linked to the asymmetries and the racist order of the imperial age. But even within the rigidly structured regulations of the ethnographic show, there was room for manoeuvre and agency. For example, Friedrich Maharero, the son of the Herero ruler Samuel Maharero, refused to wear a folklore-based costume and insisted on appearing in a suit. And the Cameroonian Bismarck Bell himself observed the visitors of the exhibition with a set of opera glasses, thus turning upside down the relationship of observer and exhibits, thereby reversing the imperial gaze.[7]

LABORATORIES OF THE MODERN?

In recent years, interest in the effects of the colonial experience has gone beyond images and representation and has focused on socio-economic and material repercussions. Did the German presence in Africa, China, and the Pacific leave an imprint on German society as well? Here, too, an idea put forward by post-colonial studies may serve as a useful starting point: this is the metaphor of the colonies as laboratories for modern societies. In many ways, the colonies were spaces in which European bureaucracy could experiment, where it could test major interventions and social reforms. The colonies were frequently seen as a quasi-empty space, an ideal place for putting social interventions into practice, including the kind of interventions that would meet with seemingly insuperable levels of resistance in Europe: urban planning, gender issues, and eugenics. This scholarly approach is based on the hypothesis that the development of European modernity cannot be taken in isolation, but must be linked to the

---

[6] Said, *Orientalism*.

[7] Nana Badenberg, 'Zwischen Kairo und Alt-Berlin. Sommer 1896: Die deutschen Kolonien als Ware und Werbung auf der Gewerbe-Ausstellung in Treptow', in: Alexander Honold and Klaus R. Scherpe (eds.), *Mit Deutschland um die Welt. Eine Kulturgeschichte des Fremden in der Kolonialzeit*, Stuttgart (Metzler) 2004, 190–200.

structures of imperial global conquest. The modern era, then, was a colonial one.

This is a highly generalizing approach that may not easily be linked to concrete colonial projects, and the laboratory trope is certainly less applicable to the short-lived German empire. Nevertheless, as a heuristic perspective it is still useful. Like the territory of Alsace-Lorraine (*Elsass-Lothringen*) or the institutions run by the Naval Office, all of which were under the direct control of the *Reich* (as opposed to state governments), the colonies were regarded as the primary test sites for social reform. As late as 1940, as part of the debate about the recovery of the colonies that had been lost after the First World War, the legal almanac *Schmollers Jahrbuch für Gesetzgebung* stated that the colonies had the advantage that one could 'start afresh, unhindered by the traditions of former times such as exist at home. This can open up a huge sphere of activity for great organizers in the administration of the colonial empire.'[8] In this regard, Germany's Chinese colony in Kiaochow, run by the Navy, was indeed a 'model colony' in which a military social utopia was to be put into practice (including a rigid policy of ethnic segregation), partly in order to provoke reforms at home. However, many of the major social programmes never progressed beyond than the planning stage, and almost none was put into practice in the colonies exactly as intended. And the concept of the 'laboratory' suggests a specific kind of rationality, and a specific kind of modernity. When we look closer, however, it becomes evident that the colonies were, rather, a screen onto which was projected a variety of divergent, and often competing, ideas about the way modern society should develop.

At one end of the spectrum, the interventions were based on utopian ideas about a social order that could be planned in detail on the basis of scientific findings. Such interventions included the large-scale immunization of the German army at the start of the First World War. The typhoid vaccine had been tested in German South-West Africa between 1904 and 1907, during the Herero war, and it led to mortality rates that were much lower than in the Franco-Prussian war

---

[8] Quoted from Dirk van Laak, 'Kolonien als "Laboratorien der Moderne"?', in: Sebastian Conrad and Jürgen Osterhammel (eds.), *Das Kaiserreich transnational: Deutschland in der Welt 1871–1914*, Göttingen (Vandenhoeck & Ruprecht) 2004, 257–79, quote on p. 263.

of 1870–1. They also included large-scale urban redesign projects; these were realized in the colonies without much consideration for local structures or the resistance of the inhabitants. Of course, German experiments in urban planning had a less marked influence on the debate in Europe than, for example, Hubert Lyautey's reorganization of Rabat and Casablanca or Le Corbusier's plans for Algiers (which included the segregation of ethnic groups in the old town) and the projects the latter realized in Chandigarh, India after the Second World War. But German city planning in Qingdao, too, was as ambitious as it was negligent of existing structures and ways of life. Six Chinese villages, home to 4,500 inhabitants, were completely torn down to make room for the planned urban conglomeration. The existing port and town structure were thoroughly transformed in an attempt to build a model colonial city.

As early as 1898, only a few months after the Kiaochow territory was formally leased to Germany, the Navy administration had already drawn up a land development plan that demarcated three distinct zones of settlement – the European living quarters and business area, the residential area with villas, and the Chinese city. Government spending concentrated on the city centre. The aim was to build a showcase of German modernity, both by developing what was seen as typical German architecture, and by furnishing the central parts of the city with the most modern technological equipment available, such as waterworks and sewage systems (Illustration 39).

One of the central elements of the development plan was the legal stipulation concerning ownership of land as introduced by Wilhelm Schrameier. Schrameier (1859–1926) had served as a translator in Shanghai and Hong Kong before assuming the post of 'commissary for Chinese affairs' and responsibility for native policy in Qingdao. His regulations foresaw a sales tax and limitations to the disposal of land, with the idea of preventing the land speculation so common in colonial boomtowns such as Shanghai. These regulations were in the fiscal interest of the colonial government, and not a form of social policy benefiting the Chinese population, as some contemporaries claimed them to be. But owing to their similarities with land reform projects by Henry George in the United States and Adolph Damaschke in Germany, they were soon appropriated as a model by the active reform movements in Germany. In 1902, Schrameier gave a

Illustration 39 The German quarter of Qingdao (here: Hohenzollern Street) was designed as a model of a modern city, fully equipped with sanitary and sewage systems, and street lighting.

talk to the German Association for Land Reform (*Bund der Bodenreformer*), and Qingdao was regularly referred to in domestic debates as an example that land reform was indeed feasible. After 1904, similar provisions were introduced in a number of German municipalities. If colonial planners and social reformers did indeed see Qingdao as a laboratory of modern city life, it could be appropriated both by the interventionist state bureaucracy and by social reform movements – including in China: Sun Yat-Sen, first president of the Republic of China after 1911, had Schrameier's book on administration in Kiaochow translated into Chinese and invited Schrameier to be an adviser in 1924. Sun was interested in Kiaochow as an example of how to realize the idea of the 'single tax' as stipulated by Henry George, and as incorporated into the welfare programme of the Kuomintang party.[9]

---

[9] Wilhelm Matzat, *Die Tsingtauer Landordnung des Chinesenkommissars Wilhelm Schrameier*, Bonn (Selbstverlag) 1985.

The measures taken in Qingdao were thus based on a vision of infrastructural order that was believed, for Germany as well, to be the way of the future. At the other end of the spectrum, there were historical actors who associated the colonies less with innovation and progress than with hierarchies and behaviours that were regarded as outdated back in the metropoles. They included adventurers like Carl Peters, who brutally indulged in fantasies of *Herrenmenschen* (members of the 'master race') in German East Africa, without any regard for the indigenous population, and whose behaviour was reminiscent of a late-medieval feudal lord. For Peters, the colonies were a place where individuals could rise above the anonymous masses of the urban centres and the mechanized world of work.

A more broadly shared ideal was that of the colonies as a site for communal life similar to (or so it was believed) that of the pre-industrial era. One contested field of these attempts to hold on to traditions was that of gender relationships. Concomitant with the emergence of settler communities, in particular in German South-West Africa, 'colonial schools' were set up specifically to prepare women interested in permanent emigration to the colonies (Illustration 40). Some of these schools survived the end of Germany's empire and continued to operate well into the Nazi period (see Illustration 41). One of the aims of these schools was to supply the predominantly male settler communities with wives and thus to ensure that they would not 'go native' by mingling with African women and adopting local customs. Therefore, the colonial school in Witzenhausen emphasized traditional values and gender roles by focusing on subordination and obedience, and by confining the role of women to the domestic sphere: 'The woman looks after the house, creates a home for the man, in which he can relax and recover from the worries and effort of work.'[10] In the German colonies, patriarchy would still reign supreme, or so at least believed many of those involved. In nationalist circles, German settlements abroad were described as strongholds of a traditional gender order at a time when the women's movement and debates about education and

---

[10] Wilhelm Breitenbach, *Über das Deutschthum in Süd-Brasilien: Eine Studie*, Hamburg (Richter) 1887, 14.

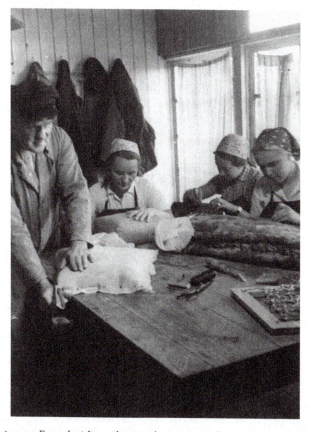

Illustration 40 For colonialist milieux and supporters of a *völkisch* nationalism, the colonies represented an ideal space to recreate notions of paternalistic community and pre-industrial values that were threatened by extinction in the urban conglomerations of modern Germany. The colonial women's schools were devised to educate middle-class women to live in the colonies and find a marriage partner among the German settler population. In the schools, the focus was on domestic and supposedly female values and skills such as, in this picture, upholstery. Some of the colonial schools carried their activities forward into the interwar period. This image is from the Colonial School for Women at Rendsburg, founded in 1926.

voting rights for women had already begun to undermine that order in Germany.

However, we should not rush to equate such ideas with backwardness and pre-modernity. They were often based on alternative

Illustration 41 The colonial school at Rendsburg was established with a focus on 'settlement purposes both at home and abroad'. Its students were to serve as 'loyal comrades to our fellow Germans far away'. In 1937, the cinematographer Paul Lieberenz, who had participated in the famous Nazi propaganda movie *Triumph of the Will*, directed by Leni Riefenstahl in 1934, produced a documentary film on the school in Rendsburg from which this image (and the preceding image) are taken. Sport had always been an element in the training of women for the empire, but this image conveys the particular emphasis placed on physical education in the Nazi period, when recruitment was only from the 'most racially sound' German women with a 'flawlessly National Socialist attitude'. After 1939, sending women overseas became impossible; instead, graduates were supposed to move to the occupied eastern territories. This was not, however, the end of colonial aspirations. A school newsletter in 1940 proclaimed that 'with the victorious end of the war . . . many female workers for the re-conquered colonies will probably be needed'.

visions of a new order for modern societies, and thus were themselves a product of the modern age. The colonial settlements would, it was hoped, take on a similar function to that ascribed to the American frontier by the American historian Frederic Jackson Turner in his

famous speech of 1893.[11] At the frontier, which Turner understood as
the boundary of civilization, the immigrants put aside their
'European' characteristics – such as hierarchies, social classes and
what Turner described as decadence – and became free and equal
citizens. The German colonies, too, for their proponents represented
a utopia in which society still meant community. There, 'class differences disappear', as one commentator stated, and 'many social problems simply solve themselves'.[12] A strand of German nationalists and
social reformers saw the colonies as the ideal location for the transformation of the German nation in the context of global mobility.

Ideas such as these had wider repercussions when they were linked
to the *Lebensreform* movement in Germany. This movement was
broad and all-encompassing and consisted of a series of diverse projects. Among them was a critique of civilization that was popular
during the Wilhelmine era and that was entranced by the idea of the
'happy children of nature' in Samoa and the utopia of a natural life
free of the inhibitions of modern civilization. The tiny 'Order of the
Sun', founded by August Engelhardt, drew dropouts and critics of
materialist civilization to New Guinea with the promise of realizing an
earthly paradise on the basis of a coconut diet.

The colonial spaces also held symbolic value for more influential
groups such as supporters of the cultural reform and homeland protection movements, and of movements such as theosophy: its members
hoped that the Pacific, India, or Africa would be a source of cultural
renewal for Germany. One such was Hans Paasche, who had fought as
an officer in the Maji-Maji war in East Africa. After his return to
Germany, he became a pacifist and created fictitious letters from the
point of view of an African 'chief' who, visiting Germany, expressed his
criticisms of civilization. This epistolary novel was widely read later on,
during the Weimar Republic era. Paasche was pleading for a return to
nature, justifying this call with an idealized vision of Africa.[13]

---

[11] Frederick Jackson Turner, 'The Significance of the Frontier in American History', in: John
Mack Faragher (ed.), *Rereading Frederick Jackson Turner: The Significance of the Frontier in
American History and Other Essays*, New York (Henry Holt) 1994, 11–30.
[12] Robert Gernhard, *Reise-Bilder aus Brasilien*, Breslau (Schottlaender) 1900, 44.
[13] Alan Nothnagle, 'Metanoia! Hans Paasche – ein lebensreformerischer Visionär', *Zeitschrift für
Geschichtswissenschaft* 45 (1997), 773–92; Werner Lange, *Hans Paasches Forschungsreise ins
innerste Deutschland: Eine Biographie*, Bremen (Donat) 1994.

GLOBAL SPHERES OF ACTION AND A GLOBAL
CONSCIOUSNESS

As we have seen, repercussions from the colonies did indeed have effects on German society, even if those effects were less pronounced than in France, Britain, the Netherlands, or Japan. But we need to go beyond a balance-sheet of colonial exports and imports. Asking about 'reverse effects' is itself part of a paradigm that is based on two separate worlds and assumes that the boundaries between the colonies and the 'mother country' were clearly drawn. But it is evident that from the end of the nineteenth century, social actors increasingly operated with a global consciousness that allowed them to link local or national issues with colonial or global contexts. For this reason, it is not enough to ask whether or to what extent the colonies changed the course of German history. Rather, we must consider the fact that the transformation of German society took place in a context in which those involved increasingly thought, and acted, in an imperial and global context.

One good example of these links is the late-nineteenth-century 'civilizing mission' that was directed not only at the colonies but also at underprivileged groups at home. In Germany, the unemployed and 'vagabonds', tramps and the 'work-shy' became the objects of social education projects. From the mid-1870s in particular, the 'work-shy' were increasingly perceived as a social problem. In 1880 approximately 1 per cent of Germany's population, i.e. some 400,000 persons, lived on the streets. The different institutions of the 'Inner Mission' – the missionary project that focused on the Christian populations within Europe and was mainly concerned with philanthropic solutions to mid-nineteenth-century social problems – catered to their needs and sought to 'elevate' and integrate them into society. The language employed differed little from the rhetoric of the civilizing mission overseas. 'Foreigners' and 'savages' were terms used to describe both tramps in Germany and 'natives' in Africa. Frequently, they were also described as 'children' who required protection. But the similarities of the groups were not a matter of discourse alone. Going beyond the linguistic similarities, there were direct links between these two bourgeois projects of 'elevation', and in part they influenced each other. Friedrich von Bodelschwingh, for example, founder of the Bethel

Institution, a Protestant (charitable) hospital for the mentally ill in Bielefeld, set up a large number of 'workers' colonies' in Germany. These were intended to allow social outcasts to become accustomed to a life of work. Labour stood at the centre of Bodelschwingh's reform project: 'Work, not alms' was the guiding principle in his philanthropic 'worker colonies': 'Education for work ... is an incomparably greater benefit than a piece of bread handed out for free.'[14] From 1890 onwards, he was also head of the Protestant Mission Society, which set up stations in German East Africa to 'educate' Africans and Christians in work and Christianity. 'The Inner and the Foreign Missions cannot be separated', he claimed.[15] His belief that missionary work would create 'light in the darkness' – the darkness of the city and the 'dark continent' of Africa equally – reveals the imperial mindset on which these philanthropic activities were based.

Similarly, the radicalization of German nationalism from the 1890s onwards is easier to understand if we view it in the context of the colonial experience. From the 1890s, nationalism in Germany was increasingly characterized by ethnic categories and social-hygiene and eugenic practices; this resulted in changes to the image of the nation and the way it was defined against its 'others'. For a long time, this superimposition of a discourse of race on to the idea of the nation was interpreted solely in terms of anti-Semitism. But while before the First World War the radicalization of anti-Semitism was still largely confined to the level of discourse, employing racial categories and implementing actual ethnic segregation were already common practice in the colonies. It is no coincidence that, in the debates about whether racial criteria should be included in the German Citizenship Act of 1913, reference was frequently made to existing practice in the colonies, most prominently the bans on 'mixed marriages'. Debates about belonging and exclusion, and

---

[14] Cited in Jürgen Scheffler, 'Die Gründungsjahre 1883–1913', in: Zentralverband Deutscher Arbeiterkolonien (ed.), *Ein Jahrhundert Arbeiterkolonien. 'Arbeit statt Almosen' – Hilfe für Obdachlose Wanderarme 1884–1984*, Bielefeld (VSH – Verlag Soziale Hilfe) 1984, 23–35, quote on p. 28.

[15] Quoted in Walther Trittelvitz, *Nicht so langsam! Missionserinnerungen an Vater Bodelschwingh*, Bethel bei Bielefeld (Anstalt Bethel) 1929, 123. See also Sebastian Conrad, '"Eingeborenenpolitik" in Kolonie und Metropole: "Erziehung zur Arbeit" in Ostafrika und Ostwestfalen', in: Sebastian Conrad and Jürgen Osterhammel (eds.), *Das Kaiserreich transnational. Deutschland in der Welt 1871–1914*, Göttingen (Vandenhoeck & Ruprecht) 2004, 107–28.

modifications of the idea of 'Germanness', were all embedded in the colonial world order. The concept of *Lebensraum*, coined by the geographer Friedrich Ratzel and, of course, influential well into the twentieth century, was another example of the geopolitical context of the national discourse.[16]

These changes in the meaning of Germanness found legal expression in, for example, the changes to citizenship law in the 1913 Act. While the law of 1870 had foreseen that citizenship ended ten years after leaving the country, this stipulation was revoked in 1913: from then on, citizenship could not expire and was even transferred to descendants. This provision was a reaction to changes in mobility. During the nineteenth century, the vast majority of emigrants had moved to the United States, presumably for good, and were considered a loss to the national fibre. The acquisition of colonies from 1884 was motivated, to a large extent, by the intention to provide emigrants with opportunities overseas without severing their ties with the German nation. In the face of political support for the colonial project, it was thus mandatory to enable Germans to settle in the colonies without risking their legal status. The modification of the durability of citizenship thus was a direct outcome of the debates about global mobility. This was no mere legal veneer, rendered insignificant by the dissolution of the colonial empire just shortly thereafter; rather, it concerned central dimensions of belonging and participation. It is instructive to note that the effects of this legal adaptation survived the end of empire. When in the 1990s large groups of descendants of former emigrants (*Aussiedler*) 'returned', as it came to be called, from the Soviet Union, they still benefited from this redefinition of Germanness drawn up under the colonial and global conditions of the early twentieth century.

---

[16] On Ratzel and his concept of *Lebensraum*, see Woodruff D. Smith, *The Ideological Origins of Nazi Imperialism*, New York (Oxford University Press) 1986, 146–50.

CHAPTER 10

Colonialism in Europe

For some years, there has been increasing discussion about the extent to which imperial expansion and colonial forms of rule were evident not only in Africa and Asia but also in Europe. The best-known examples include English control of its 'Celtic fringe' in Ireland and the role of the Hapsburg Empire in central Europe. Similar suggestions have recently been made about German history. In analytical terms, the debate about German history has two separate starting points. Firstly, Hannah Arendt's conceptual differentiation between 'continental' and 'overseas' imperialism leads to the suggestion that German expansion into Poland and Russia, especially the expansion during the Second World War, can perhaps be seen as a form of continental empire-building.[1] Secondly, the concept of 'internal colonialism' focuses on the domestic use of colonial forms of rule.

Heuristically, these perspectives have proven to be very fruitful, and they have opened up spaces for analytical questions outside the purview of traditional approaches that equated colonial territories, by definition, with overseas possessions. At the same time, it is important to be precise about the status and level of 'coloniality', and to clarify whether the links under investigation are rhetorical and metaphorical, economic, or indeed overlapping social practices. As much as it is illuminating to understand the reach and pervasiveness of colonial constellations, it is just as crucial to recognize the differences, not least the legal differences, between 'domestic colonialism' and foreign colonialism. Otherwise, there is a danger that the concept of 'colonialism' will become so broadly conceived that it covers, more or less indiscriminately, any kind of rule at all. This should be borne in

---

[1] Cf. Hannah Arendt, *The Origins of Totalitarianism*, New York (Harcourt, Brace) 1951.

mind over the following paragraphs, in which I briefly outline three current debates on the European dimension of German colonialism. They have to do with 'internal colonization' in the eastern provinces of Prussia, with the question of a link between the Herero war and the Holocaust and finally with the colonial character of Nazi expansion in eastern Europe.

'POLAND' AS AN ADJACENT COLONY

'The real German counterpart to India or Algeria was not Cameroon', the American historian David Blackbourn has recently pointed out, 'it was *Mitteleuropa*'.[2] German colonial fantasies before the First World War were not limited to Africa and the Pacific, but also extended to eastern Europe. It has been suggested, especially with regard to Polish-speaking areas, that German encounters with the European East can be read as a form of colonialism. This is a complex topic. To begin within, 'Poland' is in some ways an anachronistic term, as a sovereign Polish state ceased to exist following the three partitions in the late eighteenth century. As large parts of the Polish–Lithuanian Commonwealth had been incorporated into Prussia, large Polish-speaking groups, numbering 2.4 million people in the late decades of the nineteenth century, lived in Germany. The Polish population within Germany was very heterogeneous: it included about half a million so-called 'Ruhr Poles', who had migrated to the industrial cities of the Ruhr from the 1880s onwards, as well as the Polish-speaking majority population of the eastern provinces of Prussia, especially in Poznan, who made up almost 10 per cent of the total population of Prussia. The latter had Prussian nationality, in contrast to the seasonal workers who had been coming to Prussia from other parts of divided Poland since the 1890s. Polish–German interaction was thus an everyday reality, in particular in Prussia. Apart from these connections, German visions of and claims to 'Poland' often extended beyond the actual boundary of the Empire into the western provinces of Russia and the Austrian-ruled province of Galicia.

---

[2] David Blackbourn, 'Das Kaiserreich transnational: Eine Skizze', in: Sebastian Conrad and Jürgen Osterhammel (eds.), *Das Kaiserreich transnational: Deutschland in der Welt 1871–1914*, Göttingen (Vandenhoeck & Ruprecht) 2004, 302–24, quote on p. 322.

When assessing the 'coloniality' of German interventions in eastern Europe, it is possible to discuss different dimensions. The most obvious parallels are at the level of rhetoric and imagination. In general Prussian policies *vis-à-vis* the Polish population were aimed at 'improvement' and cultural 'betterment'. For example, Konrad von Studt, the *Oberpräsident* of Westphalia, demanded that the Polish population should be 'Germanified' so that the 'inferior elements, always liable to excesses, and in particular their female members who are equipped with dubious characteristics' would be improved and could 'benefit in full from the economic and moral superiority of Germanness'.[3] It is striking to what extent the rhetorical arsenal levelled against the Polish groups was reminiscent of the synchronous attempts to legitimize control and a 'native policy' in the overseas colonies.

The underlying rhetoric of a cultural mission was not entirely new, and it often made reference to the medieval tradition of German settlement in the east and German *Kulturträgertum* (roughly, 'carrying the banner of German culture'). One recurring trope was the derogatory concept of the 'Polish economy' (*polnische Wirtschaft*) that brought together vague ideas about cultural and social backwardness, a lack of sanitation and economic inefficiency. But even if there was a strong sense of continuity, it is important to recognize that the German–Polish encounter had been deeply transformed. Geographic and cultural difference was replaced, from the 1830s, by linear concepts of development and hierarchies of progress. In the accounts of German travellers to the Polish provinces, for example, the Poles were no longer primarily strange and different, but were increasingly characterized in a language of deprivation and backwardness. Visits to distant lands were interpreted as travels into the past, resembling what Johannes Fabian describes as the emergence of a colonizing gaze and, in his terms, the 'denial of coevalness'.[4] Again, therefore, it is instructive to note the synchronicity of this transformation on Prussia's eastern borders with a general shift towards thinking

---

[3] Quoted from Christoph Kleßmann, *Polnische Bergarbeiter im Ruhrgebiet 1870–1945: Soziale Integration und nationale Subkultur einer Minderheit in der deutschen Industriegesellschaft*, Göttingen (Vandenhoeck & Ruprecht) 1978, 63.
[4] Fabian, *Time and the Other*.

in developmental stages and concepts of temporality in Europe's relation to the colonial world.

One of the privileged sites where developmentalist tropes were linked to the notion of colonial expansion was the *Ostmarkenroman* (novel of the eastern marches). This literature, originating in the early 1890s, fused tropes from the colonial movement with the idea of *Heimat* (homeland). It depicted German Poland as a wasteland, as a landscape of colonial conquest, as a 'Wild East' with many parallels to the 'Wild West' in North America. The novels were characterized by rural settings, imbued with traditional social values, and based on a civilizing mission rhetoric that attempted to discursively maintain the border between Germans and Poles.[5] The texts bespeak a fear of non-identifiability and a lack of clearly marked boundaries typical, Ann Laura Stoler has argued, of colonial frontiers.[6]

The appropriation of the Polish-speaking territories as a form of colonial wasteland was not, however, a matter of discourse alone. Similarities can be observed on a more profound, and more material, level. In striking synchronicity, indeed, overseas colonies such as South-West Africa and the Polish-speaking provinces in eastern Prussia were subjected to policies of settlement. The redirection of outbound migration to Africa had been one of the *raisons d'être* of the colonial project, and the agitation of the colonial movement aimed at establishing large diaspora communities in 'New Germany'. At virtually the same time, the 'internal colonization' of Polish Prussia emerged as a central concern in nationalist circles, social science debates, and government policies.

Their goal was the 'internal colonization' of the regions mainly inhabited by Poles. In 1886, an Imperial Prussian Settlement Commission was formed to purchase land on which German-speaking small farmers could be resettled. The German Eastern Marches Society (*Deutscher Ostmarkenverein*) supported this 'Germanification of the soil' with propaganda and organizational measures. Demands for *Lebensraum*, the ideology on which this policy

[5] Kristin Kopp, 'Constructing Racial Difference in Colonial Poland', in: Eric Ames, Marcia Klotz, and Lora Wildenthal (eds.), *Germany's Colonial Pasts*, Lincoln (University of Nebraska Press) 2005, 76–96.

[6] Stoler, 'Rethinking Colonial Categories'.

was based, were common to the settlement projects in eastern Europe and in Germany's overseas colonies. This was not only the simple result of a common vocabulary, but also the effect of a shared problematic, as politics of settlement were presented as a solution to the problem of mobility and the emigration of Germans into the world. This was true for overseas expansion motivated by the alleged need to prevent the 'loss of national energies' to the United States and to redirect migration flows to 'New Germany' in Africa. At precisely the same time, the German Eastern Marches Society urged peasants 'not even to think about migrating to the United States' but instead to 'find a new *Heimat* in the east of the German fatherland'.[7]

Population policies in eastern Germany, in the end, were not successful and eventually strengthened, rather than weakened, Polish nationalism in the region. In comparison with the colonial settlements, however, the figures are staggering: more than 120,000 Germans were settled in the Prussian East, more than five times as many as ever lived in the entire colonial empire.

When discussing the validity of the colonial paradigm to analyse German–Polish relations in Prussia and beyond, the strongest objections concern the issue of race. It is commonly assumed that imperialism was determined by an absolute notion of racial difference, while continental expansion was predicated upon the assumption of ethnic compatibility and cultural affinities. Indeed, the differences between the colonial empire and eastern Prussia should not be played down. This is clear already from the point of view of the administration, which did not treat Poznan and Silesia as colonial territories. More importantly, assimilation was always a political and cultural option. For a long time, acculturation of the Polish-speaking population was the stated aim of governmental interventions. Social actors were frequently in a position to articulate different notions of subjecthood, nationality, and modernity and to appropriate them to their own purposes. Moreover, large groups of the Polish-speaking population possessed German citizenship (in this they differed from the migrants and seasonal workers from Galicia and Russia). This was a crucial difference when compared to the overseas empire. The colonies

---

[7] Cited in Jens Oldenburg, *Der deutsche Ostmarkenverein 1894–1934*, Berlin (Logos-Verlag) 2002, 147.

belonged to Germany according to international law, but this status did not imply German citizenship for the indigenous populations. In fact, there were virtually no cases of naturalization of colonial subjects.

The practices of separation and segregation, in other words, suggest a different quality of life under colonial conditions, compared with the more conventional forms of prejudice and repression in Prussia's eastern provinces. This is not to say, however, that the notion of 'race' did not play a role in the European context. Referring to the Polish population as the Slavic race was common practice in the *Kaiserreich*. Anton Wohlfahrt, for example, the hero in Gustav Freytag's 1855 novel *Credit and Debit*, defined himself as 'one of the conquerors who, for the sake of free labour and human culture, have taken away rule of this territory from a weaker race'.[8] The propaganda of the Eastern Marches Society was also replete with a racial vocabulary. Its frequent use was not least an attempt to banish the spectre of miscegenation and the dissolution of boundaries.

As in the overseas colonies, racial issues usually overlapped with conflict about gender roles. Polish women were typically described as the 'most effective and most dangerous opponents' because not only were they threatening to outnumber German women and the German people with their supposedly high fertility rates, but they might even 'Polonize' respectable Catholic German men by marrying them.[9] The parallels with contemporary fears about 'kaffirization' in Germany's African colonies are obvious. But just as obvious, again, were the differences: while warnings of miscegenation in the Prussian east were limited to rhetoric, they were translated into administrative practice in the colonial empire. After 1905, marriage of German citizens with indigenous partners was legally banned in South-West Africa (1912 in Samoa). A similar regulation never existed in the Polish-speaking territories of Prussia – not, that is, until the blatantly racist politics of the National Socialists during the Second World War.

The use and implementation of racial categories, then, diverged from colonial practice and was specific to the particular situation in

---

[8] Gustav Freytag, *Debit and Credit*, Charleston (BiblioBazaar) 2007, 475.
[9] Quoted from Elizabeth A. Drummond, '"Durch Liebe stark, deutsch bis ins Mark": Weiblicher Kulturimperialismus und der Deutsche Frauenverein für die Ostmarken', in: Ute Planert (ed.), *Nation, Politik und Geschlecht: Frauenbewegungen und Nationalismus in der Moderne*, Frankfurt am Main (Campus) 2000, 147–64, quote on p. 152.

Poznan and Silesia. It is equally clear, however, that notions of race increasingly coloured the discourse and practices of belonging. In this context, 'Polonization' could be perceived as a threat equally as powerful as the dangers implied by racial mixing in the colonies. To be sure: it was not the same threat. Polish women, for example, were credited with forms of agency that African women – the objects of legal provisions against miscegenation – were not associated with in colonial discourse. Moreover, 'Polonization' was frequently couched in a language of nationalism that at the time was not yet at the disposal of most social actors in the African colonies. But it would be reductionist to assume a global order in which nationalism and colonialism functioned as mutually exclusive forms of discourse and practice. Instead, it is important to recognize that in an age of high imperialism differences of nation, culture, and class, in the Prussian east, were increasingly underwritten by, and articulated with, notions of colonial difference.

Therefore, we need to go beyond a strictly territorial view of German colonialism (the *Schutzgebiete* paradigm) that assumes neatly separated spheres and asks to what extent 'repercussions' of the colonial experience impacted on the *Kaiserreich*. Instead, the 'colonial' character of Polish Prussia can be grasped only by seeing it as part of global interactions in a world deeply structured – albeit unevenly – by capitalism and imperialism. It is this larger context that enables colonial dimensions to structure social experience in highly diverse places – without, to be sure, erasing the particularities of the situation in question. Rather than looking at colonial empires as a specific form of territoriality, separated from their 'mother countries', it is more instructive to understand Polish Prussia in the framework of global modernity that was marked by colonialism globally.

COLONIALISM AND THE HOLOCAUST

Much more controversial than the question of whether German policy towards central Europe was colonial in character has been the suggestion that there was a link between the unleashing of violence in colonial wars and the policies of extermination pursued by the Nazis in the 1930s and 40s. This theory takes as its point of departure the writings of Hannah Arendt, who claimed a connection between practices of violence in the colonies and the genocidal politics of Nazi Germany, and also Frantz Fanon's suggestion that fascism can in general be understood as European imperialism turned in on itself and that it is no coincidence that it was in Germany, which lost its colonies in 1918, that fascism had its most far-reaching effects.[10]

Recent discussions of the issue have been triggered by a more general revision of the perception of the war in German South-West Africa against the Herero and Nama between 1904 and 1907. While German historians had long described these events as a 'rebellion' that was violently suppressed, the massacres are now increasingly seen as genocide. The infamous orders issued by General von Trotha to shoot any Africans on German-occupied territory, including women and children, the establishment of concentration camps, and the expulsion of the surviving Herero into the Omaheke desert where most of them starved to death led to the 'annihilation of the Herero people', as even the official German military report of 1906 blatantly stated.[11]

Historians such as Jürgen Zimmerer have recently interpreted these events as part of the longer 'prehistory of the Holocaust'. The war against the Herero and Nama was, he argues, 'an important step towards the Nazi war of annihilation'.[12] This statement implies a twofold argument. Firstly, it is based on the recognition of the structural similarities between the two events. They include the destruction of a group's economic basis for survival, the mass executions, the acceptance that huge numbers would die of thirst or starvation, the highly 'racialized' language in which the conflict was represented and fought, and the objective of annihilation. General von Trotha, who had been brought to South-West Africa because of his reputation as a particularly ruthless colonial warrior in East Africa (1894–7) and in China (1900), insisted on the extermination of the Herero even long after the war had been won. 'It was both a foolish and cruel policy to smash the [Herero] people this way', wrote Ludwig

[10] Cf. Arendt, *Origins*; Frantz Fanon, *The Wretched of the Earth*, trans. Constance Farrington, New York (Grove Press) 1963.

[11] Quoted from Jürgen Zimmerer, 'Krieg, KZ und Völkermord in Südwestafrika: Der erste deutsche Genozid', in: Jürgen Zimmerer and Joachim Zeller (eds.), *Völkermord in Deutsch-Südwestafrika: Der Kolonialkrieg (1904–1908) in Namibia und seine Folgen*, Berlin (Ch. Links) 2003, 45–63, quote on p. 45.

[12] Ibid., p. 60.

von Esstorff, an officer in the Herero campaign who had early on emerged as a critic of Trotha's strategies. 'It would have been possible to save much of their rich livestock had they been spared and taken back [into society]; they had already been sufficiently punished. I suggested this to General von Trotha, but he wanted their complete annihilation.'[13]

The similarities, on a discursive and phenomenological level, between the Herero war and parts of the genocidal politics of the Nazi period are indeed remarkable (Illustration 42). But the differences between the events are significant. In particular, the industrialized form that mass murder took in the Nazi concentration camps is without precedent in colonial Africa. To some extent, this difference

Illustration 42 The Herero war (1904–7) has emerged as the point of departure for a vibrant scholarly debate about the larger ramifications of this 'first German genocide' and the way it can be placed within continuities of German history. This picture shows men and women who fled German troops during the Herero uprising on their return to the Omaheke desert in German South-West Africa (present-day Namibia), early 1905.

[13] Cited in ibid., p. 52.

can be ascribed to the difference between a colonial plantation society with limited enforcement of authority over the colonized society, and the totalitarian state of the 1940s with its bureaucratic means of control and penetration of territory and population. But are these differences in state-formation sufficient to explain the peculiar – and differing – logic of these events? The extermination of women and children, for example, was accepted as a by-product of the war in South-West Africa, but it was highly intentional in the case of the Holocaust. Beneath the striking similarities, in other words, it is important to recognize crucial differences between the Omaheke desert and Auschwitz.

The second link that has been drawn between these two genocidal events goes beyond identifying parallels and focuses on causal relationships that locate the Holocaust in a continuity with the Herero war. What are the continuities at play here? On a very general level there are the discursive connections that turned the colonial imagination into a kind of cultural reservoir, a 'colonial archive', that social actors could mine and tap into. Its most important ingredient, in the context of this discussion, was the readiness to consign entire populations to annihilation. Jürgen Zimmerer and Joachim Zeller have described the willingness to murder entire groups of people as the 'ultimate breach of taboo', one that took place first in German South-West Africa before experiencing 'its most radical extent in the Holocaust'.[14] Without this breach of taboo overseas, it is implied, radical politics of extermination within Europe might have been unthinkable. Secondly, there were, it is argued, institutional continuities that were able to guarantee the longevity of the colonial experience. Among them are categories of knowledge perpetuated in academic disciplines and research institutions, geography and anthropology; but even more importantly eugenics and racial sciences come most readily to mind. The possible transmitters of colonial experiences would also include the educational establishments of the German military institutions, although in the absence of research this remains highly speculative. Finally, personal experiences of events

---

[14] Quoted from Robert Gerwarth and Stephan Malinowski, 'Der Holocaust als "kolonialer Genozid"? Europäische Kolonialgewalt und nationalsozialistischer Vernichtungskrieg', *Geschichte und Gesellschaft* 33 (2007), 439–66, quotes on p. 442.

in the colonies may have fed into the policies adopted in the occupations during the Second World War. One example frequently cited is that of Franz Ritter von Epp, who took part both in the Boxer and Herero wars, later became involved in the *Freikorps* (Free Corps, paramilitary organizations active during the Weimar Republic), and was made head of the NSDAP's Colonial Policy Office in the 1930s. Another is Viktor Boettcher, who was deputy governor of Cameroon before 1914 and later became *Regierungspräsident* of Poznan in the Warthegau, a German-occupied zone formed from territory annexed from Poland in 1939.

There have been various critical reactions to all these suggestions. The criticisms refer to the impact and the influence of colonial discourses, to the significance (or insignificance) of colonial experience in the biographies of soldiers and officers, and to the fact that, to date, only few institutional links have been identified. A more important point is that there was no German colonial parallel to the industrialized policy of annihilation under the Nazis. And the genocidal characteristics of the Herero war were not an inherent part of the colonial project; they were very much specific to the involvement of von Trotha – the war had been conducted very differently under Theodor von Leutwein, Trotha's predecessor. This is an important point, as the genocidal interventions in eastern Europe were more systematic and clearly hinged much less on the selection of the individuals involved. And more fundamentally, while colonial policies certainly aimed to subjugate and exploit the African population, there was no *a priori* intention to exterminate them, not least because they were regarded as a resource and a labour force. Under the Nazi policy of extermination, by contrast, utilitarian ideas were of lesser importance than ideological motives and the momentum that the spiral of violence developed.

Another important criticism of the idea that the colonial wars were precursors to the Holocaust points out that those who argue for continuity have not paid enough attention to the years between the Herero war and the Nazis' introduction of exterminatory policies. If the issue of continuity is to be discussed properly, the events of the First World War and those of the years between 1918 and 1923, in which Germany was on occasion close to civil war, must be taken into account. Instead of drawing a simple connection from 1904 to 1941, the radicalizing effects of domestic European excesses of violence must be seriously taken into account. For many members of the generation later involved in the Nazi war, these experiences were a major turning-point in their lives and had a formative character. This is clearly an important argument that also takes into account the generational gap between actors with colonial experiences, and the protagonists of the later Nazi wars. There cannot be a direct link between the Herero war and the Nazi atrocities that does not recognize the important and transformative character of the ordeals of the First World War. However, it would be equally deceiving to yield to the familiar narrative that portrays the First World War as Europe's original sin. The First World War was not the radical rupture it is often described as, but must itself be placed within the larger imperial context of the epoch. This implies that it is necessary to register, for example, the 're-importation' of the strategies of colonial warfare – the use of machine guns, gas attacks, air raids, the deployment of colonial army units – to Europe. It also suggests taking more seriously the way in which the policies that Germany pursued in the territories it occupied during the war, such as in Oberost in the northwest of the former Russian empire, were informed by experiences and analogies of occupation and foreign rule gained in colonial settings.

Overall, the suggestion of a link between colonialism and the Holocaust has brought up more questions than it has answered. It has certainly opened up new ways of seeing events and has placed German twentieth-century history in new contexts, a process that has been extremely productive. That said, this does not mean that we have to join the search for direct causal links and the quest for continuities. In the end, this may prove not to be the most promising path to pursue. As discussed above, constructing direct connections may result in oversimplifying events and in positing unwarranted equiv-alences. The links were more complex than some of these theories suggest, and in most cases, we are dealing with similarities caused by similar conditions rather than deliberate transfers or biographical continuities. Furthermore, German colonialism did not stand alone; it was an integral part of the larger European and American colonial project. Our aim therefore must not be to create a new variant of the German *Sonderweg*, the narrative of the peculiar and deviant German path into modern times, as an over-zealous fixation with the Herero war might suggest. Terribly brutal colonial wars, founded on a belief in cultural superiority and, later, on Social Darwinist theories, were also launched by other countries: infamous examples include the French colonization of Algeria, the Boer war, and the American occupation of the Philippines. Such wars were a central element of colonial rule. In discussing the relationship between colonialism and Nazi violence, therefore, it is more useful to think in terms of a shared colonial archive involving ways of behaving, rituals, forms of knowledge, and imagination, than to locate such links solely within the short-lived German colonial empire.

THE NAZI EXPANSION INTO EASTERN EUROPE

A third area of debate is the question of whether the Nazis' expansion towards the east can be seen as a form of colonial empire-building. Adolf Hitler almost suggested as much: 'The Russian space is our India', he soliloquized in September 1941; 'like the English, we shall rule this empire with a handful of men'.[15] For a long time, historians have dismissed such pronouncements, interpreting them as examples of Hitler's hubris.[16] It is only more recently that questions have been asked about whether the war and the Nazis' occupation policies in the Warthegau and the Ukraine should be placed in the broader context of colonialism.

Here, too, we can differentiate between discourse and actual practice. Nazi rhetoric and ideological agendas often contained references to European colonial empires. During an inspection trip through occupied Poland, for example, Hanns Johst, the President of the *Reich* Chamber of Literature and a friend of Heinrich Himmler, declared that 'a country that has so little feeling for systematic settlement has no claim to any sort of independent political status within the European area. It is a colonial country.'[17] References to the *Drang nach Osten* (the 'thrust towards the east'), to links with German

---

[15] *Hitler's Table Talk 1941–44: His Private Conversations*, Oxford (Oxford University Press) 1988, entry for 17 October 1941.
[16] Cf. the assessment of the literature in Wendy Lower, *Nazi Empire-Building and the Holocaust in Ukraine*, Chapel Hill (University of North Carolina Press) 2005, 3.
[17] Hanns Johst, *Ruf des Reiches – Echo des Volkes: Eine Ostfahrt*, Munich (Eher) 1944 (7th edition), 86.

medieval settlement in the east and the expansionary policies of the
Teutonic Order, were equally common. In his *Mein Kampf,* Hitler
had stressed the continuity with medieval settlements, in explicit
contrast to the overseas empire acquired after the 1880s:

We National Socialists consciously draw a line beneath the foreign policy of
our pre-War period. We take up where we broke off six hundred years ago.
We stop the endless German movement to the south and west, and turn our
gaze to the east. At long last we break off the colonial, commercial policy of
the pre-War period and shift to the soil policy of the future.[18]

These two points of references – modern colonialism, and continuities with medieval settlements – infiltrated the rhetoric of National
Socialists in different ways, and they were taken as an inspiration and a
model. But they also allowed those involved to legitimize violent
expansion and occupation by reference to a broader European history.
Carl Schmitt, the legal scholar, believed Germany had been denied its
overseas empire in 1919, and was thus compelled to expand within the
colonial space of eastern Europe.[19]

   Colonial references were not confined to the level of discourse. The
actual practice of occupational policies also exhibited some similarities
with colonial rule. One reason why these similarities were ignored for
so long is terminological. The use of the term 'occupation' has tended
to distract attention from the fact that Nazi policies in eastern Europe
were not intended as a temporary seizure of power; the Nazis were
aiming for permanent control that would allow far-reaching political,
economic, and social changes. In these plans, the role of the indigenous population was usually limited to serving as a source of cheap
labour, just as in the 'protectorates' overseas. For this reason, ethnic
segregation was practised (in the Warthegau, Germans wore distin-
guishing marks that identified them as such), and schooling for the
indigenous population was, as in the colonies, reduced to only the
most basic level of knowledge. To some extent, the former colonial
empire served as a reservoir of know-how and organizational expertise.
In 1943, German farmers from East Africa were brought to the
Warthegau, in the hope that their experiences would be of use for

---

[18] Quoted from Lower, *Nazi Empire-Building*, 3.
[19] On Carl Schmitt's vision of expansion and empire, see Julia Hell, 'Katechon: Carl Schmitt's
       Imperial Theology and the Ruins of the Future', *The Germanic Review* 84 (2009), 283–326.

Nazi settlement policies. And many private companies that had been active in the colonies made use of their networks and contacts, for example the Togo Company, which was reformed in Zhytomyr in Ukraine under the name 'Togo East'.

Despite these similarities, there were major differences between the Nazi occupation of the east and German colonial rule in Africa or in the Pacific. The most important difference is that there was no question of a 'civilizing mission' in Nazi-occupied eastern Europe. This is, indeed, a major departure from colonial practice. To be sure, it must be taken into account that German control of Ukraine, in particular, lasted only three years and took place during a global war. It could well be that if the period of German rule had lasted longer, ideological changes would have occurred. But it is nevertheless remarkable that the rhetoric of 'development', which in the colonies was in a constant state of tension with the daily violence of colonial rule, was completely absent. In fact, any ideas about 'elevating' and 'civilizing' the inhabitants of the region were explicitly rejected. The local populations were instead described as 'serf peoples' (*Helotenvolk*) and seen only as objects of exploitation. And they were treated with utmost brutality. Heinrich Himmler, the chief engineer of the Holocaust, demanded that the police forces of the SS (*Schutzstaffel* or protection squadron, the paramilitary organization of the Nazi party responsible for many of the war crimes) 'clean the territory of Ukraine for the future settlement of Germans'. Apart from the destruction and annihilation of Jews and their communities, Himmler requested that the Ukrainian civilian population be brought to a 'minimum'.[20]

These differences are important and are vital for understanding the particular characteristics of each situation. National Socialism and overseas colonialism were not one and the same. But the question is wrongly put as long as it remains within the confines of German history. When assessing the colonial dimensions of German rule in the European east, it is not enough to compare Nazi policy with the German colonial empire alone. It is more instructive to situate Nazi policy within the larger context of European settlement colonies that, in North America and Australia for example, were characterized by

[20] Quoted from Lower, *Nazi Empire-Building*, p. 8.

the brutal expulsion and annihilation of indigenous populations. In fact, North America was one of the models to which frequent reference was made in plans that saw Ukraine as a region of settlement zones and military bases.

Overall, the debate on this issue has concentrated too much on comparing (German) nineteenth-century colonialism with Nazi expansion and on looking for links between the two. But these diachronous links were in fact less important than the context of the colonial policies being pursued by other European powers at the same time. German expansion in eastern Europe took place in the geopolitical (and discursive) context of the development of political, economic, and demographic blocs in Europe from the 1920s onwards. These made use of colonial resources and settlement regions that might be located in India or Rhodesia, in Manchuria or indeed in Ukraine. The Nazis' expansion towards the east must be seen in this synchronous context, the global transformation of colonial empires.

CHAPTER II

German colonialism and its global contexts

The dynamics of German colonialism extended not only to Europe but also into the world, far beyond the 'protectorates' and overseas possessions. The formally acquired territorial colonial empire was not a separate sphere that can be understood in isolation from the increasing integration of the world – integration caused by capitalist structures, imperialist intervention, cultural exchange, and migratory flows. German colonial history was embedded in global events and linkages in many ways.

We can identify three different levels of global entanglement. Firstly, the imperialists' expansionary plans often extended beyond the existing colonial territories; there was no shortage of visions of an enlarged empire. This fact is well established and is usually mentioned in traditional accounts of colonial history. There are many examples for these larger expansionary ambitions. Most prominent among them was the media campaign by nationalist groups hailing from the educated classes and organized in the Pan-German League, for Germany to seize western Morocco. While the government and industry favoured a liberal open door policy, nationalist circles claimed Morocco to be an ideal location for German settlement. These debates fed into the two Moroccan crises of 1905 and 1911, in which Germany attempted to employ gunboat diplomacy to limit France's ambitions in the region, but ultimately failed and became increasingly diplomatically isolated. Another region of imperialist aspirations was central Africa, where protagonists of imperialism like Wilhelm Hübbe-Schleiden saw a 'German India' in the making. These proposals date from the early 1880s, but surfaced regularly in the following decades. The creation of *Mittelafrika*, centred on the Belgian Congo, was one of the official German objectives of the First

World War. In public discussion, mainly on the nationalist fringe, a series of further territorial aims were put forward, among them in South Africa and in Latin America, in particular in Brazil.

Secondly, it is possible to differentiate between strategies of formal and informal colonialism. In this way, one can distinguish Germany's actual territorial colonial empire from the regions in which it had created spheres of influence. The best-known example of German informal imperialism was the construction of the Baghdad railway. This project, entered into for reasons of status-building and foreign relations, was a symbol of Wilhelmine *Weltpolitik* ('world politics') and contemporary financial imperialism. In terms of public perception, the Baghdad railway project was at least as significant as the German colonies in Africa. *Kaiser* Wilhelm II described it as a 'gateway to the world' and a 'gateway for German work and industry that could not in the immediate future have been attained through colonialism'.[1] The idea was to create a direct connection between Berlin and Baghdad (taking thirteen days) and thus to open up the vast areas and markets around the Arabian gulf, and also India and east Asia. Internationally, the project was highly confrontational as it competed with French and particularly British interests. In Germany, by contrast, it received almost unanimous support and was also backed by the Social Democratic Party. In the press, the project was celebrated as a form of development aid for the 'sick man of Europe', the Ottoman Empire, with all the attendant connotations of paternalism and superiority of the civilizing mission rhetoric.

We help the Turks to build railways and ports. We seek to awaken their industry. We support them with our credit. We supply ships and cannons ... The 'sick man' will be cured, and so thoroughly will he be cured that he will be hardly recognizable .... One may be tempted to believe that he is properly blond, blue-eyed, and Germanic. By our loving embrace we have infiltrated him with so much German juice that it is difficult to tell him apart from a German.[2]

---

[1] Quoted from Dirk van Laak, *Über alles in der Welt: Deutscher Imperialismus im 19. und 20. Jahrhundert*, Munich (C. H. Beck) 2005, 94.

[2] *Die Welt am Montag*, 21 November 1989, quoted from Gründer (ed.), *Rassismus, Kolonien und kolonialer Gedanke*, 210.

The Baghdad railway was financed by the Deutsche Bank, and it was built by the construction company Philipp Holzmann (Illustration 43). The project was the product of overlapping desires and discourses. It fed on a scholarly interest in the region, Orientalist knowledge, and the

Illustration 43 The Baghdad railway was one of the high-prestige projects of the *Kaiserreich*. Co-financed by the Deutsche Bank and largely completed by 1914, it linked Konya in central Anatolia to Baghdad. This cartoon with the title 'Full steam ahead to Baghdad!', taken from the weekly German satirical magazine *Lustige Blätter* in 1900, caricatures the ideology of Germany's informal imperialism. It shows Georg von Siemens (1839–1901), director of the Deutsche Bank and 'founder of the Anatolian railway' in the guise of an Ottoman stationmaster asking to 'Make way for German cultural work in the Orient!' In 1915, the railway was used to deport Armenians and was thus instrumental in the Armenian genocide.

myth of the archaeologist Heinrich Schliemann, who in the 1870s had unearthed the ancient city of Troy. It was driven by political ambitions in Asia minor, grand schemes of economic expansion, and plans of German settlement. Alongside the railway tracks, Pan-Germans intended 'to settle tens and even hundreds of thousands of our peasants on Ottoman territory'.[3] On loftier grounds, the investment into infrastructure was presented as part of an overarching cultural mission, fuelled by the *Kaiser*'s ambition to emerge as a world monarch, beyond religious strife and conflict. These visions corresponded, on a more material level, with the deployment of German military advisers through which the German *Reich* secured its influence in Ottoman politics.

From the point of view of the Ottoman Sultan Abdul Hamid II, the Baghdad railway was primarily an attempt to bring foreign capital into the country. The background was the financial crisis of the Ottoman Empire, which since 1881 had been exploited by the European powers to exert financial control over the region. At the same time, the extension of the railway to the Arabian Gulf was to be the start of massive investments into infrastructure and into the industrialization of his empire. Not least, the railway had a strategic value for the Ottoman military. In 1915/16, it was used for the forced deployment of Armenians and was thus instrumental in the Armenian genocide.

On a third, more fundamental level, both formal and informal colonialism were part of the contemporary process of global integration. There is agreement among historians to regard the decades before the First World War as a zenith in the history of globalization. Germany was affected by this process in many ways and many contemporaries saw it as a characteristic of their era. The history of colonialism is closely linked to the process of globalization. Global entanglements – the mobility of goods, people, ideas, and institutions – took place, before the First World War, under conditions of colonialism. The world economy was based on the use, sometimes violent exploitation, of the labour, raw materials, and demand of non-European societies. Colonialism was a central ingredient of the political world order – and also of the legal and ideological legitimation of

---

[3] Heinrich Schnee, *Als letzter Gouverneur in Deutsch-Ostafrika: Erinnerungen*, Heidelberg (Quelle und Meyer) 1964, 26.

that order. Projects of 'modernization' in both the colony and the metropole were thus shaped by colonialism, as were the processes of cultural interaction and appropriation. Globalization around 1900, then, was directly structured by the asymmetrical relationships of the colonial situation even beyond the effects of formal colonial empires and informal colonial claims. For that reason the specific character of global interactions before the First World War can be described as 'colonial globality'.

A GERMAN ALABAMA IN TOGO

The overlaps between these different dimensions of globality are very evident in one particular example that has recently been analysed by the American historian Andrew Zimmerman. This was the attempt to establish a German cotton industry in Togo. In 1900, Baron Beno von Herman was commissioned by the Colonial Economic Committee (*Kolonialwirtschaftliches Komitee*) to bring four graduates of the Tuskegee Normal and Industrial Institute of Alabama to Africa 'to teach the negroes there how to plant and harvest cotton in a rational and scientific way'.[4] This initiative was part of an overall attempt to introduce a more systematic, more sustainable form of colonialism after the initial phase of exploitation by private capital. This new approach, which was to be founded on scientific principles, focused on the central role of indigenous 'human capital' in colonial development policy (see Illustration 44).

German colonial reformers were interested in students from Tuskegee because they assumed that race relations in the American South could be a model for Germany's African colonies. German administrators and social scientists were particularly interested in Booker T. Washington, the head of the Tuskegee Institute, who instilled his ideas about natural hierarchies in his African American students. Washington assumed that once slavery had been abolished, the next step would be to educate African Americans to lead a

---

[4] Quoted in Andrew Zimmerman, 'A German Alabama in Africa: The Tuskegee Expedition to German Togo and the Transnational Origins of West African Cotton Growers', *American Historical Review* 110 (2005), 1362–98, quote on p. 1380. See also Andrew Zimmerman, *Alabama in Africa: Booker T. Washington, the German Empire, and the Globalization of the New South*, Princeton (Princeton University Press) 2010.

Illustration 44 This picture shows Togolese men pulling wagons of cotton. The wagon covers bear the initials 'KWK', for *Kolonialwirtschaftliches Komitee*, the organization that sponsored the Tuskegee expedition to Togo. The KWK was an organization that was known for its efforts to modernize and rationalize colonial production, infrastructure, and exploitation. These principles notwithstanding, and because of the difficulty of keeping draft animals alive in Togo, humans were often required to take their place on animal-drawn farm equipment. As Andrew Zimmerman observes: 'Ironically, the progress of Togolese cotton production could involve a regression of humans to the work roles of animals' (Zimmerman, 'A German Alabama in Africa', 1385).

Christian life and become manual workers and small farmers; gradually, over a long period of time, they would then be able to attain the status of citizens. Washington's conservative views on social and 'race' relations corresponded to the imperialist belief in control and segregation. Three of his books were translated into German and read in Germany as user's manuals for Africa, even though they dealt only with the southern states of the USA. 'We are interested in Dr Washington's book mainly in terms of the possibilities for development for Africans.'[5] For this reason, graduates of Tuskegee were believed to be the ideal candidates to communicate a project of modernization that would not undermine the political or 'racial'

[5] Max Größer, 'Die Emporentwicklung der Neger nach den Methoden des Booker T. Washington', *Zeitschrift für Missionswissenschaft* 8 (1918), 113–30, quote on p. 123.

order of the colonies. For his part, Washington supported imperialism because he believed Africa to be backward and he assumed that a 'civilizing mission' was necessary – and partly because he was convinced that the German 'way of treating Negroes in Africa . . . could be a model for other nations'.[6]

When the experts from Tuskegee arrived in Togo in 1904, a cotton production school was set up under the leadership of John W. Robinson to train young Togolese men to grow cotton for the European market. For a number of years, cotton production grew strongly. But the introduction of new forms of production had huge impacts on local forms of cultivation and local social structures. Many producers insisted on retaining established forms of mixed cultivation and resisted the creation of export-oriented cotton monocultures. And among the Ewe people in southern Togo, cultivating and spinning cotton had generally been women's work. German and American experts attempted to change this domestic division of labour, which was linked to the common practice of having separate households for women and men, and to replace it with what they believed to be the morally and economically superior model of patriarchal monogamy and field labour by men.

The population bitterly resisted the colonial powers' interference in recruitment, schooling, and labour and social practices. As a result, the authorities increasingly attempted to compel cooperation. The use of violence became more and more common, although often unsuccessful. Even the cotton school, where children were to be prepared for the new forms of work, was attended only by students forced to do so. When, in 1907, two students turned up of their own free will, this was such an extraordinary event that Governor Zech ordered an investigation. Overall, attempts to create 'a German Alabama in Africa' were a failure, in that Germany never imported more than 0.5 per cent of its cotton from its colonies.

But the Togo cotton project allows us to identify some of the structures and different levels of contemporary transnational linkages. Firstly, the project formed part of German colonial policy, to which the expectation of commercial gain was central. At the turn of the

---

[6] Quoted from Sven Beckert, 'Von Tuskegee nach Togo: Das Problem der Freiheit im Reich der Baumwolle', *Geschichte und Gesellschaft* 31 (2005), 505–45, quote on p. 519.

century, the German cotton industry was the third-largest in the world. Whole regions of Germany, such as Saxony and present-day Alsace, were dominated by the production of cotton, and it was Germany's most important export. Bismarck himself declared, somewhat exaggeratedly, 'I have been engaged in colonial politics mainly for the opportunity of securing our own cotton production.'[7] Secondly, the project is also an example of the importance of the concept of the 'civilizing mission' to the colonial project. Talk of 'elevating' and development was commonplace, and work was regarded as the most important way of 'civilizing' Africans. At the same time, it is clear that the concept of modernization upon which these ideas were based itself assumed a gendered, racially structured order and a very specific type of subjectivity linking the individual with the state and the global market.

Thirdly, the transfer of Afro-American expertise illustrates the broader transnational context in which German society was embedded. This includes German fascination with the work ethic of the United States, one of the *Kaiserreich*'s most important economic and political rivals; it is this rivalry that forms one of the political backgrounds of the Togo project. Fourthly, this project embodied a hope that the social order of the American South – also known as 'New South', following the American Civil War and the abolition of slavery and the plantation system could be a model for ethnically segregated labour relationships in agriculture, not just in the colonies but also, in the medium term, in the Polish-speaking parts of east Prussia. These overlaps between the New South, east Prussia, and colonial Togo illustrate the global perspective in which sociological debates about labour, mobility, and modernization at the turn of the century took place. And fifthly, the Togo project was also linked to the global restructuring of the production of raw materials after the end of the slave trade. In cotton production, as elsewhere, slave-based plantations were to be replaced by plantations based on supposedly free labour. But the reality was otherwise, characterized by an increasing level of state intervention and new forms of bonded labour, particularly – but not only – in the colonies.

---

[7] Quoted from ibid., 516.

DIMENSIONS OF COLONIAL GLOBALITY

Finally, I wish to examine in a slightly more systematic fashion the extent to which the *Kaiserreich* was embedded in pre-1914 colonial globality. The following typology is an analytical construction, as it is almost impossible to separate out these different dimensions in historical reality. The integration of Germany into global contexts is evident, firstly, on the level of foreign policy, which, from the 1890s onwards, was focused on expanding Germany's sphere of influence. In the Wilhelmine era, politics had become *Weltpolitik*, especially under Chancellor Bernhard von Bülow (1900–9). Telegrams to Bad Ems and Bad Gastein were replaced by gunboats to Agadir and to the Taku forts – examples of the broadened horizons of Wilhelmine politics. After Prussia defeated France in 1871, Prussian military advisers were in demand around the world. The best known was Otto Liman von Sanders in the Ottoman empire whose appointment in 1913 triggered the last major diplomatic crisis on the international scene before the outbreak of the war, but Prussian experts could also be found in Chile, in China, and in Japan; Jacob Meckel regarded the Japanese victory over China in 1895 as due in large part to his efforts. Wilhelm II was described in Germany as the 'Travelling Kaiser'. In 1898, he went to Jerusalem for three weeks, where he consecrated the Christian Church of the Redeemer, publicly stated that he was in favour of the migration of Jews to Palestine and that he would work towards that end. In Damascus he gave the famous speech in which he promised the three hundred million Muslims of the world that he was their friend. There is a wealth of other examples that demonstrate how German politics no longer felt itself to be limited to European affairs.

Weltpolitik was embedded in a transformed vision of world order that emerged in the closing decades of the nineteenth century (see Illustration 45). Many political decision-makers regarded it as an established fact that the system of a European equilibrium had been superseded by a system of world equilibrium. In the long term, it was believed, only nations that had their own 'world empire' would be able to secure their own status. Of course, *Weltpolitik* was always rooted in European power politics and thus had a European base. In particular, it was to a large extent an attempt to break British

~C Geographifches. ℈~

Wenn das gute Wetter ſich hält, ſoll nächſtens die Façade unſeres Erdballs friſch geſtrichen werden, da an manchen Stellen die alte Farbe ſchlecht gehalten hat.

Illustration 45 The formation of the German colonial empire was part of a new phase of world politics (*Weltpolitik*) in which newly founded and consolidated states vied with older colonial powers for spheres of influence. This woodblock print by E. Spott with the title 'Geographical news' shows Americans, Russians, and Germans making new claims for territorial possessions. 'If the good weather persists', the painters exclaim, 'the façade of the globe will soon be painted anew because in some regions the old paint has not lasted very well'. First published in the satirical magazine *Kladderadatsch*, 23 March 1884.

hegemony and make Germany a 'world empire' which would, according to widely held hopes, play its part in determining world events. Territorial expansion was on the agenda, and even British observers recognized this: Sir Eyre Crowe in the British Foreign Office conceded that 'it would be neither just nor politic to ignore the claims to a healthy expansion which a vigorous and growing country like Germany has a natural right to assert in the field of legitimate endeavour'.[8] Naval policy, which occupied much of the *Reich*'s

---

[8] Sir Eyre Crowe, 'Memorandum on the Present State of British Relations with France and Germany, January 1, 1907', in: G. P. Gooch and Harold Temperley (eds.), *British Documents on the Origins of the War*, vol. III, London (HMSO) 1928, 418.

internal and foreign policy debate from 1897 onwards, was the most conspicuous result of the competition with Great Britain which the *Kaiserreich* felt it faced in the new area of *Weltpolitik*. And as 'world empires' were inconceivable without colonies and the global projection of power, foreign policy attention was increasingly directed to locations outside Europe. Germany got involved in China and Samoa, organized military patrols along the coasts of Venezuela and Chile, and acted as an agent for negotiations about the colonial claims of Belgium and Portugal.

Secondly, in economic terms, Germany was highly involved in the process of globalization – in many areas its involvement was exceeded only by that of Great Britain. The use of the term 'world economy' and the setting-up of the Kiel Institute for the World Economy in 1911 are indications that contemporaries were well aware of this. By 1914, foreign trade made up 34 per cent of national income – a level that was attained again only in the 1960s. In the years leading up to 1914, the German empire had become one of the most dynamic exporting powers. This had effects on the balance of trade and also helped to determine which areas of manufacturing in Germany grew most strongly. The chemicals industry, in particular, was focused strongly on export business. Before the First World War it exported 35 per cent of its production (transported mainly on British ships). The electrical and metal industries and consumer manufacturing also produced large amounts for export.

Conversely, it was one of the consequences of the transformation of Germany into an industrial state that imports of raw materials grew in importance. The effects on agricultural production were considerable. While the new industries produced for the world market, landowners and peasants in the agrarian regions of eastern Prussia came to see themselves as victims of global economic integration. Wool was imported from Australia and South Africa; wheat used for bread was grown on the North American prairies and also in Russia, Canada, and Argentina. The reduction in transatlantic transportation costs made it possible that grain from Chicago arrived at inland port cities like Mannheim at a lower price than its Prussian competitor via Berlin. This changed the geography of the world economy, and it radically transformed the structure of eastern Prussian agriculture. The crisis in the grain market was countered, very successfully, with the expansion of highly profitable sugar beet cultivation. In 1880, the value of sugar exports had already surpassed that of machinery or chemical products. The indirect effects of these structural adjustments – labour-intensive beet cultivation led to the recruitment on a mass scale of cheap Polish workers from neighbouring provinces in Russia and Galicia – illustrate the degree to which local, regional, and transnational processes were always interlinked.

These links with the global market could not be separated from the colonial world order, even if this was not always obvious within Germany. In fact, almost three-quarters of German exports went to Europe, mostly to Britain, but a large proportion also went to the United States. Smaller markets such as Argentina, Egypt, Morocco, China, and Japan all became increasingly important but never reached the level of Germany's European trading partners. Most capital investment took place within Germany or Europe and there was little in the German colonies – in fact, there was more German investment in British colonies than in 'New Germany'. Even though Britain and the USA remained central to Germany's international economic interlinkages, this phenomenon involved an indirect link to world trade flows impossible to understand without taking into account the colonial structure of the global economy: British free trade imperialism, the 'unequal contracts' established by the use of force, and the exploitative integration of colonial economies.

Part cause and part consequence of economic interaction, migration – the third level of global integration under consideration – was one of the forms through which large segments of the population experienced global entanglement first hand. Mobility continued to be the privilege of individual 'globetrotters' (a contemporary neologism) like Heinrich Schliemann, who not only famously discovered ancient Troy in the 1870s, but also travelled extensively to St Petersburg, San Francisco, Peking (today's Beijing), and Edo (Tokyo). At the same time, it was a mass phenomenon that transformed whole cities and regions. For a long time, scholarship has treated the three waves of German migration in the nineteenth century as chapters of a continuing process. However, the third wave of transatlantic migration between 1880 and 1883, which led more than two million people mainly to the United States, was not just the sequel to the earlier movements of 1846–7 and 1864–73. It was the result of very specific circumstances, related to the effects of industrialization, to the long economic slump of what was at the time called the 'Great Depression', and to the pressures of the world market. As a result, migration emerged as a central field of public debate. The alleged 'loss of national energies' was pitted against the advantages of migration as a 'safety valve' that ridded the Empire of 'revolutionary elements'. Among the explicit goals of the early colonial movement, therefore, was the redirection of population flows to the colonies – so that Germans would remain Germans, albeit overseas, and not deteriorate into what was called 'fertilizer of the peoples' (*Völkerdünger*) in contemporary parlance, a comment on the allegedly too rapid assimilation of Germans in the United States. Before 1914, however, there never lived more than 20,000 Germans in the colonies – small even in comparison to the tiny German principality of Schwarzburg-Sondershausen.

The much larger German communities abroad that were outside the colonial empires, which, along with those in the USA, included groups in southern Brazil (Illustration 46), Australia, and the Middle East, all formed part of the German colonial imagination. Eduard von Liebert, the governor of German East Africa, went so far as to proclaim that 'The German nation [*Deutschtum*] abroad is our most important colony.'[9] The links were not just imaginary. The contemporary debate about mobility almost unanimously agreed that the different migratory flows of the era – immigration from Russia and Galicia, migration from eastern Europe to the USA via Bremen and Hamburg, emigration to the USA and colonial settlement projects – were directly linked. And the organizational and legal conditions of mobility were structured in line with the colonial world order: well-off Germans travelled to Latin America via the Hamburg–Amerika-Linie or Norddeutscher Lloyd, while the boilermen below deck were from India or Java. Stefan Zweig later remembered that before 1914, 'the world belonged to all human beings. Everyone could go wherever he wanted and stay as long as he wanted.'[10] But this hardly applied to the African inhabitants of German South-West

---

[9] Quoted from Karl A. Wettstein, *Brasilien und die deutsch-brasilianische Kolonie Blumenau*, Leipzig (Friedrich Engelmann) 1907, 1.

[10] Stefan Zweig, *Die Welt von Gestern: Erinnerungen eines Europäers*, Frankfurt am Main (Fischer) 1970, 465.

Illustration 46 Latin America had been a destination for German emigrants throughout
the nineteenth century, even if no more than 5 per cent of the *Auswanderer* settled in
the region. Most of them (more than 200,000) moved to Brazil in spite of restrictive
Prussian emigration policies after 1859. They were lured by the prospects of allegedly
uninhabited land and bountiful nature, and by proactive immigration measures on the
part of the Brazilian government that aimed at reinforcing the European elements in a
politics of *embranquecimento* (whitening). Bordering on Uruguay, the most southern
province of Rio Grande do Sul was home to 150,000 *Auslandsdeutsche* (roughly 15 per
cent of the total population of the province) in 1914. Brazil was present in Germany
through the many travelogues that reported from this new 'promised land'. In these texts,
the German settlements were typically represented as 'fountains of youth' that were
immune to the kind of degeneration often associated with modern civilization (Karl
A. Wettstein, *Mit deutschen Kolonistenjungens durch den brasilianischen Urwald!
Selbsterlebtes. Eine Reise nach und durch Südbrasilien und seine deustchvölkischen kolonien*,
Leipzig (Engelmann) 1910, 195). 'If you want to know and appreciate the power and energy
of the German nation', one travelogue claimed, 'then you have to follow the Germans to
the far end of the world, into the swamps and jungles of Latin America' (Karl Leonhardt,
'Die deutschen Kolonien im Süden von Chile', *Das Auswandereproblem* 5 (1912), 7–53,
quote p. 16).

Africa, who had to keep passes and identification certificates on their
person because any movement by an individual outside what the
German administration considered their 'tribal area' was to be controlled and, where possible, prevented. And Chinese 'coolies' hired as

labourers for German Samoa were legally regarded as 'natives' while Japanese citizens were treated as equal to Europeans. The flows of mobility so characteristic of globalization before 1914 were deeply shaped by the colonial structures of the times.

Fourthly and finally, Germany's involvement in the cultural flows of globalization also bore the traces of colonial hierarchies. Here, too, the extent of German cultural influence went further than the reach of its territorial possessions. German institutions were imported into a large number of countries, translated, adopted, and modified. In the sciences, in particular, Germany became the starting-point for vigorous intellectual transfer. The Humboldtian university model was adopted, with some modifications, in Europe, the USA, and Japan. German medicine, Oriental studies, linguistics, sociology, and historical studies were among the most successful exports of German universities, and many members of modernizing elites from Asia and the Americas spent time studying in Germany.

It is important to note, however, that the concept of cultural diffusion only partially captures the meaning of this dimension of the globalization of the *Kaiserreich*. 'Germany' for many intellectuals and political commentators outside of Europe denoted not only the geographical origin of cultural achievements, but also referred to a model of social development that was set apart from other trajectories of modernization associated with France, Great Britain, and the United States. As a result, in the eyes of non-western elites Germany frequently appeared more unified than it might have looked from contemporary Munich or Karlsruhe – and more homogeneous, certainly, than from the perspectives of Jews and Social Democrats. The general appeal of the German version of modernization resulted in a vogue of political and cultural borrowing in which not only particular forms of knowing, but in a very general sense the cultural capital of 'Germany' was tapped into. The German constitution is a case in point. Interpreted as the institutional expression of a 'third way' between absolutism and democracy, it served as a model for other countries like Meiji Japan in 1889. In late-comer societies like Japan from the 1880s and Turkey after 1908, 'Germany' was evoked as a blueprint for modernization, promising a form of development that would articulate modernity with indigenous cultural traditions. The notion of the German

Sonderweg (special path) between east and west, so influential during the First World War and ever since, thus clearly had its equivalent in the way imperial Germany was appropriated globally.

It is useful to remember that in the early twentieth century, these processes of cultural exchange operated within an imperialist framework: belief in a European cultural mission and the concept of the gradual 'elevation' of backward societies were part and parcel of an overarching colonialist discourse. Differences between regions and cultures were seen as a temporal rift. As evolutionist ideas became widespread, such ideas became predominant, supported as they were by liberal, Social Darwinist, and racializing world-views. All cultural transfers and appropriations – from national constitutions to art, from philosophies to fashions – took place in this context. This does not mean that these borrowings were always in the same direction. Van Gogh hoped to find solutions to problems of artistic representation in the woodblock prints of Hiroshige, and Picasso borrowed from African art. In addition, the award of the Nobel Prize for Literature to Rabindranath Tagore in 1913 can be seen as an expression of the positive view of Asian 'spirituality' in European intellectual circles. But even here, non-European cultures were understood to represent an unspoilt state that, while seen as positive, was located within the hegemonial understanding of time.

A typical example was the work of Ludwig Riess. In 1887, this twenty-six-year-old historian was hired by the Japanese government to establish the teaching of history at the University of Tokyo. Riess had done some copying work for Leopold von Ranke, the elderly doyen of German historians, and was thus regarded as Ranke's student. He stayed in Japan for fifteen years, setting up a faculty of history, a historians' association, and a journal based on the German *Historische Zeitschrift*, with summaries of all articles in German. These innovations were introduced in the face of a tradition of historiography in Japan that stretched back over a thousand years; but the hegemony of the western academic system seemed to render it suddenly worthless. The new discipline of history, understood as a science, was based on the idea that the nation was the subject of history and in particular on a new concept of time. And the concept of 'development' linked historical thinking directly with the colonial order, which was also based on the categories of backwardness and progress.

The *Kaiserreich* was itself an integral part of colonial globality before the First World War. The country's own colonies were less important to it than was the case for France, Holland, Japan, and in particular Britain, whose colonial empires lasted longer and where the relationships between the colonies and the metropole were more intense and more important for the countries' self-image. Until 1914, and even afterwards, western Europe remained Germany's foremost point of reference. But this does not mean that colonial structures were of no importance to the *Kaiserreich*. Europe was itself increasingly bound up in global linkages that were shaped, in different ways, by the asymmetries of the colonial order. Germany was equally enveloped in these processes. These connections were particularly important because they coincided with a fundamental transformation of German society and a zenith in the development of European modernity. Around the turn of the century, several of the basic social, economic, and cultural structures, terminologies, and conflicts developed that would shape western industrialized societies, including Germany, for much of the twentieth century. For this reason, the effects of global and colonial interactions during this era – on structures of economic dependency, on categories of academic knowledge, on cultural hierarchies, and on gender and 'race' relations – were of long-lasting importance.

CHAPTER 12

Memory

The end of Germany's formal colonial rule did not put an end to colonialism. This was true quite literally for the German colonies: in 1919, the German colonial empire was dissolved on the grounds that 'Germany's failure in the field of colonial civilization', as the indictment of the Allied powers read, 'has become all too apparent to leave the thirteen to fourteen million natives again to the fate from which the war has liberated them'.[1] Liberation, however, did not imply sovereignty. Instead, the former colonies became mandates of the newly founded League of Nations and were transferred to the victorious powers (mainly France and England but also Japan, Belgium, and Portugal). In terms of international law they were no longer colonial territories, but in terms of the practice of rule, there was little difference. Moreover, colonial structures continued well into the post-war period. After 1945, and even after decolonization, the now-independent nations were still characterized by colonial modes of dependence, colonial world views and memories of the colonial era.

Colonialism had its after-effects in Germany, too, even if they differed markedly from the situation in the former colonies and followed a dynamic of their own. After 1918, the territorial empire was a thing of the past, but it lived on in the German imagination and in some expansionist projects at least until the Second World War. Social and economic structures and discursive patterns shaped by the colonial influence continued to affect German society in a number of ways and were still apparent even in post-1945 West Germany.

[1] Quoted from Hans Poeschel, *Die Kolonialfrage im Frieden von Versailles: Dokumente zu ihrer Behandlung*, Berlin (Mittler & Sohn) 1920, 87.

COLONIAL REVISIONISM

The Treaty of Versailles marked the formal end of German colonial rule but not the end of German colonial ambitions. This is evident, for example, in the huge crowds that turned out to welcome home General Paul von Lettow-Vorbeck's colonial army from German East Africa in March 1919 (Illustration 47). Germany's military resistance in Africa was interpreted in the nationalist press as another instance of an army undefeated before the public's failure to answer their 'patriotic calling' forced the soldiers to capitulate, and thus fed into the myth of the 'stab in the back' (*Dolchstoßlegende*) so prevalent in the 1920s.

Illustration 47 On 2 March, 1919, the remainders of the German troops in East Africa returned to Berlin. They included the last governor of the colony, Dr Heinrich Schnee, about thirty officers and more than 100 further troops, and were led by General Paul von Lettow-Vorbeck (centre, on horse back). The 'undefeated heroes of East Africa', as the popular slogan had it, were greeted by a large nationalist crowd as they marched through the Brandenburg Gate as well as by official representatives of the city and the *Reich*. In the interwar period, Lettow-Vorbeck emerged as a powerful symbol of colonialist propaganda. His book *Heia Safari!*, a hagiographic account of the war in German East Africa, was an immensely popular reference point for colonial revisionism. Lettow-Vorbeck himself had to resign after participation in the ultra-nationalist *Kapp Putsch*, an attempted coup that occupied the capital in early 1920.

When Lettow-Vorbeck and governor Heinrich Schnee approached on their horses, the *Frankfurter Zeitung* reported, 'Cheering broke out, and the cheers went on and on – cheers of such heart-breaking ardour as Berlin has seldom, if ever, seen before.'[2] This episode suggests that in the interwar period, colonial issues continued to achieve a broad consensus across political boundaries. During the Weimar Republic, the *Reichstag* was rarely as unanimous as in its demands for the restitution of German colonial territories. On 1st March 1919, the Weimar National Assembly (*Weimarer Nationalversammlung*) that drew up the constitution of the Weimar Republic had called for the 'Restoration of Germany's colonial rights', with a majority vote of 414 to seven.

Despite this broad level of consensus, however, colonial revisionism as a political project remained a side issue. There were more pressing interests in foreign policy, in particular the issue of the eastern borders of Germany, and the lobby groups of colonial enthusiasts remained small and had very limited influence. Outside the realm of high politics, colonialism was more important in its effects on the popular imagination. The myth of benevolent German colonial rule was kept alive, a myth personified in the supposedly 'loyal *askaris*', the African members of the *Schutztruppe* (armed forces) in German East Africa. Ethnographic shows were still held and the new medium of film also helped to satisfy a hunger for all things colonial and exotic. Many cities put on 'colonial weeks' that drew thousands of visitors. Commercial products such as 'Kaba' hot chocolate and the 'Afri-Cola' beverages cashed in on the allure of the exotic and racialized stereotypes. Most importantly, colonial literature did not decline in popularity; in fact, the number of publications actually increased after 1918. Some of the best-known examples of the genre included the memoirs of the hero of Germany's last stand in East Africa, Lettow-Vorbeck's *Heia Safari!*, and Hans Grimm's 1926 novel *Volk ohne Raum* ('Nation without Space'), which provided the influential slogan for the Nazi expansion in eastern Europe and by 1945 had sold over 650,000 copies.

Colonial interactions were not limited to the imagination and to fiction. German settlers from the colonies moved back, and new

[2] *Frankfurter Zeitung*, 5 March 1919, evening edition, cover page.

migratory flows developed from the colonial world to Germany. After 1919, the mandate powers dispossessed German farmers, confiscated German companies, and expelled the Germans from the colonies. An exception was South Africa, the mandate power for former German South-West Africa, which allowed about half of the German settlers to stay. Beginning in the mid 1920s, German settlers again moved back into the former colonial territories, and by the early 1930s, some 4,000 of them had again settled in New Guinea, Cameroon, and Tanganyika (former German East Africa). Attempts to record the history of the returning settlers, and research into the ways in which they had an impact on Weimar Germany, has only just begun.

While German revisionists were busy demanding a restoration of Germany's colonial status, Berlin became home to anti-colonial activists from other colonies who hoped to profit from the popular German criticisms of British and French imperialism typical of the Weimar period. In the interwar period, it was not unusual for anti-colonialists to move to Europe as the empires' centres were much safer spaces for their political work than in their home countries, where 'seditious activities' were punished much more severely. The influx of anti-colonial nationalists to Germany began during the war when activists from India and elsewhere hoped to benefit from cooperation with their enemy's enemy. The German government, in turn, had established an intelligence bureau for the East (*Nachrichtenstelle für den Orient*) that engaged in propaganda schemes and plotted anti-British uprisings in different locations. As Germany was stripped of its colonial possessions after 1919, and as Berlin formed one of the centres of the Communist International, Berlin appeared to many anti-colonial political leaders as the appropriate location for their activities. It was no accident that the League against Imperialism, founded in 1927, was based in Berlin. The anti-colonialists included intellectuals such as the Indian nationalist M. N. Roy, who was active in communist circles and was in close contact with individuals like August Thalmeier, the chairman of the Communist Party of Germany in 1923/4; and Mohammad Nafi Celebi (1901–33), a student from Syria who campaigned from Berlin for Islamic–Arab nationalism.

A separate phenomenon was the African colonial troops recruited by France and used in the French occupation of the Rhineland (Illustration 48). Colonial troops – from Africa and India in particular – had played

Illustration 48 The use of colonial troops was a common feature of the First World War. When about 30,000 African troops were deployed as part of the occupation of Germany, however, they became the object of a highly racialized discourse in the German public sphere. While the East African *askari*, the African members of the *Schutztruppe* (armed forces), were celebrated for their loyalty and prowess, German foreign minister Wilhelm Solf, former governor of Samoa, protested against the 'racially shameful (*rassenschänderisch*) use of coloureds on the European front'. Racialized propaganda against the 'horrors on the Rhine' (*Schrecken am Rhein*) was common in the press and also, as in this image, in artistic production. Soon, the protests spread to other European countries. In April 1920, the British socialist newspaper *Daily Herald* published an editorial with the title 'Black Scourge in Europe: Sexual Horror let Loose by France on Rhine', and protest notes were signed by the British Labour Party, the Swedish premier, and the Pope.

an important part in the British and French war effort. Germany also had relied on African soldiers, in particular in Lettow-Vorbeck's drawn-out struggle in East Africa, but had not deployed them in Europe. As a result, the nationalist right represented Germany as the last defender of European 'racial purity' and accused France of breaking a civilizational taboo. In German newspapers and soon also in parts of the European press, the presence of between thirty and forty thousand Africans on German soil led to a hysterical campaign against the 'Disgrace on the Rhine' (*Schmach am Rhein*) and the supposed humiliation of the German nation, indeed, of the 'culture and morals of Western civilization', by the 'uncivilized' occupying forces.[3] 'For German women', indeed, as a joint declaration of the German national assembly warned in 1920, 'these savages are a terrible danger'.[4] The rhetoric employed tapped into political anxieties in an era of economic crisis as well as into racialized world views, fears of social degradation, gendered notions of social order, and a set of desires expressed in the frequently pornographic images of the campaign. In the second volume of his programmatic book *Mein Kampf*, Adolf Hitler interpreted the French decision to deploy African troops as a Jewish strategy aiming to 'destroy the white race as a result of the necessarily ensuing bastardization, to topple them from their cultural and political heights, and to rise to a position of masters themselves'.[5] In 1937, more than four hundred of the children fathered by these soldiers in relationships with German women were forcibly sterilized – evidence of the close relationship between colonial hierarchies, racial categories, and the eugenic policies of the Nazis.[6]

Colonial projects continued under Nazi rule (see Illustration 49). The programme of the NSDAP included a demand for the restitution of Germany's colonial empire. The *Reichskolonialbund* (*Reich* Colonial

[3] Quoted from Christian Koller, '*Von Wilden aller Rassen niedergemetzelt*': *Die Diskussion um die Verwendung von Kolonialtruppen in Europa zwischen Rassismus, Kolonial- und Militärpolitik (1914–1930)*, Stuttgart (Steiner) 2001, 215.

[4] Quoted from Fatima El-Tayeb, *Schwarze Deutsche: Der Diskurs um 'Rasse' und nationale Identität 1890–1933*, Frankfurt am Main (Campus) 2001, 160.

[5] Adolf Hitler, *Mein Kampf*, München (Franz Eher Nachfolger) 1943, 357.

[6] Cf. Reiner Pommerin, *Sterilisierung der Rheinlandbastarde: Das Schicksal einer farbigen deutschen Minderheit 1918–1937*, Düsseldorf (Droste) 1979; Tina M. Campt, *Other Germans: Black Germans and the Politics of Race, Gender, and Memory in the Third Reich*, Ann Arbor (University of Michigan Press) 2004.

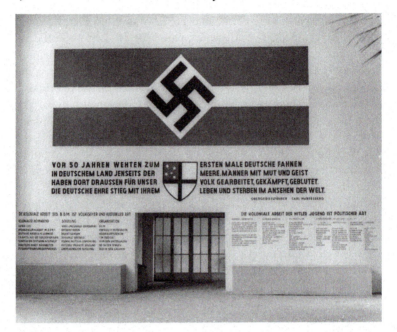

Illustration 49 In the interwar years, colonial exhibitions abounded and kept colonial revisionism alive among nationalist milieux. This image stresses the colonial ambitions of the League of German Girls (*Bund Deutscher Mädel*) and the Hitler Youth (*Hitlerjugend*), the two youth organizations of the National Socialist Party. In the early years of Nazi reign, colonial claims remained vague and unspecific. After the outbreak of war, Hitler ordered systematic planning for a large colonial empire in central Africa, ranging from the Atlantic to the Indian ocean. Different from what was now perceived as the failed colonial politics of the *Kaiserreich*, the Nazi empire was to be based on a rigid politics of racial segregation and intended as a site of reckless economic exploitation. With the beginning of the war in Russia, however, colonial ambitions in Africa were increasingly marginalized.

Association), founded in 1933, had over two million members by 1940 – huge numbers in comparison with the forty-three thousand who had been members of the German Colonial Society on the eve of the First World War. Novels and films with colonialist content were extremely popular. Among them were *Germanin* (1938), a movie about a German scientist who invents a medical treatment for sleeping sickness and thus represents Germany as the good colonizer; *Carl Peters* (1940) with Hans Albers, and *Ohm Krüger* (1941) with the Afro-German Louis Brody in leading roles. Large sums of money were

spent on colonial research and colonialist propaganda. After the outbreak of the Second World War, and further sparked by Rommel's
campaign in the North African desert, many institutions developed
full-scale plans for the re-seizure of the territories lost in the First
World War, and a 'Colonial Blood Protection Act' was also drafted in
preparation for the planned resuscitation of the colonial empire. This
colonial revisionism was supported by small but vociferous communities of Germans in the former colonies (Illustration 50). These
visions notwithstanding, the main object of the expansive desires of
the Nazi leadership was clearly not Africa, but eastern Europe. In the
1920s, Hitler himself had excluded the acquisition of colonial territories
overseas for another hundred years. In 1943, during the war against the

Illustration 50 The *völkisch* ideology of the Nazi regime was met with the approval of large
groups in the colonial settlement communities. After 1919, about half of the German
population of South-West Africa, mostly government officials and members of the
military and police were forced to repatriate. Among the remaining settlers, the
preservation and construction of 'Germanness' emerged as a central concern. This was
reinforced when in the 1930s large numbers of Boers, so-called 'poor whites', immigrated
from South Africa and turned the German settlers into a minority among the white
population. This image shows the celebration of 1 May 1939, in Windhoek. 1 May was a
national holiday in Germany from 1933, when the Nazi regime appropriated the holiday in
their quest to gain support from the workers' movement.

Soviet Union and the implementation of policies of annihilation in eastern Europe, the plans for overseas expansion were shelved once and for all.

COLONIAL MEMORIES IN GERMANY AFTER 1945

After the Second World War, plans for territorial expansion were no longer of any relevance in Germany. But this does not mean that projects for imperial intervention had lost all their attractiveness. 'The world has by no means all been given away', the journalist A. E. Johann claimed as late as the 1950s; 'On the contrary! The world is currently being divided up anew. For Europe, and in particular for Germany, the sizzling and rapidly developing Africa is offering yet inconceivable opportunities.'[7] During the first few years after the war, France and Britain, in particular, invested in new infrastructural projects in their colonies to such an extent that historians have described it as a 'second colonization'. The plans by western European governments to jointly develop 'Eurafrica', in which German planners were also involved, were part of this process. Structures of dependency and hierarchies from the colonial era were thus still influential. This was particularly the case for development aid, to which the Federal Republic contributed from the late 1950s. Development aid took place in the context of the Cold War and was described by Kurt Birrenbach, a member of the *Bundestag* for the CDU (the conservative Christian Democratic Union, the largest political party in West Germany), as a 'battle [against the eastern bloc] for the underdeveloped countries' and one which it was essential to win.[8] But connections formed during the imperial age remained important: the former German colonies received a considerable amount of West German development aid (although this pattern was less pronounced than in Britain and France, which sent 90 per cent of their development aid to their former colonies).

[7] Quoted from Dirk van Laak, *Imperiale Infrastruktur: Deutsche Planungen für eine Erschließung Afrikas 1880 bis 1960*, Paderborn (Schöningh) 2004, 345.
[8] Quoted from Bastian Hein, *Die Westdeutschen und die Dritte Welt: Entwicklungspolitik und Entwicklungsdienste zwischen Reform und Revolte 1959–1974*, Munich (Oldenbourg) 2006, 38.

For a long time, positive references to the German colonial era were still commonplace and some groups, such as the 'Association for Germans Abroad' (*Verein für das Deutschtum im Ausland*), continued in existence. The *Bundeswehr* (Federal Armed Forces) continued to observe a number of colonial traditions such as the annual guard of honour and wreath-laying by veterans of the colonial wars at the Lettow-Vorbeck barracks in Hamburg. More widespread than such events were continuities in perception that were never made explicit. This applies in particular to popular culture: the Sarotti Moor (the figure of an African servant used in chocolate advertising) and Bernhard Grzimek's films about Africa (in which the Wilhelminian longing for a 'place in the sun' is translated into an exotic 'place for animals') are evidence of a continuing fascination with and nostalgia for the colonial era. Another example was the creation, in 2005, of an 'African village' in Augsburg zoo. Although this plan met with considerable criticism and the 'exhibiting' of Africans in a zoo was seen as a continuation of the colonial-era ethnographic shows, the zoo's director refused to be dissuaded, insisting 'that Augsburg zoo is exactly the right place to communicate an atmosphere of the exotic'.[9]

This is not to say, however, that critical attitudes towards colonialism did not also have an important place in the public sphere of West Germany. The institution of development aid, for example, was criticized from the 1960s onwards by groups who saw it as reinforcing dependencies and as a kind of neo-colonialism. Resistance to imperialism was also an important concept for the New Left of the 1950s and 1960s, and it fed into the protests of 1968. Many of those on the left put their hopes in the newly independent countries of the Third World, which they saw as a driving force for renewal through revolution – a renewal of which the European workers, the traditional subjects of left-wing hopes for revolution, no longer seemed capable. In a way, for the reformist Left, the colonial subjects had become the agents of change that would also transform societies in Europe. Speaking for the 'socialist forces in Europe,' and reporting on events in Havana, the left-wing journal *Sozialistische Politik* drew the 'conclusion that the revolution in Cuba and in Latin America is also theirs. The colonial revolution needs

---

[9] Quoted from www.ag-friedensforschung.de/themen/Rassismus/afrikaschau.html, accessed 10 November 2010.

the working classes of the industrialized states, and they need the colonial revolution.'[10] German political activists began to travel to the countries in which an anti-colonial movement was fighting for national independence. 'Suitcase carriers' helped Algeria in its war of independence against France; activists travelled to Havana and held demonstrations against the Vietnam war and the neo-imperialist system. An anticolonialist perspective remained influential even after 1968 and can still be seen today, for example in parts of the anti-globalization movement.

The GDR, in its official statements, radically distanced itself from any form of colonialism; this stance formed an integral part of the state's self-image. From the 1960s onwards, East German historians critically analysed the history of German colonialism. But in official rhetoric anti-imperialism was always part of and subordinated to the ideology of anti-capitalism; even the border between the two Germanies was described as an 'anti-imperialist protection wall'. Research on the extent to which colonial stereotypes and structures continued to exist in the GDR – in popular culture, comics, and films, or in development aid and migration policies – is still in its infancy.

Germany's colonial past was to a large extent ignored by the official remembrance policies of the Federal Republic. If colonies were mentioned at all it was mainly in terms of their absence – for example in 1998, when the influential conservative politician Gerhard Mayer-Vorfelder explained the decline of the German soccer team by reference to the lack of a reservoir of talent from the former colonies (in contrast with France). To date, no official critical remembrances of the colonial era, such as monuments or museums, have been created, and even local attempts to have streets with colonialist names re-designated have met with little success. Petersallee in Berlin, for example, named after Carl Peters, now so infamous for his violent cruelty in German East Africa, still bears his name – although, after an intense debate, it is now supposedly named after a previously obscure local politician called Hans Peters.

One of the few events that brought the colonial past to the attention of a wider public was a lawsuit filed in Washington by the Herero people demanding reparation by the German government and by a number of private companies for the Herero war. This provoked some

---

[10] Felipe Olmos, 'Die Kubanische Revolution', *Sozialistische Politik* 1 (1960), 6–7.

debate on the issue within Germany, especially in 2004, the anniversary of the war. However, while Gerhard Schröder and Joschka Fischer as chancellor and foreign minister went on official state visits to Namibia, there was no official apology for the war, partly to avoid financial repercussions. It was only in August 2004 that the minister for development, Heidemarie Wieczorek-Zeul, on a visit to Windhoek, issued an emotional plea for 'forgiveness for our guilt' in a war 'that we would today describe as genocide' (Illustration 51).

Illustration 51 On the occasion of the centenary of the Herero war, a commemorative event was held in Ohamakari, Namibia, to recall the Battle of Waterberg in 1904, the decisive battle in the German campaign against the Herero. Among the 4,000 guests was the German federal minister for economic cooperation and development Heidemarie Wieczorek-Zeul, who in her speech apologized for the atrocities of the German military. This image shows Wieczorek-Zeul in June 2002 together with Sam Nujoma, president of the Republic of Namibia, on a visit in Berlin. Nujoma led the SWAPO party that looked critically on the claims of the Herero. The lawsuits filed by the representatives of the Herero in the United States asking for reparations from the German federal government and individual German companies have not yet been admitted to hearings in court. In Germany, one of the most recent initiatives has been the motion by the leftist party *Die Linke* in June 2008 asking the *Bundestag* for acknowledgment and compensation for colonial crimes; this was turned down by a large majority vote.

This was by no means the accepted official view, as can be seen from a strategy paper by the German Foreign Office; in typical style, it describes Germany's 'colonial past as comparatively less encumbered'[11] than that of other European nations. And the speaker of the CDU/CSU parties (the CSU, Christian Social Union, is the sister party of the CDU in Bavaria) on development topics, Christian Ruck, issued a press statement warning: 'The emotional outburst of the minister for economic cooperation could cost the taxpayer millions.'[12]

REMEMBRANCE OF THE COLONIAL ERA IN THE FORMER COLONIES

In the former colonies, the colonial era usually has a major place in cultural and public memory. This general assessment, however, requires qualification and differentiation. In China, for example, there is now little evidence of the short-lived German presence in Kiaochow as a haunting past. Not only was Germany a minor power, but with China's current economic growth and geopolitical strength, anti-imperialist impulses have faded into the background. Since the 1990s, the colonial architecture of Qingdao has been promoted to tourists, like Tsingtao beer, which originated with the Germania brewery in 1903. In some countries, official political discourse includes even positive memories of German colonial rule. In 1960, the last German governor of Togo, Grossherzog von Mecklenburg, then ninety years of age, was invited to the celebrations of Togolese independence. In general, this idealization of the German colonial era, which can also be found in Samoa and partly in Cameroon, says less about the realities of German rule and more about the attempts of particular groups in the former colonies to distance themselves from the countries that followed the Germans as colonial rulers after 1918.

---

[11] Wieczorek-Zeul quoted in *Frankfurter Allgemeine Zeitung*, 16 August 2004, p. 2. The quote from a strategy paper by the German Foreign Office is in Henning Melber, '"Wir haben überhaupt nicht über Reparationen gesprochen": Die namibisch-deutschen Beziehungen – Verdrängung oder Versöhnung?', in: Jürgen Zimmerer and Joachim Zeller (eds.), *Völkermord in Deutsch-Südwestafrika: Der Kolonialkrieg (1904–1908) in Namibia und seine Folgen*, Berlin (Ch. Links) 2003, 215–25, quote on p. 223.

[12] Quoted from Andreas Eckert, 'Der Kolonialismus im europäischen Gedächtnis', *Aus Politik und Zeitgeschichte* 2008, no. 1, 31–8.

By contrast, in Namibia and Tanzania debates about remembrance focus mainly on the traumatic elements of the colonial past. A variety of different perspectives are taken and competing images of the past are linked to differing present-day interests and claims. In Tanzania, memory of the Maji-Maji war has played a crucial role for the nationalist movement in the post-war period. The Tanganyika African National Union (TANU), founded by Julius Nyerere and Oscar Kambona in 1954, placed itself explicitly within the tradition of resistance against German rule that was interpreted as a pro-national event. The Maji-Maji war seemed a particularly appropriate point of reference as it had not been fought by a single group and thus lent itself as a narrative that bridged the interests of the more than 120 ethnic groups in Tanzania.

In Namibia, the Herero remembrance culture focuses on the 1904–7 war (Illustration 52). Every August, a remembrance ceremony is held and a ceremonial procession visits a number of important places

Illustration 52 Since Samuel Maharero was buried there in 1923, Herero delegations from all over Namibia have congregated annually in Okahandja in late August to celebrate 'Herero Day'. They sport uniforms that allude to German and British army uniforms but are invested with layers of new meaning in the context of the commemorations. The appropriation of symbols of colonial rule can be read as strategies of 'mimicry' and subversive re-enactment that challenge the power of the colonial past over the present. This image was taken in August 1994.

of remembrance, including the grave of Samuel Maharero, the leader in the war. This procession, which includes symbols and rituals taken from the former colonial rulers, is part of the grieving process, but it is also an expression of the political claims of the Herero, who form the largest ethnic group in the country. It conjures up a level of cultural cohesion among the Herero that has long been undermined by social and ethnic differences. Since 1990, when Namibia became independent from South Africa, the Namibian government has been made up of the SWAPO (South West Africa People's Organization), which developed from an organization of the Ovambo people from northern Namibia. For this government, Herero remembrance can be useful for foreign-policy purposes but domestically represents a threat. In 1990, the government introduced a 'Heroes Day' dedicated to all victims of colonialism and of the wars of liberation. By doing so it was attempting to counteract the centrifugal forces of the debate about the relevance of the past and to establish its own interpretative hegemony. Accordingly, President Nujoma refused to support the Herero lawsuit. In addition to these two influential positions, there are a number of other groups in Namibia that have their own perspectives on the past. They include a small German-speaking minority which, for a long period, continued to make positive references to the colonial period. In 2003, however, their annual celebration to mark the German military victory at Waterberg was banned.

Remembrance of the colonial era is a controversial issue everywhere and it enters into many debates that are concerned with the present day as well as with the past. It includes the question of whether the political and economic difficulties of many African states can be causally linked to the history of the slave trade, colonial interventions, and their after-effects. The problematic of failing states in Africa, too, has raised the issue of possible path-dependencies. To give just one example of this kind of argument, the Uganda-born sociologist Mahmood Mamdani has emphasized that in many African states the status of 'indigenous' remains, well after the end of formal colonialism, the condition for access to rights and power. 'If we look at the definition of citizenship in most African states, we will realize that the colonial state lives on, albeit with some reforms. My point is that in privileging the indigenous over the nonindigenous we turned the colonial world upside down, but we did not change it.'

Mamdani describes a political culture of legal entitlements that make ethnic categories not only the resource of cultural identity, but also the basis for civil and political claims. Given the intensified rates of mobility and migration in a capitalized economy, increasing numbers of people now live on the territory of a different ethnic group but carry the claims to minority rights with them. The problem of competing legal orders and limited state penetration of society and population, so familiar from the colonial era, thus continues in aggravated form. Mamdani goes so far as to 'suggest we go beyond the conventional thought that the real crime of colonialism was to expropriate the indigenous, and consider that colonialism perpetrated an even greater crime. That greater crime was to politicize indigeneity, first as a settler libel against the native, and then as a native self-assertion.'[13]

The afterlife of colonialism is a huge issue that will remain contested for some time to come. Just as interesting for the historian is to analyse to what extent this debate itself, and the different arguments that support it, is used in current political conflicts. One example among many is the conflict about the dispossession of white settlers, which is ongoing in the former British colony of Zimbabwe and also in Namibia. In this debate, the overlaps between political interests and cultures of remembrance, social differences, and the construction of ethnic differences are immediately obvious. Such conflicts show that decolonization is a lengthy process and one that was by no means completed at the moment of political independence, but rather continues into our post-colonial and globalized present.

---

[13] Mahmood Mamdani, 'Beyond Settler and Native as Political Identities: Overcoming the Political Legacy of Colonialism', *Comparative Studies in Society and History* 43 (2001), 651–64, quotes on p. 658, p. 664. See also Mamdani, *Citizen and Subject*.

CHAPTER 13

Selected readings

CHAPTER 1: INTRODUCTION

In the wake of Said, *Orientalism*, published in 1978, and particularly since the 1990s, the field of colonial studies has undergone dramatic transformations. For a good account of the changes in perspective over the past century, see the lucid and well-informed overview by Patrick Wolfe, 'History and Imperialism: A Century of Theory, from Marx to Postcolonialism', *American Historical Review* 102 (1997), 388–420. Good introductions into the field of post-colonial studies are provided by Leela Gandhi, *Postcolonial Theory: A Critical Introduction*, New York (Columbia University Press) 1998 and Robert Young, *Postcolonialism: An Historical Introduction*, Oxford (Blackwell) 2001. One of the seminal and frequently cited works of this new strand of scholarship is Dipesh Chakrabarty, *Provincializing Europe: Postcolonial Thought and Historical Difference*, Princeton (Princeton University Press) 2000. For critical perspectives, see Arif Dirlik, *The Postcolonial Aura: Third World Criticism in the Age of Global Capitalism*, Boulder (Westview Press) 1997; and recently Frederick Cooper, *Colonialism in Question: Theory, Knowledge, History*, Berkeley (University of California Press) 2005. For fresh perspectives, see also Ann Laura Stoler, Carole McGranahan and Peter Perdue (eds.), *Imperial Formations*, Santa Fe (School for Advanced Research Press) 2007.

For overviews of the history of colonialism that also provide the context of German colonialism, see the older study by David K. Fieldhouse, *The Colonial Empires: A Comparative Survey from the Eighteenth Century*, 2nd edition, London (Macmillan) 1982 [1966] and the more recent book by H. L. Wesseling, *The European Colonial Empires 1815–1919*, Harlow (Pearson Longman)

2004. For a more analytical approach, see the outstanding textbook by Jürgen Osterhammel, *Colonialism: A Theoretical Overview*, Princeton (Wiener) 1997, and the concise and very useful *Empire: A Very Short Introduction* by Stephen Howe, Oxford (Oxford University Press) 2002.

Good reviews of the older literature on German colonialism can be found in Klaus J. Bade, 'Imperialismusforschung und Kolonialhistorie', *Geschichte und Gesellschaft* 9 (1983), 138–50 and Jost Dülffer, 'Deutsche Kolonialherrschaft in Afrika', *Neue Politische Literatur* 26 (1981), 458–73. For the cultural turn since the late 1990s, see Sebastian Conrad, 'Doppelte Marginalisierung: Plädoyer für eine transnationale Perspektive auf die deutsche Geschichte', *Geschichte und Gesellschaft* 28 (2002), 145–69 and Andreas Eckert and Albert Wirz, 'Wir nicht, die Anderen auch: Deutschland und der Kolonialismus', in: Sebastian Conrad and Shalini Randeria (eds.), *Jenseits des Eurozentrismus: Postkoloniale Perspektiven in den Geschichts- und Kulturwissenschaften*, Frankfurt am Main (Campus) 2002, 372–92. Overviews of the most recent literature include David Ciarlo, 'Globalizing German Colonialism', *German History* 26 (2008), 285–98, and Ulrike Lindner, 'Plätze an der Sonne? Die Geschichtsschreibung auf dem Weg in die deutschen Kolonien', *Archiv für Sozialgeschichte* 48 (2008), 487–510.

CHAPTER 2: COLONIALISM BEFORE THE COLONIAL EMPIRE

The pre-history of German colonialism has not been the object of many extensive studies. Hans Fenske provides informative overviews: 'Die deutsche Auswanderung in der Mitte des 19. Jahrhunderts. Öffentliche Meinung und amtliche Politik', *Geschichte in Wissenschaft und Unterricht* 24 (1973), 221–36 and 'Imperialistische Tendenzen in Deutschland vor 1866. Auswanderung, überseeische Bestrebungen, Weltmachtträume', *Historisches Jahrbuch* 97/98 (1978), 336–83. The history of the *Texasverein* is taken up by Harald Winkel, 'Der Texasverein: Ein Beitrag zur Geschichte der deutschen Auswanderung im 19. Jahrhundert', *Vierteljahrsschrift für Sozial- und Wirtschaftsgeschichte* 55 (1968), 348–72. For discussions of the emerging colonial movement since the 1870s, the best account is Klaus J. Bade, *Friedrich Fabri und der Imperialismus der Bismarckzeit: Revolution, Depression, Expansion*, Freiburg (Atlantis) 1975. Much of this older literature will be replaced by Bradley D. Naranch, *Beyond the Fatherland: Colonial Visions, Overseas Expansion, & German Nationalism, 1848–1885*, Ph. D. diss., Johns Hopkins University 2006.

The debate on Orientalism in Germany was sparked, as elsewhere, by Edward Said, *Orientalism*. Critical responses that stress the close interplay between academic and popular forms of knowledge and colonial power in Germany include Zantop, *Colonial Fantasies*; Nina Berman, 'K.u.K. Colonialism: Hofmannsthal in North Africa', *New German Critique* 75 (1998), 3–27, and Kamakshi P. Murti, *India: The Seductive and Seduced 'Other' of German Orientalism*, Westport (Greenwood) 2001.

CHAPTER 3: PRESSURE GROUPS, MOTIVATIONS, ATTITUDES

The best current synthesis of the groups and motives leading up to 1884 is Matthew P. Fitzpatrick, *Liberal Imperialism in Germany: Expansionism and Nationalism, 1848–1884*, New York (Berghahn) 2008. See also Naranch, *Beyond the Fatherland*.

For an analysis of different factors and motives leading to Germany's decision to embark on formal colonialism, the best point of departure is still Woodruff D. Smith, *The Ideological Origins of Nazi Imperialism*, New York (Oxford University Press) 1986. In the book, Smith differentiates two main strands of ideological thinking that developed out of two sets of ideas embedded in German liberalism: *Weltpolitik*, focused on the role of the state in securing and encouraging Germany's economic expansion; and *Lebensraum*, focused on emigration as a source of problems for German national culture. Other important analyses of the decision to enter the colonial arena can be found in Wehler, *Bismarck und der Imperialismus*, which was the first to explore the notion of social imperialism, and Bade, *Friedrich Fabri und der Imperialismus der Bismarckzeit*. An interesting and recently re-published contemporary source for this debate is Friedrich Fabri, *Bedarf Deutschland der Colonien? Eine politisch-ökonomische Betrachtung*, Lewiston (Mellen) 1998 [1879].

On deportation, see the very empirical overview by Cathrin Meyer zu Hogrebe, *Strafkolonien – 'eine Sache der Volkswohlfahrt'? Die Diskussion um die Einführung der Deportation im Deutschen Kaiserreich*, Münster (LIT) 1999, and specifically on the 'Madagascar plan', Magnus Brechtken, *'Madagaskar für die Juden': Antisemitische Idee und politische Praxis 1885–1945*, Munich (Oldenbourg) 1997. The role of political parties and associations has not seen much interesting scholarship in recent years. The best book in this context is Roger Chickering, *We Men Who Feel Most German: A Cultural Study of the Pan-German League 1886–1914*, Boston (Allen & Unwin) 1984. From the older literature, see also Hans-Christoph Schröder, *Sozialismus und Imperialismus: Die Auseinandersetzung der deutschen Sozialdemokratie mit dem Imperialismusproblem und der 'Weltpolitik' vor 1914*, Hanover (Verlag für Literatur und Zeitgeschehen) 1968 and Elfi Bendikat, *Organisierte Kolonialbewegung in der Bismarck-Ära*, Heidelberg (Kivouvou) 1984. A broad history of criticisms of colonial rule, ranging from the eighteenth through to the twentieth centuries and looking comparatively at European colonial powers and the United States is Benedikt Stuchtey, *Die europäische Expansion und ihre Feinde: Kolonialismuskritik vom 18. bis in das 20. Jahrhundert*, Munich (Oldenbourg) 2010. Specifically on Germany, see also Maria-Theresia Schwarz, *'Je weniger Afrika, desto besser': Die deutsche Kolonialkritik am Ende des 19. Jahrhunderts*, Frankfurt am Main (Lang) 1999. See also the interesting sections on colonial scandals in Frank Bösch, *Öffentliche Geheimnisse: Skandale, Politik und Medien in Deutschland und Großbritannien 1880–1914*, Munich (Oldenbourg) 2009.

CHAPTER 4: THE GERMAN COLONIAL EMPIRE

The recent overview by Winfried Speitkamp, *Deutsche Kolonialgeschichte*, Stuttgart (Reclam) 2005, is a very good and concise introduction to the history of the German colonial empire. For a glimpse of the state of the art and recent discussions in the field, the most important volume is without doubt Geoff Eley and Bradley Naranch (eds.), *German Cultures of Colonialism*, Durham (Duke University Press) 2012 (forthcoming). Good points of departure for an overview continue to be two older works, Woodruff D. Smith, *The German Colonial Empire*, Chapel Hill (University of North Carolina Press) 1978 and Gründer, *Geschichte der deutschen Kolonien*. For a good and very accessible collection of primary sources, consult Gründer (ed.), *Rassismus, Kolonien und kolonialer Gedanke*.

Most former German colonies are now the subject of recent studies and overviews that supplement the older literature of the 1970s. For German South-West Africa, the best current account is Jürgen Zimmerer, *Deutsche Herrschaft über Afrikaner: Staatlicher Machtanspruch und Wirklichkeit im kolonialen Namibia*, Münster (LIT) 2001. See also Jakob Zollmann, *Koloniale Herrschaft und ihre Grenzen: Die Kolonialpolizei in Deutsch-Südwestafrika 1894–1915*, Göttingen (Vandenhoeck & Ruprecht) 2010, with a focus on the colonial police force. Less convincing is Udo Kaulich, *Die Geschichte der ehemaligen Kolonie Deutsch-Südwestafrika 1884–1914: Eine Gesamtdarstellung*, Frankfurt am Main (Lang) 2001. Among the older works, Helmut Bley, *Southwest Africa under German Rule*, Evanston (Northwestern University Press) 1971 and the book by the East German historian Horst Drechsler, *'Let Us Die Fighting': The Struggle of the Herero and Nama against German Imperialism (1884–1915)*, London (Zed Press) 1966 remain the most useful.

For Cameroon, see in particular the work by Andreas Eckert, *Grundbesitz, Landkonflikte und kolonialer Wandel: Douala 1880 bis 1960*, Stuttgart (Steiner) 1999, and the long-term perspectives in Ralph A. Austen and Jonathan Derrick (eds.) (1999), *Middlemen of the Cameroon Rivers: The Duala and their Hinterland, c. 1600–c. 1960*, Cambridge (Cambridge University Press) 1999; and Martin Njeuma (ed.), *Introduction to the History of Cameroon: Nineteenth and Twentieth Centuries*, New York (Macmillan) 1989, all from an African/Africanist perspective. For recent work on German colonialism in Cameroon, see Stefanie Michels, *Imagined Power Contested: Germans and Africans in the Upper Cross River Area of Cameroon 1887–1915*, Münster (LIT) 2005; Monika Midel, *Fulbe und Deutsche in Adamaua (Nord-Kamerun) 1809–1916: Auswirkungen afrikanischer und kolonialer Eroberung*, Frankfurt am Main (Peter Lang) 1990. These are complemented by the older studies by Karin Hausen, *Deutsche Kolonialherrschaft in Afrika: Wirtschaftsinteressen und Kolonialverwaltung in Kamerun vor 1914*, Zurich (Atlantis) 1970, focusing on the German bureaucracy, and Helmuth Stoecker (ed.), *Kamerun unter deutscher Kolonialherrschaft*, 2 volumes, East Berlin (Rütter and Loening) 1960 and East Berlin (Deutscher Verlag der Wissenschaften) 1968, with a focus on exploitation and repression.

The best work on Togo continues to be Trutz von Trotha, *Koloniale Herrschaft: Zur soziologischen Theorie der Staatsentstehung am Beispiel des 'Schutzgebietes Togo'*, Tübingen (Mohr) 1994, characterized by a sociological and analytical approach. See also Peter Sebald, *Togo 1884–1914: Eine Geschichte der deutschen 'Musterkolonie' auf der Grundlage amtlicher Quellen*, Berlin (Akademie) 1988.

A large number of studies have been devoted to the German colony in East Africa, most recently Pesek, *Koloniale Herrschaft in Deutsch-Ostafrika*. Among the older works, see in particular Detlef Bald, *Deutsch-Ostafrika 1900–1914: Eine Studie über Verwaltung, Interessengruppen und wirtschaftliche Erschließung*, Munich (Weltforum) 1970; John Iliffe, *Tanganyika under German Rule 1905–1912*, Cambridge (Cambridge University Press) 1969, and Ralph A. Austen, *Northwest Tanzania under German and British Rule: Colonial Policy and Tribal Politics, 1889–1939*, New Haven (Yale University Press) 1968. For a biography of the general who led Germany's drawn-out retreat in the First World War in East Africa, see Eckard Michels, *'Der Held von Deutsch-Ostafrika'. Paul von Lettow-Vorbeck: Ein preußischer Kolonialoffizier*, Paderborn (Schöningh) 2008. See also the biography of the colonial pioneer Carl Peters: Arne Perras, *Carl Peters and German Imperialism 1856–1918. A Political Biography*, Oxford (Clarendon Press) 2004. A fascinating study of the uprising against the agents of the German East Africa Company in 1888 is Jonathon Glassman, *Feasts and Riot: Revelry, Rebellion and Popular Consciousness on the Swahili Coast, 1856–88*, Portsmouth, N. H. (Heinemann) 1995. Glassman shows to what extent the anti-colonial uprising was also the product of multiple tensions within coastal societies over access to wealth derived from the caravan trade, over the status of slaves, and over the rituals and formal offices of power.

For Kiaochow, clearly the best work – and one of the finest studies of German colonialism in general – is Mühlhahn, *Herrschaft und Widerstand*. Mühlhahn is a German historian of China who is able to use a multitude of sources and to demonstrate the complexities of social interactions. Among the older works, see John E. Schrecker, *Imperialism and Chinese Nationalism: Germany in Shantung*, Cambridge, Mass. (Harvard University Press) 1971. For the Pacific possessions, see Hermann J. Hiery, *Das Deutsche Reich in der Südsee*

1900–1921: Eine Annäherung an die Erfahrungen verschiedener Kulturen, Göttingen (Vandenhoeck & Ruprecht) 1995 as well as the useful, albeit somewhat encyclopedic and sometimes positivistic handbook Hermann J. Hiery (ed.), *Die deutsche Südsee 1884–1914: Ein Handbuch*, Paderborn (Schöningh) 2001. For older works in English, see John A. Moses and Paul M. Kennedy (eds.), *Germany in the Pacific and Far East 1870–1914*, St Lucia (University of Queenland Press) 1977, and Peter J. Hempenstall, *Pacific Islanders under German Rule: A Study in the Meaning of Colonial Resistance*, Canberra (Australian National University Press) 1978.

CHAPTER 5: THE COLONIAL STATE

An important moment for the inauguration of a modern state system in Africa was the Berlin Africa conference in 1885 that established many of the rules of the international state system. The best account can still be found in Stig Förster (ed.), *Bismarck, Europe, and Africa: The Berlin Africa Conference 1884–1885 and the Onset of Partition*, Oxford (Oxford University Press) 1988. For a general study of the evolution of state power in Africa, from pre-colonial times to the post-colonial state, see Jeffrey Herbst, *States and Power in Africa: Comparative Lessons in Authority and Control*, Princeton (Princeton University Press) 2000. Reflections on the question of whether the colonial state was a strong or a weak state can be found in Bruce J. Berman, *Control and Crisis in Colonial Kenya: The Dialectic of Domination*, London (James Currey) 1990, and Frederick Cooper, 'Conflict and Connection: Rethinking Colonial African History', *American Historical Review* 99 (1994), 1516–45. An interesting typology of the levels of state control and its limits is discussed by the German sociologist Trutz von Trotha, 'Was war der Kolonialismus? Einige zusammenfassende Befunde zur Soziologie und Geschichte des Kolonialismus und der Kolonialherrschaft', *Saeculum* 55 (2004), 49–95; see also Trotha, *Koloniale Herrschaft*. Interesting comparative insights can be gleaned from Osterhammel, *Colonialism*.

The question of how the European state model has been adopted, appropriated, and transformed in the colonial world is discussed in Wolfgang Reinhard (ed.), *Verstaatlichung der Welt? Europäische Staatsmodelle und außereuropäische Machtprozesse*, Munich

(Oldenbourg) 1999. Aspects of the legal dimension of this process, with a strong focus on the German colonial empire, are taken up in Rüdiger Voigt and Peter Sack (eds.), *Kolonialisierung des Rechts: Zur kolonialen Rechts- und Verwaltungsordnung*, Baden-Baden (Nomos) 2001. There is a large, and growing, literature from legal historians, frequently focusing on the intricacies of legal principles and procedures at the expense of issues of power and socio-political context. One of the better works in this field is Norbert Berthold Wagner, *Die deutschen Schutzgebiete: Erwerb, Organisation und Verlust aus juristischer Sicht*, Baden-Baden (Nomos) 2002. On the *Kolonialrat* (Colonial Council), see Hartmut Pogge von Strandmann, *Imperialismus vom grünen Tisch: Deutsche Kolonialpolitik zwischen wirtschaftlicher Ausbeutung und 'zivilisatorischen' Bemühungen*, Berlin (Ch. Links) 2009. A meticulous if somewhat empiricist case study of the making of the colonial state is Florian Hoffmann, *Okkupation und Militärverwaltung in Kamerun: Etablierung und Institutionalisierung des kolonialen Gewaltmonopols*, 2 volumes, Göttingen (Cuvillier-Verlag) 2007. For a social history of the higher echelons of the German colonial bureaucracy, see the now classical work by Lewis H. Gann and Peter Duignan, *The Rulers of German Africa 1884–1914*, Stanford (Stanford University Press) 1977. See also Lewis H. Gann and Peter Duignan, *African Proconsuls: European Governors in Africa*, New York (Free Press) 1978. On the case of Togo, see Bettina Zurstrassen, *'Ein Stück deutscher Erde schaffen': Koloniale Beamte in Togo 1884–1914*, Frankfurt am Main (Campus Verlag) 2008, which focuses exclusively on the German administration and neglects African agency.

For an understanding of the workings of the colonial state, the general works cited in Chapter 3 provide the best point of entry into a large literature. In addition, two recent and stimulating works have discussed particular aspects of the colonial state. Michael Pesek's *Koloniale Herrschaft in Deutsch-Ostafrika* analyses the traditional structures, like the caravan system, within which the early colonial state in East Africa had to operate. Pesek describes the colonial state – in particular before 1907 – as a weak state and puts the focus on the fragility of colonial rule *vis-à-vis* a colonial population that proved difficult to control. George Steinmetz, in his magisterial *The Devil's Handwriting*, offers an in-depth and comparative discussion of the colonial state in three different German colonies. Steinmetz argues that the pre-colonial images, in particular ethnographic studies, to a large extent worked as a framework within which the dynamics of later colonial rule must be understood.

The three major colonial wars are also discussed in the context of the general literature cited above. In addition, several recently published volumes that specifically focus on colonial wars deserve mention: a particularly interesting account, from the point of view of a historian of China, is provided by Paul A. Cohen, *History in Three Keys: The Boxers as Event, Experience, and Myth*, New York (Columbia University Press) 1997. See also Joseph W. Esherick, *The Origins of the Boxer Uprising*, Berkeley (University of California Press) 1987. Susanne Kuß and Bernd Martin (eds.), *Das Deutsche Reich und der Boxeraufstand*, Munich (Iudicium) 2002 is devoted entirely to the Boxer war in China. Most of the articles, however, are written in a somewhat positivistic tone and set out to prove the particular and unparallelled brutality of the German forces. Geared to a more general audience is Mechthild Leutner and Klaus Mühlhahn (eds.), *Kolonialkrieg in China: Die Niederschlagung der Boxerbewegung 1900–1901*, Berlin (Ch. Links) 2007. On the Herero war, see Jürgen Zimmerer, Joachim Zeller and Edward Neather (eds.), *Genocide in German South-West Africa: The Colonial War (1904–1908) in Namibia and its Aftermath*, Monmouth (Merlin Press) 2008 with controversial theses discussed below in Chapter 8. See also Jan-Bart Gewald, *Herero Heroes: A Socio-Political History of the Herero of Namibia 1890–1923*, Oxford (James Currey) 1998; Jon M. Bridgeman, *The Revolt of the Hereros*, Berkeley (California University Press) 1981; Andreas H. Bühler, *Der Namaaufstand gegen die deutsche Kolonialherrschaft in Namibia von 1904–1913*, Frankfurt am Main (IKO) 2003; Casper W. Erichsen, *'The Angel of Death Has Descended Violently Among Them': Concentration Camps and Prisoners-of-War in Namibia, 1904–08*, Leiden (African Studies Centre) 2005.

The best volume on these issues, going beyond the confines of the German colonial empire, is Thoralf Klein and Frank Schumacher (eds.), *Kolonialkriege: Militärische Gewalt im Zeichen des Imperialismus*, Hamburg (Hamburger Edition) 2006. See also Susanne Kuß, *Deutsches Militär auf kolonialen Kriegsschauplätzen: Eskalation von Gewalt zu Beginn des 20. Jahrhunderts*, Berlin (Ch. Links) 2010, who analyses the way in which the setting of colonial wars, including the colonial career of large groups of military officers, was contributory to the escalation of violence. Specifically on the involvement of native soldiers and colonial troops, see Thomas

Morlang, *Askari und Fitafita: 'Farbige' Söldner in den deutschen Kolonien*, Berlin (Ch. Links) 2008.

CHAPTER 6: ECONOMY AND WORK

The standard narrative of German economic colonialism is short and concludes by stating that in the context of the German economy, the colonies did not matter much. This verdict is supported by, and typically based on, Francesca Schinzinger, *Die Kolonien und das Deutsche Reich: Die wirtschaftliche Bedeutung der deutschen Besitzungen in Übersee*, Stuttgart (Steiner) 1984. At the same time, it should be clear that the gradual incorporation of the colonial territories into the world economy, and the complex interactions of older and newer structures of production, remain important and interesting fields of research. That this may even be fruitful for an understanding of German economic policy, beyond the balance sheet of import and export, is interestingly argued by Dirk van Laak, *Imperiale Infrastruktur*.

For economic development in the colonial territories, the best place to start is the comprehensive works mentioned in Chapter 3. A few studies have particularly focused on economic interactions and thus deserve especial mention. Among them is the superb *Vom Sklavenhandel zum kolonialen Handel: Wirtschaftsräume und Wirtschaftsformen in Kamerun vor 1914*, Zurich (Atlantis) 1972, by Albert Wirz. See also Andreas Eckert, *Grundbesitz, Landkonflikte und kolonialer Wandel*. For East Africa, see Rainer Tetzlaff, *Koloniale Entwicklung und Ausbeutung: Wirtschafts- und Sozialgeschichte Deutsch-Ostafrikas 1885–1914*, Berlin (Duncker & Humblot) 1970. Also useful are Ralph Erbar, *Ein 'Platz an der Sonne'? Die Verwaltungs- und Wirtschaftsgeschichte der deutschen Kolonie Togo 1884–1914*, Stuttgart (Steiner) 1991 and Gerd Hardach, *König Kopra: Die Marianen unter deutscher Herrschaft 1899–1914*, Stuttgart (Steiner) 1990. One of the best works on the colonial economy, even if very factual and not informed by a larger theoretical framework, is Juhani Koponen, *Development for Exploitation. German Colonial Policies in Mainland Tanzania 1884–1914*, Helsinki (Tiedekirja) 1994.

In recent years, the focus has shifted to an interest in work and work relations. David Northrup in his book *Indentured Labor in the*

Age of Imperialism 1834–1922, Cambridge (Cambridge University Press) 1995 is the best point of entry into this debate, even if he does not focus on the German empire. The best work on the reorganization of work and the work-place under conditions of colonialism is Thaddeus Sunseri, *Vilimani: Labor Migration and Rural Change in Early Colonial Tanzania*, Portsmouth, N. H. (Heinemann) 2002. Interesting also is Jan-Georg Deutsch, *Emancipation without Abolition in German East-Africa c. 1884–1914*, Oxford (James Currey) 2006 on the long after-life of slavery and the slow emergence of a labour market in German East Africa.

CHAPTER 7: COLONIAL SOCIETY

The fundamental tension between the civilizing mission and the colonial politics of difference is, implicitly and explicitly, discussed in large parts of the theoretical literature on colonialism. See, for example, Frederick Cooper and Ann Laura Stoler (eds.), *Tensions of Empire: Colonial Cultures in a Bourgeois World*, Berkeley (University of California Press) 1997; Ann Laura Stoler, *Carnal Knowledge and Imperial Power: Race and the Intimate in Colonial Rule*, Berkeley (University of California Press) 2002; Partha Chatterjee, *The Nation and its Fragments*. The concept of the civilizing mission is comparatively taken up in Boris Barth and Jürgen Osterhammel (eds.), *Zivilisierungsmissionen: Imperiale Weltverbesserung seit dem 18. Jahrhundert*, Constance (UVK) 2005.

For the German colonies, see the literature mentioned above in Chapter 3. Particularly illuminating discussions can be found in George Steinmetz, *The Devil's Handwriting* who discusses, among many other things, strategies of going native; and Birthe Kundrus, *Moderne Imperialisten*. On the example of Kiaochow, see the interesting arguments in Mühlhahn, *Herrschaft und Widerstand*. See also Felix Axster, 'Die Angst vor dem Verkaffern: Politiken der Reinigung im deutschen Kolonialismus,' *Werkstatt Geschichte* 14 (2005), 39–53.

For some of the more traditional aspects of colonial policy mentioned, there is an older literature to start with. This is true for the role of the Christian missions and their relationship *vis-à-vis* both the state and the local population. See Klaus J. Bade (ed.), *Imperialismus und Kolonialmission: Kaiserliches Deutschland und koloniales Imperium*,

Wiesbaden (Steiner) 1982; Horst Gründer, *Christliche Mission und deutscher Imperialismus: Eine politische Geschichte ihrer Beziehungen während der deutschen Kolonialzeit 1884–1914 unter besonderer Berücksichtigung Afrikas und Chinas*, Paderborn (Schöningh) 1982; and recently Thorsten Altena, *'Ein Häuflein Christen mitten in der Heidenwelt des dunklen Erdteils': Zum Selbst- und Fremdverständnis protestantischer Missionare im kolonialen Afrika 1884–1918*, Münster (Waxmann) 2003. Fairly traditional, sometimes bordering on the apologetic, are the treatments of educational politics such as Chun-Shik Kim, *Deutscher Kulturimperialismus in China: Deutsches Kolonialschulwesen in Kiautschou (China) 1898–1914*, Stuttgart (Steiner) 2004 and Ingo T. Krause, *'Koloniale Schuldlüge'? Die Schulpolitik in den afrikanischen Kolonien Deutschlands und Britanniens im Vergleich*, Hamburg (Dr Kovac) 2007.

More recently, discussions have focused on issues of race and gender. In particular, the prohibition of 'mixed marriages' has received great attention. The best account is Lora Wildenthal, *German Women for Empire 1884–1945*, Durham (Duke University Press) 2001. The older and less academic study by Martha Mamozai, *Herrenmenschen: Frauen im deutschen Kolonialismus*, Reinbek bei Hamburg (Rowohlt) 1982 can still be mined for interesting aspects and episodes. Katharina Walgenbach, *Die weiße Frau als Trägerin deutscher Kultur* is informed by more recent theoretical discussions on gender, race, and whiteness. Beyond the more circumscribed issue of 'mixed marriages', interesting insights into the role of race in the construction of the colonial order can be gleaned from Robbie Aitken, *Exclusion and Inclusion: Gradations of Whiteness and Socio-Economic Engineering in German Southwest Africa, 1884–1914*, Bern (Peter Lang) 2007.

Increasing attention has also been paid, in recent years, to the German overseas populations. Jürgen Becher has reconstructed urbanization and the development of cities in German East Africa in his *Dar es Salaam, Tanga und Tabora: Stadtentwicklung in Tansania unter deutscher Kolonialherrschaft 1885–1914*, Stuttgart (Steiner) 1997. The settlers in East Africa, and their conflicts with both missions and the colonial government, are discussed by Philippa Söldenwagner, *Spaces of Negotiation: European Settlement and Settlers in German East Africa 1900–1914*, Munich (Meidenbauer) 2006. On settler communities, see also the interesting collection of essays by Krista O'Donnell, Renate Bridenthal, and Nancy Reagin (eds.), *The Heimat Abroad: The Boundaries of Germanness*, Ann Arbor (University of Michigan Press) 2005. Daniel J. Walther's study *Creating Germans Abroad: Cultural Policies and National Identity in Namibia*, Athens (Ohio University Press) 2006 has a strong focus on the development of German settler communities after the end of the German empire.

CHAPTER 8: KNOWLEDGE AND COLONIALISM

Reflections on the complex interplay of knowledge and power in the colonial context owe much to the works of Edward Said and Michel Foucault (*Discipline and Punish*). The problematic has been influentially discussed by Bernard S. Cohn in his study on South Asia, *Colonialism and its Forms of Knowledge: The British in India*, Princeton (Princeton University Press) 1996, even if studies in the wake of Cohn have tended to put less emphasis on the disciplining power of the colonial state. See also Gyan Prakash, *Another Reason: Science and the Imagination of Modern India*, Princeton (Princeton University Press) 1999.

In the context of the German empire, the most interesting work has been produced on the colonial dimensions of disciplinary histories. Among the best works in this context are studies of anthropology, most notably Andrew Zimmerman, *Anthropology and Antihumanism in Imperial Germany*, Chicago (University of Chicago Press) 2001 and Glenn H. Penny, *Objects of Culture: Ethnology and Ethnographic Museums in Imperial Germany*, Chapel Hill (University of North Carolina Press) 2002; see also Glenn H. Penny and Matti Bunzl (eds.), *Worldly Provincialism: German Anthropology in the Age of Empire*, Ann Arbor (University of Michigan Press) 2003. Rainer F. Buschmann, *Anthropology's Global Histories: The Ethnographic Frontier in German New Guinea, 1870–1935*, Honolulu (University of Hawai'i Press) 2009 has a stronger focus on the fieldwork dimension of anthropology. See also the magisterial study on German *Orientalistik* by Suzanne Marchand, *German Orientalism in the Age of Empire: Religion, Race, and Scholarship*, Cambridge (Cambridge University Press) 2009.

Full of insights, and combining an interest in academic discourse with analysis of political debate, is the study by Pascal Grosse on eugenic discourse in his *Kolonialismus, Eugenik und bürgerliche Gesellschaft in Deutschland 1850–1918*, Frankfurt am Main (Campus) 2000. The fact that disciplinary and scholarly knowledge was never insulated and instead embedded in broader and more popular forms of knowing is beautifully demonstrated in the more than fifty vignettes assembled in Alexander Honold and Klaus R. Scherpe (eds.), *Mit Deutschland um die Welt: Eine Kulturgeschichte des Fremden in der Kolonialzeit*, Stuttgart (Metzler) 2004.

For further studies on academic disciplines, see Wolfgang Eckart, *Medizin und Kolonialimperialismus: Deutschland 1884–1945*, Paderborn (Schöningh) 1996; Jürgen Zimmerer, 'Im Dienste des Imperiums: Die Geographen der Berliner Universität zwischen Kolonialwissenschaften und Ostforschung', *Jahrbuch für Universitätsgeschichte* 7 (2004), 73–100; Woodruff D. Smith, 'Anthropology and German Colonialism', in: Arthur J. Knoll and Lewis H. Gann (eds.), *Germans in the Tropics: Essays in German Colonial History*, 39–57; Paul J. Weindling, *Health, Race and German Politics between National Unification and Nazism 1870–1945*, Cambridge (Cambridge University Press) 1989; Niels C. Lösch, *Rasse als Konstrukt: Leben und Werk Eugen Fischers*, Frankfurt am Main (Lang) 1997.

The importance of early geographical explorations for the dynamics of rule in East Africa are stressed by Pesek, *Koloniale Herrschaft in Deutsch-Ostafrika*. On explorations and travelling, see also Cordelia Essner, *Deutsche Afrikareisende im neunzehnten Jahrhundert: Zur Sozialgeschichte des Reisens*, Stuttgart (Steiner) 1985. Christoph Marx, in his '*Völker ohne Schrift und Geschichte*': *Zur historischen Erfassung des vorkolonialen Schwarzafrika in der deutschen Forschung des 19. und frühen 20. Jahrhunderts*, Stuttgart (Steiner) 1988 has looked at representations of pre-colonial Africa in German historical scholarship. The links to the natural sciences are discussed in Susanne Köstering, *Natur zum Anschauen: Das Naturkundemuseum des deutschen Kaiserreichs 1871–1914*, Cologne (Böhlau) 2003, and in Lewis Pyenson, *Cultural Imperialism and Exact Sciences: German Expansion Overseas 1900–1930*, New York (Lang) 1985. A maverick position is taken by Russell A. Berman in his *Enlightenment or Empire: Colonial Discourse in German Culture*, Lincoln (University of Nebraska Press) 1998 in which he sees post-Romanticist Germany as part of the colonized world *vis-à-vis* France and Great Britain.

CHAPTER 9: THE COLONIAL METROPOLE

The call to understand colonies and metropole within one integrated analytical field has been forcefully put forward by Ann Laura Stoler and Frederick Cooper, 'Between Metropole and Colony: Rethinking a Research Agenda', in: Frederick Cooper and Ann Laura Stoler (eds.), *Tensions of Empire: Colonial Cultures in a Bourgeois World*, Berkeley (University of California Press) 1997, 1–56. This approach has been employed most of all in the context of British history. For a good overview on this kind of work, see Kathleen Wilson (ed.), *A New Imperial History: Culture, Identity, and Modernity in Britain and the Empire 1660–1840*, Cambridge (Cambridge University Press) 2004; Catherine Hall (ed.), *Cultures of Empire: A Reader: Colonisers in Britain and the Empire in the Nineteenth and Twentieth Centuries*, Manchester (Manchester University Press) 2000; and Catherine Hall and Sonya O. Rose (eds.), *At Home with the Empire: Metropolitan Culture and the Imperial World*, Cambridge (Cambridge University Press) 2006.

In the context of German colonialism, the repercussions of the colonial project on the metropole have first been taken up in the pioneering volume by Sara Friedrichsmeyer, Sara Lennox, and Susanne Zantop (eds.), *The Imperialist Imagination: German Colonialism and its Legacy*, Ann Arbor (University of Michigan Press) 1998. More recent research can be found in the collected volumes by Birthe Kundrus (ed.), *Phantasiereiche: Zur Kulturgeschichte des deutschen Kolonialismus*, Frankfurt am Main (Campus) 2003; Sebastian Conrad and Jürgen Osterhammel (eds.), *Das Kaiserreich transnational: Deutschland in der Welt 1871–1914*, Göttingen (Vandenhoeck & Ruprecht) 2004; Eric Ames, Marcia Klotz, and Lora Wildenthal (eds.), *Germany's Colonial Pasts*, Lincoln (University of Nebraska Press) 2005. For the latest contributions to the topic, see Michel Perraudin and Jürgen Zimmerer (eds.), *German Colonialism and National Identity*, London (Routledge) 2011.

Most work concerned with gauging the impact of colonialism on German society has focused on the realm of culture, both high and more popular. On the subject of advertising and popular colonial consciousness, see David Ciarlo, *Advertising Empire: Race and Visual*

Culture in Imperial Germany, Cambridge, Mass. (Harvard University Press) 2011; on this topic, see also the richly illustrated Joachim Zeller, *Bilderschule der Herrenmenschen: Koloniale Reklamesammelbilder*, Berlin (Ch. Links) 2008. On ethnographic shows (*Völkerschauen*), see Anne Dreesbach, *Gezähmte Wilde: Die Zurschaustellung 'exotischer' Menschen in Deutschland 1870–1940*, Frankfurt am Main (Campus) 2005. On popular culture more broadly, see, for example, Nina Berman, *Orientalismus, Kolonialismus und Moderne: Zum Bild des Orients in der deutschsprachigen Kultur um 1900*, Stuttgart (Metzler) 1996; Alexander Honold and Oliver Simons (eds.), *Kolonialismus als Kultur: Literatur, Medien, Wissenschaft in der deutschen Gründerzeit des Fremden*, Tübingen (A. Francke) 2002; Ulrich van der Heyden and Joachim Zeller (eds.), *Kolonialmetropole Berlin: Eine Spurensuche*, Berlin (Berlin Edition) 2002; and Ulrich van der Heyden and Joachim Zeller (eds.), '. . . *Macht und Anteil an der Weltherrschaft': Berlin und der deutsche Kolonialismus*, Münster (Unrast) 2005. On the issue of migration, see Marianne Bechhaus-Gerst and Reinhard Klein-Arendt (eds.), *Die (koloniale) Begegnung: AfrikanerInnen in Deutschland 1880–1945 – Deutsche in Afrika 1880–1918*, Frankfurt am Main (Lang) 2003. A first glimpse into the role of colonial exhibitions, and also the lure of exotic products, can be gleaned from Robert Debusmann and Janos Riesz (eds.), *Kolonialausstellungen – Begegnungen mit Afrika?*, Frankfurt am Main (IKO) 1995. See also Dreesbach, *Gezähmte Wilde* and Joachim Zeller, *Weiße Blicke. Schwarze Körper: Afrika(ner) im Spiegel westlicher Alltagskultur*, Erfurt (Sutton) 2010.

CHAPTER 10: COLONIALISM IN EUROPE

The debate about German colonialism in Europe is a very recent one, and the literature on some of these questions still has a probing and exploratory character. One of the central points of departure remains Hannah Arendt, *The Origins of Totalitarianism*, New York (Harcourt, Brace) 1951. See also Pascal Grosse, 'From Colonialism to National Socialism to Postcolonialism: Hannah Arendt's *Origins of Totalitarianism*', *Postcolonial Studies* 9 (2006), 35–52. A recent collection of essays dealing with some of the questions discussed in this chapter is Robert L. Nelson (ed.), *Germany, Poland, and Colonial Expansion to the East: 1850 Through the Present*, New York (Palgrave Macmillan) 2009.

On the question of the colonial dimensions of Prussia's and imperial Germany's policies in the European east before the First World War, there are to date only a few first probings of the terrain. See the suggestive article by Philipp Ther, 'Deutsche Geschichte als imperiale Geschichte: Polen, slawophone Minderheiten und das Kaiserreich als kontinentales Empire', in: Sebastian Conrad and Jürgen Osterhammel (eds.), *Das Kaiserreich transnational: Deutschland in der Welt 1871–1914*, Göttingen (Vandenhoeck & Ruprecht) 2004, 129–48 as well as the dissertation by Kristin Kopp, *Contesting Borders: German Colonial Discourse and the Polish Eastern Territories*, Ph.D. diss., University of California, Berkeley 2001 with a strong focus on literature. See also Kopp, 'Constructing Racial Difference in Colonial Poland'. For a first attempt at synthesis, see Sebastian Conrad, 'Internal Colonialism in Germany: Culture Wars, Germanification of the Soil, and the Global Market Imaginary', in: Eley and Naranch (eds.), *German Cultures of Colonialism*.

The debate on the continuities between the Herero and Nama wars and the Holocaust has been primarily initiated by Jürgen Zimmerer, drawing on Arendt and on earlier works like Drechsler, *Südwestafrika unter deutscher Kolonialherrschaft* and Helmut Bley, *Kolonialherrschaft und Sozialstruktur in Deutsch-Südwestafrika: 1894–1914*, Hamburg (Leibniz) 1968. See, for example, Jürgen Zimmerer, 'Colonialism and the Holocaust: Towards an Archeology of Genocide', in: A. Dirk Moses (ed.), *Genocide and Settler Society: Frontier Violence and Stolen Indigenous Children in Australian History*, New York (Berghahn) 2004, 49–76 as well as Jürgen Zimmerer, 'Kein Sonderweg im "Rassenkrieg": Der Genozid an den Herero und Nama 1904–08 zwischen deutschen Kontinuitäten und der Globalgeschichte der Massengewalt', in: Sven O. Müller and Cornelius Torp (eds.), *Das deutsche Kaiserreich in der Kontroverse*, Göttingen (Vandenhoeck & Ruprecht) 2009, 323–40. See also the collected volume edited by Zimmerer, Zeller, and Neather, *Genocide in German South-West Africa*; Benjamin Madley, 'From Africa to Auschwitz: How German South West Africa Incubated Ideas and Methods Adopted and Developed by the Nazis in Eastern Europe', *European History Quarterly* 33 (2005), 429–64. A popularizing synthesis of the continuity thesis is David Olusoga and Casper W. Erichsen,

The Kaiser's Holocaust: Germany's Forgotten Genocide and the Colonial Roots of Nazism, London (Faber & Faber) 2010.

For critical perspectives that cast doubt on the construction of long-term continuities, see in particular Birthe Kundrus, 'Continuities, Parallels, Receptions: Reflections on the "Colonization" of National Socialism', *Journal of Namibian Studies* 1 (2008), no. 4, 25–46, Pascal Grosse, 'What Does German Colonialism Have to Do with National Socialism? A Conceptual Framework', in: Ames, Klotz, and Wildenthal (eds.), *Germany's Colonial Pasts*, 115–34, and Gerwarth and Malinowski, 'Der Holocaust als "kolonialer Genozid"?'. A good summary of the debate can be found in Matthew P. Fitzpatrick, 'The Pre-History of the Holocaust? The *Sonderweg* and *Historikerstreit* Debates and the Abject Colonial Past', *Central European History* 41 (2008), 477–503. For the latest statements in this ongoing debate, see Volker M. Langbehn (ed.), *German Colonialism: Race, the Holocaust, and Postwar Germany*, New York (Columbia University Press) 2011.

Stimulating critical syntheses of recent scholarship on the Nazi empire and ways to read the Nazi empire as part of a larger history of colonialism without losing sight of the distinctiveness of the Nazi version of racial empire are Mark Mazower, *Hitler's Empire: Nazi Rule in Occupied Europe*, London (Penguin) 2008, and Shelley Baranowski, *Nazi Empire: German Colonialism and Imperialism from Bismarck to Hitler*, Cambridge (Cambridge University Press) 2010. The best empirical case study is Lower, *Nazi Empire-Building*. See also David Furber, *'Going East': Colonialism and German Life in Nazi-Occupied Poland*, Ph.D. diss., University of New York at Buffalo 2003; Furber, 'Near as Far in the Colonies: The Nazi Occupation of Poland', *International History Review* 26 (2004), 541–81; Jürgen Zimmerer, 'The Birth of the "Ostland" out of the Spirit of Colonialism: A Postcolonial Perspective on Nazi Policy of Conquest and Extermination', *Patterns of Prejudice* 39 (2005), 197–219; Diemut Majer, 'Das besetzte Osteuropa als deutsche Kolonie (1939–1944): Die Pläne der NS-Führung zur Beherrschung Osteuropas', in: Micha Brumli, Susanne Meinl, and Werner Renz (eds.), *Gesetzliches Unrecht: Rassisches Recht im 20. Jahrhundert*, Frankfurt am Main (Campus) 2005, 111–34. For critical views, see the articles by Kundrus and Gerwarth/Malinowski cited in this chapter. On the question of institutional continuities within the German army, see the critical remarks in Isabel V. Hull's important study *Absolute Destruction: Military Culture and the Practices of War in Imperial Germany*, Ithaca (Cornell University Press) 2005.

CHAPTER 11: GERMAN COLONIALISM AND ITS GLOBAL CONTEXTS

The history of globalization, and in particular Germany's involvement in the globalization process in the late nineteenth century, is only now beginning to emerge as a topic of research for historians of Germany. Among the few recent works that explicitly aim to understand imperial Germany within the context of colonialism and globalization are Conrad and Osterhammel (eds.), *Das Kaiserreich transnational*; Cornelius Torp, *Die Herausforderung der Globalisierung: Wirtschaft und Politik in Deutschland 1860–1914*, Göttingen (Vandenhoeck & Ruprecht) 2005; and Sebastian Conrad, *Globalisation and the Nation in Imperial Germany*, Cambridge (Cambridge University Press) 2010.

It is important to note, however, that many of the themes discussed in this chapter were dealt with in the older literature, even if the connections to the structured process of globalization were not always spelled out explicitly. A good point of departure for many issues of *Weltpolitik* is van Laak, *Über alles in der Welt*. Apart from the general literature on foreign policy, Sönke Neitzel, *Weltmacht oder Untergang: Die Weltreichslehre im Zeitalter des Imperialismus*, Paderborn (Schöningh) 2000 is also useful. Interesting also are works that show to what extent political thinking in Germany was already operating with a global consciousness. See, in particular, the fine studies by Smith, *The Ideological Origins of Nazi Imperialism*; Rüdiger vom Bruch, *Weltpolitik als Kulturmission: Auswärtige Kulturpolitik und Bildungsbürgertum in Deutschland am Vorabend des Ersten Weltkrieges*, Paderborn (Schöningh) 1982; and, still important, Heinz Gollwitzer, *Die Gelbe Gefahr: Geschichte eines Schlagworts, Studien zum imperialistischen Denken*, Göttingen (Vandenhoeck & Ruprecht) 1962.

For Germany's role in the emerging world economy, a good point of departure is still Wolfram Fischer, *Expansion, Integration, Globalisierung: Studien zur Geschichte der Weltwirtschaft*, Göttingen (Vandenhoeck & Ruprecht) 1998; see also the older study by Wilfried

Spohn, *Weltmarktkonkurrenz und Industrialisierung Deutschlands 1870–1914: Eine Untersuchung zur nationalen und internationalen Geschichte der kapitalistischen Produktionsweise*, Berlin (Olle & Wolter) 1977. As interesting examples for case studies, see Hartmut Berghoff, *Zwischen Kleinstadt und Weltmarkt: Hohner und die Harmonika 1857–1961*, Paderborn (Schöningh) 1997 and Boris Barth, *Die deutsche Hochfinanz und die Imperialismen: Banken und Außenpolitik vor 1914*, Stuttgart (Steiner) 1995. On migration, there are a number of interesting works. The best overviews are offered in Klaus J. Bade, *Migration in European History*, Malden (Blackwell) 2003 and Dirk Hoerder and Jörg Nagler (eds.), *People in Transit: German Migrations in Comparative Perspective 1820–1930*, Cambridge (Cambridge University Press) 1995. On the role of German diasporas and their impact on debates in Germany see Klaus J. Bade (ed.), *Deutsche im Ausland – Fremde in Deutschland: Migration in Geschichte und Gegenwart*, Munich (C. H. Beck) 1992; O'Donnell, Bridenthal and Reagin, *The Heimat Abroad*; and Malte Fuhrmann, *Der Traum vom deutschen Orient: Zwei deutsche Kolonien im osmanischen Reich 1851–1918*, Frankfurt am Main (Campus) 2006.

CHAPTER 12: MEMORY

The after-life of colonialism in the Weimar Republic and during National Socialism has been the subject of a number of older studies, mainly focusing on high politics and political strategies. Among them, see Wolfe W. Schmokel, *Dream of Empire: German Colonialism 1919–1945*, New Haven (Yale University Press) 1964; Klaus Hildebrand, *Vom Reich zum Weltreich: Hitler, NSDAP und koloniale Frage 1919–1945*, Munich (Fink) 1969; Jost Dülffer, 'Kolonialismus ohne Kolonien: Deutsche Kolonialpläne 1938', in: Franz Knipping and Klaus-Jürgen Müller (eds.), *Machtbewußtsein in Deutschland am Vorabend des Zweiten Weltkrieges*, Paderborn (Schöningh) 1984, 247–70; Alexandre Kum'a N'Dumbe III, *Was wollte Hitler in Afrika? NS-Planungen für eine faschistische Neugestaltung Afrikas*, Frankfurt am Main (IKO) 1993; Karsten Linne, *Deutschland jenseits des Äquators? Die NS-Kolonialplanungen für Afrika*, Berlin (C. H. Links) 2008. The best newer study is Dirk van Laak, *Imperiale Infrastruktur*, with its focus on technological and economic strategies and projects. Interesting aspects of economic planning are also discussed in Karsten Linne, *'Weiße Arbeitsführer' im 'kolonialen Ergänzungsraum': Afrika als Ziel sozial- und wirtschaftspolitischer Planungen in der NS-Zeit,* Münster (Monsenstein & Vannerdat) 2002. The presence of Africans and African Germans is the subject of Peter Martin and Christine Alonzo (eds.), *Zwischen Charleston und Stechschritt: Schwarze im Nationalsozialismus,* Hamburg (Dölling & Galitz) 2004.

For the colonial nostalgia in the Weimar Republic, see Jared Poley, *Decolonisation in Germany: Weimar Narratives of Colonial Loss and Foreign Occupation,* Bern (Peter Lang) 2005. For this period, a special focus of the literature has been on the presence of African soldiers as part of the occupying force in the Rhineland; these have been the subject of a number of recent studies. A good point of departure for these debates is Koller, *'Von Wilden aller Rassen niedergemetzelt'.* Much more ambitious analytically, and informed by current theories of race and gender, is Tina M. Campt, *Other Germans: Black Germans and the Politics of Race, Gender, and Memory in the Third Reich,* Ann Arbor (University of Michigan Press) 2004. But see also Iris Wigger, *Die 'Schwarze Schmach am Rhein': Rassistische Diskriminierung zwischen Geschlecht, Klasse, Nation und Rasse,* Münster (Westfälisches Dampfboot) 2007 and the older study by Reiner Pommerin, *Sterilisierung der Rheinlandbastarde: Das Schicksal einer farbigen deutschen Minderheit 1918–1937,* Düsseldorf (Droste) 1979. A strong focus on race and gender is also present in El-Tayeb, *Schwarze Deutsche* and Sandra Maß, *Weiße Helden, schwarze Krieger: Zur Geschichte kolonialer Männlichkeit in Deutschland 1918–1964,* Cologne (Böhlau) 2006. A broad panorama is presented in Patricia Mazon and Reinhild Steingröver (eds.), *Not So Plain as Black and White: Afro-German Culture and History, 1890–2000,* Rochester, N.Y. (University of Rochester Press) 2005.

The impact of colonial fantasies and projects in the postwar period is only now emerging as an interesting scholarly subject. Among the first attempts to chart this terrain, see van Laak, *Imperiale Infrastruktur.* Foreign policy issues are discussed, with a political science perspective, in Ulf Engel and Hans-Georg Schleicher, *Die beiden deutschen Staaten in Afrika: Zwischen Konkurrenz und Koexistenz 1949–1990,* Hamburg (Institut für Afrika-Kunde) 1998.

Development aid, currently becoming a contested field, is described in the somewhat empiricist account of Bastian Hein, *Die Westdeutschen und die Dritte Welt: Entwicklungspolitik und Entwicklungsdienste zwischen Reform und Revolte 1959–1974*, Munich (Oldenbourg) 2006. An interesting but rather sketchy account of 'good-willed' attempts to embark on modernization projects, such as by medical doctor Albert Schweitzer (1875–1965), who received the Nobel Peace Prize in 1952 for his 'civilizing' projects in Africa, is Nina Berman, *Impossible Missions? German Economic, Military, and Humanitarian Efforts in Africa*, Lincoln (University of Nebraska Press) 2004.

The memory of colonialism, too, is a field that is very much in the making. An early and convincing study is Gesine Krüger, *Kriegsbewältigung und Geschichtsbewußtsein: Realität, Deutung und Verarbeitung des deutschen Kolonialkriegs in Namibia 1904–1907*, Göttingen (Vandenhoeck & Ruprecht) 1999, which puts the focus on the early decades of remembering the war, and mainly from a Herero perspective. See also Casper W. Erichsen (ed.): *'What the Elders Used to Say': Namibian Perspectives on the Last Decade of German Colonial Rule*, Windhoek (John Meinert Printing) 2008; André du Pisani, Reinhart Kößler, and William A. Lindeke (eds.), *The Long Aftermath of War: Reconciliation and Transition in Namibia*, Freiburg (Arnold Bergstraesser Institut) 2010; Larissa Förster, *Postkoloniale Erinnerungslandschaften: Wie Deutsche und Herero in Namibia des Kriegs von 1904 gedenken*, Frankfurt am Main (Campus) 2010.

One of the earlier works on colonial memory in Germany is Joachim Zeller, *Kolonialdenkmäler und Geschichtsbewußtsein: Eine Untersuchung der kolonialdeutschen Erinnerungskultur*, Frankfurt am Main (IKO) 2000. See also contributions to Perraudin and Zimmerer (eds.), *German Colonialism and National Identity* as well as the edited volumes by Helma Lutz and Kathrin Gawarecki (eds.), *Kolonialismus und Erinnerungskultur: Die Kolonialvergangenheit im kollektiven Gedächtnis der deutschen und niederländischen Einwanderungsgesellschaft*, Münster (Waxmann) 2005; Steffi Hobuß and Ulrich Lölke (eds.), *Erinnern verhandeln: Kolonialismus im kollektiven Gedächtnis Afrikas und Europas*, Münster (Westfälisches Dampfboot) 2007; Langbehn (ed.), *German Colonialism*.

Index

CPSIA information can be obtained
at www.ICGtesting.com
Printed in the USA
BVOW06s2152200217

476724BV00007B/51/P